WINGED CHARIOT

Dedicated to the memory of the forgotten dead of the raid on St Nazaire.

Sergeant Hilary Rolfe Parfitt, RAFVR
(Observer)

Flight Sergeant Archie William Taylor, RAAF
(Pilot)

Beaufighter ND-Y, 236 Squadron, RAF
Killed in action against Ju 88 and who have no known grave.

Also to the memory of
Sergeant Douglas Murton Colledge, RAFVR
(Observer)

Whitley KN-G, 77 Squadron, RAF
Killed when his aircraft crashed in Yorkshire returning from the raid.

Flying Officer W.D.S. Bow, RAFVR
(Captain)
Sergeant L.K. Newman, RAF
(Wireless Op/Air Gunner)
Flying Officer J.W.G. Potter, RAFVR
(Observer)
Pilot Officer D.M. Stein, RAFVR
(Pilot)
Sergeant H.M. Tookey, RAFVR
(Wireless Op/Air Gunner)
Sergeant D.A. Young, RAFVR
(Wireless Op/Air Gunner)

Crew of Whitley V WL-X, 612 Squadron, RAF
Killed when their aircraft crashed near Roscanvel while on an anti-submarine sweep.

And all those who flew in support of Operation Chariot.

To Andy

WINGED CHARIOT

A Complete Account of the RAF's Support Role
during the Audacious Commando Raid on St
Nazaire, March 1942

Best wishes

Peter Lush

Peter Lush

Foreword by Air Chief Marshal
Sir Patrick Hine, GCB, GBE

Grub Street • London

Published by
Grub Street
4 Rainham Close
London
SW11 6SS

Copyright © Grub Street 2016
Copyright text © Peter Lush 2016

A CIP record for this title is available from the British Library

ISBN-13: 9-781-910690-24-6

The moral right of the author, Peter Lush, has been asserted.

Printed and bound by Finidr, Czech Republic

CONTENTS

Foreword 6

Acknowledgements 8

Introduction 10

Prologue 12

Chapter 1 Plans and Provisos 13

Chapter 2 Bomber Command 27

Chapter 3 Coastal Command 35

Chapter 4 The Men from the PRU and the Women too 43

Chapter 5 Bay Watch 58

Chapter 6 Of Bombers and Bases 70

Chapter 7 The Best Laid Schemes 77

Chapter 8 Fire Down Below 98

Chapter 9 Enter the Luftwaffe 112

Chapter 10 From Dawn to Dusk 118

Chapter 11 Guests of the Third Reich 139

Chapter 12 Reports and Recriminations 148

Epilogue 154

Appendices:

1. Summary of Sorties Flown 158

2. Operation Chariot – Combined Plan 160

3. Bomber Command Order No. 141 172

4. Report by Group Captain A.H. Willetts 176

Bibliography 180

Sources 182

Index 184

FOREWORD

I have much enjoyed reading *Winged Chariot*; Peter Lush's very detailed account of the RAF's participation in the St Nazaire raid of March 1942 is well balanced and reflects meticulous research. The narrative makes clear that overall the RAF deserves much credit: for creating the model of St Nazaire, which was of vital importance to the raiding commandos; for the provision of constant and timely photographic intelligence of the target area; for patrolling above the Task Force on its outward passage to St Nazaire; and for its protection from air attack throughout its return to UK bases. The only real focus of criticism at the time (and ever since) has been on the RAF's so-called diversionary air raid, the objective of which was to put sustained pressure on the enemy's defences during the Task Force's final approach and the commando raid itself. From the evidence presented in this account of the air raid, I believe such criticism to be fairly based. The question is why did that happen?

The author rightly cites the poor weather over the target on the night and the rigid constraints placed on the RAF's bomber crews for the attack on French targets as the two main reasons. They were indeed vital factors, and as the chiefs of staff committee at their meeting on 24 March 1942 had decreed that Operation Chariot should not be undertaken unless the diversionary bombing raid could be carried out (successfully presumably), they should have been raised beforehand with the Chief of Combined Operations (Mountbatten) and the commander-in-chief Plymouth (Admiral Forbes, the flag officer responsible for implementing Operation Chariot). Someone in the air chain of command should have made clear that the bombing constraints and bad weather in combination would make it virtually impossible to achieve the desired aim of the diversionary air raid. Had that been done, and given the political importance attached to the St Nazaire operation (none more so than by Winston Churchill himself), the bombing constraints may well have been temporarily lifted, thus making the aim of the diversionary raid more achievable. As it was, unrealistic expectations of the impact of the air raid went unchallenged and Higher Command decided to leave it to the Task Force commander (himself probably unaware of the limitations facing the RAF bomber crews) to decide once at sea whether or not the operation should proceed. Reading between the lines, he did not need much encouragement.

The failure to appoint an air commander for Operation Chariot was a major omission that has been highlighted by the author. Group Captain 'Fred' Willetts, a talented officer, did his best as the air advisor on Mountbatten's staff in acting as an air liaison officer with the Ministry of Defence, HQ Plymouth and HQ Bomber Command, but the importance of the operation called for a single air commander on Admiral Forbes' staff (he did have naval and military commanders) with the responsibility for exercising operational control over all air resources allotted to Operation Chariot. Two of his top priorities would have been to ensure that Higher Command were given a realistic appreciation of the capabilities of the bomber crews and urged to press for raising the bombing restrictions, and then that all the crews involved were fully briefed on the purpose and significance of the St Nazaire raid and understood the essential nature of the support task they had been given. It is at least arguable that had they known, and despite the constraints and foul weather, the crews would have recognised the importance of staying in the target area in numbers throughout the whole of the planned diversionary air raid (2330-0400 hours). What real difference that would actually have made is very difficult to assess but the Wellington crews in particular could certainly have stayed in the target area longer, thereby helping to occupy some of the enemy air defences. All that said the presence of aircraft overhead and around St Nazaire ahead of the Task Force's arrival did serve as a distraction and strengthened the enemy's belief until almost the last moment that an attack against the port would not come from the sea.

Peter Lush has scrupulously sought to put the diversionary air raid into the broader perspective of the RAF's considerable overall contribution to Operation Chariot, and he has put 'flesh on the bones' by giving the reader a lot of information about the RAF operational commands and units involved, and about what happened to some of those who took part in the operation. Some readers may feel that at times he strays too far from the core subject but many others, particularly those with little knowledge of the RAF during World War II, will conclude that such diversion adds to the book's overall interest and appeal. I believe that the author is to be congratulated on telling fully and objectively the part that the RAF played in the successful St Nazaire raid, one that captured the British public's imagination at a time when there was very little good news about the war. Those that took part from all three services, and especially those who made the final sacrifice, should be remembered with pride and gratitude by all those of our nation who are alive today and able to read through this book of such a courageous contribution towards final victory over Nazi Germany.

Air Chief Marshal Sir Patrick Hine, GCB, GBE

ACKNOWLEDGEMENTS

Of the many books that have been written about the raid on St Nazaire there are three which have driven my desire to add this volume to the list. My near obsession with studying this raid was sparked in 1968 when I first read *The Greatest Raid of All*, Lucas Phillips' masterly account. The flames were fanned in 1998 with the appearance of Jim Dorrian's *Storming St Nazaire* which to me is the definitive work on the subject. His knowledge is encyclopaedic and his willingness to give help and advice unstinting. Jim has also provided two plans within the text and with his wife, Sandie, has painstakingly proof-read the manuscript, saving me from many errors. I was finally moved to write this account when reading the draft of *Into the Jaws of Death* for Dr Robert Lyman. I was particularly taken by his wealth of background detail, the Chariot flotilla not entering the Loire until page 203 of his book. Robert has also supplied a generous reference for the jacket of this book for which I am most grateful.

This book is research based and so I am particularly indebted to my old friend Nick Fear whose familiarity with the National Archives has enabled him to find and extract the many documents on which I have relied. He has relieved me of many hours of toil. The staff at both the RAF Museum at Hendon and the Air Historical Branch have also been most helpful while at the Medmenham Collection Mike Mockford has aided and advised beyond the call of duty and Christine Halsall, whose own book *Women of Intelligence* is a must-read for students of wartime photo reconnaissance, advised on and corrected the chapter about the PRU. Various archive websites have yielded little nuggets and I am grateful to David Fell (103 Squadron), Peter Gulliver (51 Squadron) and Michael Hayes (RAF Harrowbeer). I am much indebted to David Ray of the Colditz Society for information regarding prisoner of war camps.

I knew from the beginning that the role of the RAF was a difficult subject within the St Nazaire Society and so I am grateful to them for giving me the platform of their annual lunch to address members on the subject and I also thank my fellow members of the committee for their support and encouragement in adding this book to the story of Operation Chariot.

I have been much moved by the willingness of people to share their own research and nowhere has this been more evident than in France where Gildas Saouzanet, Marcel Burel, Arnaud Théron and the staff of the *Mairie* at Roscanvel have provided priceless material on the aircraft losses on the Crozon peninsula, while the books of Luc Braeuer and Bernard Petitjean have been a rich source of information on the fortress that was St Nazaire. They have all contributed photographs as has Lajla Johansson with her fine picture of St Eval church. I am indebted to Ann Talbot whose wizardry with several of the photographs has ensured that they have been in a condition fit for reproduction. Ann also took the portrait that adorns the jacket of this book.

In Australia, Sandra Playle did much sterling work on unearthing the story of Archie Taylor and pointing me in the direction of his nephew, Michael Dunbavan. In Canberra, my good friend Zoe Larkin trawled the archives of the Australian War Memorial to find details of Alister Currie and, I suspect, to catch the research bug. I also found relatives of

ACKNOWLEDGEMENTS

Hilary Parfitt 'down under'.

The technical language and acronyms of the services are an enduring mystery to me so the help and advice of two retired squadron leaders, Colin Pomeroy and Ian Coleman for the RAF and of Frank Stanton for the navy was indispensable. Christopher Jary and John Travell have kindly read the manuscript and offered welcome criticism and advice. Doug Killick and Martin Gleeson have willingly shared their knowledge on the loss of Blenheim Z6103 on the beach at Morgat.

Descendants of participants gave freely of their time and family archives which enabled me to add personal reminiscences to the narrative. Sue Pendry, the daughter of Brian Nation, tail gunner in 51 Squadron, gave permission to include his photograph and an extract from previous correspondence. Alex Price, the grandson of Arthur Price, a member of the crew of Blenheim Z6103, allowed me free use of his grandfather's archive, which enabled me to add detail of life in captivity and the long march to freedom in 1945, and also permission to use the photograph of his wedding. Brian Lang gave details and a photograph of his uncle, Desmond Bow.

The Cornish airfields from where so many of the sorties were flown are long since closed so I am indebted to Commander Jason Phillips OBE Royal Navy, Commander Air & Training, RNAS Culdrose, who arranged for me to visit Predannack where standing with my thoughts in the control tower was an eerie experience, and to Wing Commander Guy Bazalgette, station commander, RAF St Mawgan, initially a satellite to St Eval, for enabling me to meet his officers and give a talk on the raid.

For three years the manuscript of this book has accompanied me around the world, parts being written on cruises and much being corrected on long holidays in Australia. I cannot express too highly, therefore, my thanks to my wife, Tess, for her acceptance, with much tolerance, that this had to be written. She has been a constant source of encouragement, as have her family in Perth, WA.

Air Chief Marshal Sir Patrick Hine, GCB GBE, has contributed a generous foreword for which I am immensely grateful. His reading of the manuscript brought forth blemishes which I was able to address, resulting in a much clearer recitation of the planning process for the raid. His patient advice was much appreciated.

Finally, and most importantly, my focus has always been very much on the two airmen, Archie Taylor and Hilary Parfitt, who gave their lives in action during the withdrawal from St Nazaire. I have been moved beyond measure to have been in touch with nieces and nephews who have willingly shared family memories and photographs. Michael Dunbavan, the nephew of Archie Taylor, read and corrected the pen-picture of his uncle and provided his picture in uniform. Ann Inglis, John Parfitt and Lynne Parfitt-Green, gave me access to family photographs and biographical details of their uncle, Hilary Parfitt. I hope I have repaid them all by increasing their knowledge of the heroic circumstances in which their uncles died and ensuring that those two brave men will no longer be forgotten.

INTRODUCTION

I little realised, when C.E. Lucas Phillips' book, *The Greatest Raid of All*, came into my possession in the late 1960s, how the raid on St Nazaire would become the constant thief of my leisure hours. Nor, in my wildest dreams, could I have imagined that one day I would sail into St Nazaire on the bridge of HMS *Campbeltown* with the sons of Beattie and Tibbits.

I have walked the dockyard at St Nazaire every year for over thirty years now, guiding interested parties around the scene of that great enterprise. I have devoured every book I could find about the raid and watched repeatedly the documentaries. I have met and become friends with many of the survivors. Yet there has always been a gap in the story, something about which little has ever been written – the participation of the Royal Air Force.

The raid on St Nazaire, code-named Operation Chariot, took place on 28 March 1942. It was an enterprise planned and carried out by combined operations and yet, although there was a naval commander and an army commander appointed, no similar commander was put in post for the Royal Air Force, that task being handled with great efficiency by Group Captain A.H. Willetts who was air assistant combined operations (AACO) and who would act as liaison officer between commander-in-chief, Bomber Command, commander-in-chief, Plymouth, and the Air Ministry. In the event, for reasons beyond their control, the RAF's diversionary raid was not only deemed a failure but actually judged to have been counter-productive. The restrictive conditions, imposed by Churchill to avoid French civilian casualties, and the weather, beyond anyone's control and which was 10/10ths cloud layered over the target, combined to preclude any chance of success. Little wonder, then, that the books and documentaries have little to say on the part played by the Royal Air Force.

In reality, in addition to the diversionary bombing raid on the night of 27/28 March, there was no hour of daylight, from the departure of the flotilla of little ships from Falmouth in the afternoon of 26 March until after the return to England of the last survivors three days later, when there was not an aircraft engaged on some sortie or another in support of the Chariot force. Contrary to the sparse coverage given to their role, research shows how extensive it really was. A total of nineteen squadrons were involved, putting into the air more than 100 aircraft crewed by 500 RAF personnel who flew more than 650 hours. Seven aircraft were lost, nine airmen lost their lives and three their liberty. It was, therefore, no small effort and one that deserves its place in history.

At this remove in time and due to the enormous casualty rate amongst aircrew in World War II few, if any, of those who flew at that time survive and so research is restricted mainly to official documents. Yet even those sources appear to skirt over the operation, one history of 4 Group detailing bombing raids on 26/27 March and 28/29 March, but no mention of the raid on St Nazaire in between, even though the group provided twenty-seven aircraft and crews.

The information I have given on the units which took part is certainly not a definitive history, neither is it intended to be, but is hopefully sufficient in detail to lend both context and perspective to the situation in which the RAF found itself in March 1942, and to the various RAF units whose normal day to day activities gave assistance to the enterprise. The experiences of those squadrons whilst flying on the operation – sweeping, bombing, protecting, searching – make for fascinating reading and theirs is a story that should be told and given its true place in the annals of both the raid on St Nazaire and the Royal Air Force.

Peter Lush
Dorchester
2016

PROLOGUE

INFORMATION

1.   A night operation by naval and military forces has been
planned and will shortly take place against a certain sea port in
enemy occupied territory.

2.   It is essential to the plan that the enemy's attention
should, so far as is possible, be diverted during the approach of
the forces from the sea and during the operations on shore. This can
best be achieved by bombing the seaport before the time of landing,
thereby causing the population to take shelter and the defences to
turn their attention upwards and by continuing the attack during the
operations and for some time after they are completed in order to
keep as many people as possible still in shelters and to disorganise
any efforts the enemy may make to minimise the damage.

Bomber Command Operation Order No. 141[1]

On the night of 27/28 March 1942, sixty-two aircraft of Bomber Command flew to the
'certain seaport' of St Nazaire to provide the diversion but they were constrained by orders
that made their mission all but impossible. Circling overhead without bombing served
merely to arouse the suspicions of the defenders who were now alert and at their posts. As
a result few bombs were dropped.

All that has been written about the raid on St Nazaire has thus cast the RAF as the villain
of the piece and even today the popular conception is that the diversionary raid was a failure.
But is this assessment fair or even accurate? What of the other support flown to sweep the
Bay of Biscay? What of the search for survivors? Of these little or nothing has been written.

Operation Chariot would not have been as successful without the involvement of the
RAF. It is a part of their history in which they can take much pride. It is time for the myth
of RAF failure to be dispelled.

---

[1] The full text of this order can be found at Appendix 3.

CHAPTER 1

PLANS AND PROVISOS

'My soul, sit thou a patient looker-on;
Judge not the play before the play is done:
Her plot hath many changes; every day
Speaks a new scene; the last act crowns the play.'

Francis Quarles – Epigram, *Respice Finem*

On Empire Day, Saturday 24 May 1941, after a brief action south of the Denmark Strait, HMS *Hood*, the pride of the Royal Navy, had been sunk by the *Bismarck* in company with *Prinz Eugen*. Of *Hood's* complement of 1,419 men, only three were to survive. This swift naval victory had been greeted with great jubilation by the crews of the German ships but a calmer mood prevailed on the bridge of the *Bismarck* where, at 0632 hours, Admiral Lütjens sent a message to his Northern Command saying, "Have sunk battle cruiser, probably *Hood*."

Then, after a frantic chase across the great wastes of the North Atlantic, *Bismarck* had in her turn been sent to the bottom. When first damaged, Admiral Lütjens had found it necessary to send a further message to Group North, detailing his condition.

1. E. engine-room IV out of action.
2. Port stokehold leaking, but can be held. Bows leaking severely.
3. Cannot make more than 18 knots.
4. Two enemy radar scanners observed.
5. Intend to run into St Nazaire. No loss of men.

The importance of the French port to the German Kriegsmarine had been brought into sharp relief, for the Normandie dock at St Nazaire was the only one on the western seaboard of Hitler's *Festung Europa* that could accommodate the huge German capital ships – including the *Tirpitz*, which at that time was working up in the Baltic before moving to Norway in January 1942 to await her chance to break out into the Atlantic.

The town of St Nazaire, situated on the north bank of the Loire between the river and a huge swamp, has always depended on the sea for its livelihood by way of fishing and shipbuilding. Because of its position on the Atlantic coast it had an importance in both world wars. In 1917 it was the port through which American troops entered France on their way to the Western Front and they greatly improved the infrastructure of the port and added refrigeration facilities. In 1940 it was the port at which, following the evacuation at Dunkirk, those British forces which had been driven west by the oncoming German army had embarked for passage back to England. Here on 17 June 1940, occurred the greatest maritime disaster in British history when a crowded *Lancastria* was sunk with the loss of thousands of lives.

Between the wars the shipbuilding industry was depressed, but in 1934 the government commissioned the building of the huge liner SS *Normandie* and to accommodate her it was necessary to build the Forme Ecluse Louis Joubert, the dry dock that was to become, in March 1942, the focus of Operation Chariot, the raid on St Nazaire.

The town would pay a dreadful price for its involvement in WWII, for when the Germans refused to surrender the U-boat base following the Normandy invasion they were blockaded by the Allies and the town was not liberated until the last day of the war, 8 May 1945. By this time it had long since been evacuated and laid waste and there were said to be fewer than twenty people living there. From a population of 43,281 in 1936 it had recovered after the war to only 11,802 by 1946.

Churchill's biggest nightmare was the U-boat threat and the struggle to defeat it in what became known as the Battle of the Atlantic. It was the only battle of the war that he feared he might lose. "Battles might be won or lost," he said, "but our power to fight, to keep ourselves alive, rested on the outcome of the struggle for control of the Atlantic." Although the *Bismarck* had been sunk, there was still the *Tirpitz*, and on 25 January 1942, Churchill sent a minute to the chiefs of staff – "No other target is comparable to it ....The whole strategy of the war turns at this period on this ship, which is holding four times the number of British ships paralysed...."

The significance of the Normandie Dock at St Nazaire had already registered itself at the Admiralty. The Director of Plans (DoP) had originated a minute on 25 July 1941, in which it is integral to our story to observe that the support of the Royal Air Force would be required. "The target and the majority of the passage is outside fighter cover but the port can be reached easily by bombers", it noted, and "diversionary bombing could be arranged". The RAF was involved from the very beginning. Things now moved quickly to progress the plan. The Director of Naval Intelligence (DNI) noted his concurrence on 25 July and the Director Operations Division (Home) (DOD[H]) suggested, on the 30th, that commander-in-chief, Plymouth should be given the information contained in the DNI's minute and requested to carry out an investigation.

Thus, on 10 August 1941, less than three months after the loss of the *Hood*, Admiral of the Fleet Sir Charles Forbes, commander-in-chief, Plymouth, received, by Command of Their Lordships, a letter requesting that, "consulting the director of combined operations as necessary, you will investigate the possibility of an operation against St Nazaire, with the object of attacking the caissons of the entrance lock leading to the basin and the U-boats and shipping therein".

Within a fortnight, on 23 August, Forbes had sent his 'remarks' to the director of combined operations and the DNI. This was the first tentative plan for an attack on St Nazaire and differed in two important respects from what became the final operation. Firstly, it included an attack on the U-boats and shipping in the docks and, secondly, the initial suggestion from the DoP being that the operation should wait until September, when the nights were longer allowing for safe passage, that the attack should take place at 'first light'. No doubt the latter reflected their lordships' advice that, "German officers sleep outside the town and do not reach their offices till 0800 or 0900 hours and a surprise attack before this hour would have a good chance of success".

What did not differ from the final plan, and which would be included in every subsequent variation along the way, was the recognition that a diversion from the air to distract attention and get as many defenders as possible to ground would be essential, although it was accepted that this would need very careful coordination. Also recognised was the need for strong fighter protection to cover the withdrawal.

It is worthwhile at this point to consider Operation Archery, the raid on Vaagso. Carried out three months before Chariot, on 27 December 1941, it was the first time all three services had combined to mount a raid against a defended coast. The operation had started at dawn and so entailed different planning criteria, including fighter cover, but the principle of diversionary bombing was established. During an earlier raid on the Lofoten Islands it was realised that such missions could be jeopardised if carried out in the absence of air cooperation.

Some of the personnel most closely involved in Archery were to be similarly involved in Chariot and much was gained from the experience. Both Brigadier Haydon, the military force commander, and Group Captain Willetts, the RAF planner were to become, as we shall see, advisors to Combined Headquarters and as such would also be at the forefront of planning for Operation Chariot. Indeed, Willetts would fly to St Nazaire as he had to Vaagso. Over it all stood Mountbatten, by then settling into his new role as director of combined operations. To the men detailed for Operation Archery, Mountbatten would remark, "Nobody knows quite what is going to happen and you are the ones who are going to find out". Find out they did. The RAF provided air cover and diversionary raids for over seven hours during which they lost eleven aircraft and thirty-one aircrew. The learning process would be continued at St Nazaire.

In addition to the valuable experience gained in respect of air cooperation, the operation against Vaagso provided another priceless piece of intelligence for Chariot. Captured during the raid was the German code book which enabled Signalman Pike, in MGB 314, to use the correct recognition signal to delay fire being opened on Chariot Force as it approached its goal at St Nazaire.

In response to Admiral Forbes' request for further information the DNI replied on 5 September with details of the defences and plans and photographs, the latter showing that the services of the RAF through their Photographic Reconnaissance Unit were already a significant factor in the raid through the planning process. Later, from the same source, a fine model of the docks would be produced, but by the time it was delivered on 15 October this first plan had been dropped. Before that, however, and after all the information requested in Forbes' letter of 23 August had been supplied, a meeting was convened at the Admiralty for 19 September.

Prior to the meeting, Admiral Forbes prepared a discussion document which put a little flesh on the bones of his original remarks and incorporated the information he had requested from the directors of combined operations and Naval Intelligence. None had been requested of the RAF, but the proposed air diversion was now described as "an air attack on St Nazaire to be delivered at ?0430 [sic] if on 21 October [the raid was still planned to take place at first light], to drive the enemy to ground during the carrier's final approach and during the passage of the Eurekas[2] to the shore. Very careful timing is essential." With men storming ashore it would have to be very careful indeed.

The meeting duly took place at the Admiralty with Admiral A.J. Power, assistant chief of the naval staff (ACNS), in the chair and produced a four-page report which included

---

[2] Shallow draft boats for landing troops in amphibious assaults, designed by Andrew Jackson Higgins.

the observation that "it should be possible for Bomber Command to arrange a heavy-scale bombing attack on St Nazaire at a critical time during the operation, and aircraft might well be used to confuse the enemy's RDF cover". No RAF officer was present at the meeting and Bomber Command had yet to be consulted.

In forwarding the report of the meeting to the Admiralty, Admiral Power noted the main opinions expressed which were at odds with those of the commander-in-chief. Of importance to the future involvement of the RAF in the operation was that it was felt to be almost impossible to envisage it taking place in daylight. The operation was not dead yet, however, and C-in-C Plymouth was to be asked to work out a detailed plan based on the findings of the meeting.

Admiral Forbes' reply was sent on 15 October in terms that were far from enthusiastic. He thought the plan had a negligible chance of achieving surprise, entailed the sacrifice of the landing party and endangered valuable ships for a small chance of success. "I do not feel that the importance of the operation is sufficient to justify this risk." This assessment did not convince the director of plans, Captain Charles Lambe, but as C-in-C Plymouth would be the flag officer responsible for seeing the operation through and was clearly not totally committed to it, he bowed to the inevitable and recommended that all planning should cease. Director of operations agreed, but crucially kept the flame alive by suggesting it be referred to the new director at combined operations, Lord Mountbatten. Admiral Power also agreed, writing on the 25th, "There is much under consideration at the moment, but the project is so important that the ACO[3] should be asked to study the matter at his earliest convenience", and it was duly referred thither on 28 October. From now on, the planning of the operation would cease to be a purely naval preserve and the army and the RAF would now have a seat at the table.

Churchill had recently appointed Lord Louis Mountbatten to the post of director of combined operations in succession to Admiral Keyes, and he had taken up his appointment the previous day. Churchill's injunction to Mountbatten was to "be offensive" and the new director, shortly to be re-designated chief of combined operations (CCO), quickly gathered around him a group of like-minded individuals. Appointing an advisor from each of the three services he chose Captain John Hughes-Hallett, RN, from the Royal Navy and Brigadier J.C. Haydon, DSO MC, from the army and from the Royal Air Force came an officer, in the person of Group Captain A.H. Willetts, of whom we shall see a great deal as the plans for the raid on St Nazaire were developed.

Mountbatten's earliest convenience, it would appear, was early February 1942. Churchill had written his memo on Tirpitz to the Chiefs on 25 January 1942 and when at a meeting the following day with the First Lord of the Admiralty, Sir Dudley Pound, he again visited the subject it was quite clear that the spectre of this great ship would haunt his thinking for as long as the Normandie Dock was available to it. Only the disablement of this facility would exorcise the ghost.

The next day, the 27th, Captain Charles Lambe, the deputy director of plans who had recommended the abandonment of planning for the raid back in October, had luncheon with Mountbatten, to whom the baton had been passed at that time. No doubt Lambe was surprised that nothing had been done and prodded Mountbatten, an old friend, into action for Mountbatten put his naval advisor on to the job without further delay and his outline

---

[3] Advisor on Combined Operations, i.e. Mountbatten, soon to be redesignated director, then chief..

plan was sent to the vice-chief of the naval staff on 7 February.

Now that Royal Air Force officers were to be involved in the planning for the operation it is an opportune time to meet them. In his position as AACO, Group Captain Willetts would be in an invidious position. With no air force commander appointed he would find himself with responsibility but no power, acting only as an intermediary with Headquarters, Bomber Command.

Alfred Henry Willetts was born at Southwark on 8 May 1904 and passed through the RAF Cadet College at Cranwell to be commissioned as a pilot officer on 16 May 1925. At the outbreak of war he had reached the rank of squadron leader and on 1 March 1940 was promoted wing commander. On 5 November 1941, by then an acting group captain, he was appointed Assistant Advisor Combined Operations (Air)

Willetts, known to his friends as 'Fred', was fair of complexion and somewhat slight of stature and although having a reserved demeanour was nevertheless charming and very able. A keen and dedicated pilot, having taken over as base commander at RAF Oakington, five miles north-west of Cambridge later in the war, the lure of flying nearly proved fatal. He was to fly safely on the raids on both Vaagso and St Nazaire, but on the night of 24 August 1943, he was not so lucky. Going along for the ride, he flew in a 7 Squadron Lancaster of Pathfinder Force piloted by Squadron Leader Charles Lofthouse, who later recalled that they were early over Berlin and were losing a couple of minutes in a turn when they were hit. The aircraft caught fire and could not be controlled. Giving the order to bale out Lofthouse remembered that Willetts "was out through the nose escape hatch like a rat out of a trap", followed by the rest of the crew.

Spending the rest of the war in captivity Willetts was senior British officer at Stalag Luft III during the successful 'Wooden Horse' escape and later at Oflag 64, Moosburg, when it was relieved by the Americans on 29 April 1945. He retired from the RAF on 24 January 1946, retaining the rank of group captain and he died in Mallorca in July 1971. For his part in organising the air plan for the Vaagso raid he had been awarded the Distinguished Service Order. The citation read, "Group Captain Willetts flew in the leading Hampden bomber and much of the success which attended the operation may be attributed to his skill and devotion to duty". He was clearly the right man to steer through the RAF's contribution to Operation Chariot.

Wing Commander Charles Elworthy was on the air staff responsible for operations at HQ Bomber Command. Born in New Zealand and educated at Marlborough College and Trinity College, Cambridge, he was called to the Bar at Lincoln's Inn in 1933 and joined the reserve of air force officers. Granted a commission in the Auxiliary Air Force in January 1935, he advanced to a permanent commission in the Royal Air Force in March 1936.

At the beginning of World War II, Elworthy was involved in a training role. By April 1940, now a squadron leader, he became chief flying instructor with 13 Officer Training Unit. Joining 82 Squadron as a flight commander in August 1940, he became the squadron's commanding officer the following December. Early 1941 saw him in the thick of the action. He was awarded an Air Force Cross (1 January 1941), a Distinguished Flying Cross (7 March 1941) and a Distinguished Service Order (22 April 1941), the last for attacking and setting on fire an enemy tanker.

In May 1941, Elworthy embarked on a series of staff appointments and in October that year, as a wing commander, he transferred to Headquarters, Bomber Command where he would be intimately involved in the planning for Operation Chariot. He had already established a reputation as a most able commander, and his earlier training as a barrister undoubtedly helped him to become a brilliant staff officer as well. Elworthy would go on to hold the post of chief of the air staff and later, as a marshal of the Royal Air Force, become chief of the defence staff. Following retirement from the RAF in April 1971, he held a number of high profile appointments, including Constable and Governor of Windsor Castle and Lord Lieutenant of Greater London. Created Baron Elworthy in 1972 and a Knight of the Garter in 1977, he later returned to his native New Zealand where he died in April 1993.

Senior air staff officer (SASO) at HQ Bomber Command, Air Vice-Marshal Robert 'Bob' Saundby was born in Birmingham in April 1896. He left King Edward's School in 1913, but it would be three years before he took up flying. He first worked for the London and North Western Railway before joining the Royal Warwickshire Regiment Territorial Force as a private soldier when war broke out in 1914. He trained as an officer and, on being commissioned, spent six months in the front line before transferring to the Royal Flying Corps in January 1916.

Having gained his wings he embarked on a distinguished flying career, claiming five victories and officially qualifying as an 'ace'. He was also present in the action in which the Red Baron shot down and killed Major Lanoe Hawker, VC. Following a shared victory in June 1917, he was awarded a Military Cross. Having joined the newly-formed Royal Air Force in 1918, Saundby progressed slowly through the ranks and spent three years in Iraq where he flew as co-pilot to Arthur Harris, then a squadron leader. Whilst in Iraq he was awarded a DFC.

Back in England he was posted to RAF Worthy Down as a flight commander in 58 Squadron, serving again with Arthur Harris, now a wing commander and commanding the squadron. Another officer at Worthy Down at that time who was also destined for high office was Wing Commander Charles Portal, then commanding 7 Squadron.

In November 1940 Saundby became senior air staff officer (SASO) at Headquarters, Bomber Command where later he served again under Arthur Harris. It is here that we shall see him closely involved in the planning for Operation Chariot.

Within a year of the end of World War II Saundby had been retired from the RAF on medical grounds. Knighted in January 1944, he held an MC, DFC and AFC, together with several foreign decorations. He was four times mentioned in despatches. In retirement he lived in Hampshire, where he died in September 1971.

On 31 January 1942, Mountbatten had asked his naval advisor, Captain John Hughes-Hallett, to draft the plan which had now been sent to the vice-chief of the naval staff. Compared to the plan prepared and subsequently dropped in 1941 this one contained a more credible method for transporting the troops and was now to be a night-time operation. No fighter cover would therefore be needed and the sole requirement for RAF support in the raid itself would be a diversionary bombing raid, although Mountbatten was still "consulting with my air commodore on this aspect" and assured the VCNS that it would not be overlooked.

A meeting was held at Combined Operations Headquarters (COHQ) on 19 February 1942, at which Group Captain Willetts was the only RAF officer present, although Wing Commander the Marquis of Casa Maury attended in his capacity as senior intelligence officer at Combined Operations. Casa Maury had a fat file of information on St Nazaire, gleaned mainly from RAF bombing raids and reconnaissance by the PRU, but also including contributions from SOE and the Resistance. The file was to prove a gold mine. It was agreed that Brigadier Haydon, the military advisor to Combined Operations (MACO), and Group Captain Willetts would discuss the diversion plan following the meeting.

In his draft plan, which Mountbatten sent to the chiefs of staff on 7 February, Hughes-Hallett included, under forces required, "units from Bomber Command as requisite to carry out a diversionary raid" and later added:

> "An essential feature of the plan is that a heavy air raid should be carried out on the dock area during the last phase of the approach and throughout the operation. The objective of this raid will start by being the same area as that in which the demolitions are to be carried out, and will shift to an adjacent area before the landings take place."

The basics of the RAF raid itself had been set out and would change only in the details. However, there would be much discussion and some acrimony, at both COHQ and HQ Bomber Command, before the final operation order was agreed.

When sending the plan to vice-chief of the naval staff, Mountbatten covered his delay – he had been instructed the previous October – with a plea that he had not been shown the docket as he was "submerged in the work of taking over and reorganisation". As the raid now planned to use the high spring tides that occurred in March and April, the delay caused no damage, but a hectic period of activity would now ensue to meet the deadline.

Brigadier Haydon and Group Captain Willetts met, as agreed, to discuss the bombing diversion and, following a conversation with Wing Commander Elworthy at Bomber Command, Willetts received the first suggested scale of support and diversion. Twenty-five bombers were to attack the dockyards with high explosive bombs from Z-1h30m to Z-15m (Z had yet to be identified). The attack was then to switch to the town at Z-15m when thirty-six bombers would drop 250-lb incendiaries until Z+2h. The 250-lb incendiary was felt to be more suitable as, this being a diversion, they put up a better pyrotechnic display and made more noise than the 4-lb bomb. Also, compared with high-explosive bombs they would cause fewer casualties. This level of bombing would go through several transformations before being finalised.

A second meeting was convened at COHQ on 26 February at which Mountbatten was able to announce the approval of the chiefs of staff for the operation. Among those attending this meeting were an unwitting Commander R.E.D. Ryder who arrived late, but just in time to hear Mountbatten announce that he would be the naval force commander, and Lieutenant Colonel Charles Newman, of the Essex Regiment and 2 Commando, who had been appointed military force commander and who was already privy to the plan. Also present was Admiral Forbes, C-in-C Plymouth, who would be in charge of the whole operation. Having been the cause of dropping the earlier plans in 1941 he now gave this new outline plan his approval. This meeting was notable for the RAF in that it spelt out the convoluted arrangements for control of their contribution.

    11. It was agreed that no RAF force commander was
    necessary, and that C-in-C Plymouth, naval force commander
    and military force commander should deal with the AACO,

Group Captain A.H. Willetts, who in turn would deal direct
with AOC in C Bomber Command. C-in-C Plymouth would deal
direct with 10 Group in the matter of fighter cover, but
Group Captain Willetts stated that he would also approach
Fighter Command with a view to obtaining special long-
range fighter cover.

This was the invidious position into which Willetts was placed, but with several groups and many squadrons involved from widespread airfields he had no force as such to command. Indeed, the make-up for the RAF contribution would not be finally determined until twenty-four hours before Chariot Force sailed from Falmouth. The crews to fly the sorties would be those who were on duty at the time. Nevertheless, as we shall see, in the aftermath of Chariot the lack of a force commander for the RAF was considered to have been a mistake and such a position would be filled in future operations.

The Chariot committee met again at COHQ on 3 March when Willetts was not present but he sent his assistant, Squadron Leader Keeling. Also present was Wing Commander J.W. Tomes representing the Department of Plans at the Air Ministry. Ryder and Newman presented their outline plan and agreed to contact Willetts regarding the air cooperation. Keeling outlined the air plan and then received from Newman a request that low-flying aircraft should operate over the harbour for fifteen minutes either side of 'Z' hour. This request appears quite impractical. Although Beaufighters had the range to reach St Nazaire, with naval forces landing troops below they could have done more harm than good. Fighter cover had been arranged at Vaagso but that had been a daylight operation as would have been the raid that was planned for St Nazaire in 1941. However, on 19 March, C-in-C Plymouth requested a squadron of Beaufighters be placed under the orders of Air Officer Commanding 19 Group, Coastal Command and this was done, but nothing more was heard of Newman's suggestion. In the event, the Beaufighters would be used to cover the withdrawal of the survivors of the action.

A last meeting was held in Plymouth on 10 March and was a purely naval affair although a suggestion was put forward for an air raid on St Nazaire the night before Chariot. It was felt this would keep the defenders out of their beds, making them less alert during the diversionary raid the following night. At this time, Chariot was due to take place on the night of 28/29 March and Ryder's decision to sail a day early would have led to the cancellation of any air raid that had been planned in this respect. As it happened, a raid by twenty-seven Whitleys did take place on the night of 25/26 March, during Ryder's first night at sea, in which one aircraft was lost. Of the crew of six, only two would survive, one of whom, the Australian rear gunner Alister Currie, we shall meet later in our story.

The planning meetings were now at an end and the Combined Plan (Short title: CHAR ONE)[4], although itself undated, was circulated on 16 March. Apart from the addition of four torpedo-carrying MLs of the 7th Flotilla to add some teeth to the force and of some refinements to the timing of the fuses to detonate the charge in *Campbeltown*, no alterations to this concise document would be made. However, the detail of the RAF raid, to be planned by the RAF themselves, would endure several metamorphoses. It was set out in outline in paragraph 46:

---

[4] The full text of the combined plan can be found at Appendix 2.

OUTLINE AIR SUPPORT PLAN

46.   (a) The critical time is from 0100-0300 hours,
with the attack at its heaviest scale between 0100
and 0200 hours while the Force is approaching the
objective and when the troops are first ashore.

(b) From 2330-0045 hrs: Heavy bombs
                          M.P.I. on the Town

(c) From 0100-0300 hrs: Maximum number of sorties
                          using light bombs and
                          incendiaries. M.P.I. on
                          the Town (and NOT the
                          Dock area.)

(d) From 0300 hrs for the remaining hours of
darkness; small raids to prevent the sounding of
the ALL CLEAR. MPI in dock area.

(e) A PRU to be flown at the latest moment prior
to the operation in order to ascertain position
of shipping in the harbour, etc. These photographs
to be given to the Force Commanders before sailing.

The aim was stated as distracting attention from the main assault forces, disorganising local defences and delaying repairs until the fall of the tide.

The flight by a PRU Spitfire from St Eval would return with photographic evidence of activity in St Nazaire which had consequences for the raiders. These consequences we shall see as the operation unfolds. For now we must look at the tortuous haggling which took place at Bomber Command before the final level of bombing would be confirmed in Bomber Command Operation Order No. 141, issued as late as 25 March. A tentative suggestion had already been put forward by the Ops 1(b) at Bomber Command, Wing Commander Elworthy. On 18 March he sent a minute to the SASO:

'SASO

At enclosure 3B is CCO'S plan for Operation "CHARIOT". The outline Air Plan is detailed in para. 46.

2.   The distance between St Nazaire and the English Coast
        is approximately 230 miles. Nautical twilight[5] on the
        material dates will be 0530 BST. The last aircraft
        should therefore leave the target area at 0400 hrs.
3.   The bombing required then falls into three phases:
        (a) 2330–0045 Medium-scale attack with heavy bombs.
        (b) 0100–0300 Heavy-scale attack with light bombs & incendiaries.
        (c) 0300–0400 Light-scale attack on dock area.
4.   If full cooperation is agreed, I would suggest that
        a force of about 100 aircraft is necessary, divided
        into forces of thirty, sixty and ten respectively for the three waves.
5.   The nights chosen for the operation are during the full

---

[5] Nautical twilight occurs when the geometrical centre of the sun is between 6 degrees and 12 degrees below the horizon.

*moon period but cloud conditions may nevertheless make
accurate identification and bombing of the town to the
exclusion of the docks, a difficult matter. G/C Willetts
appreciates this but has said that the landing force would
sooner risk being hit by one of our own bombs than do
without the bombing diversion.*

6.   *I presume we shall need authority from the Air Ministry
before we can lay on an incendiary attack on the town
of St Nazaire.*

7.   *Perhaps SOE might be able to assist with a beacon
in the town to act as an aiming point.*

S.C. Elworthy,
Ops.

18/3/42
1(b)'

This was a well-considered attempt to put some flesh on to the skeleton of the diversionary bombing attack and carried forward the outline plan that had been floated by Willetts after his meeting with Brigadier Haydon. It now contained proposals for three phases of bombing with a consequent increase in bomber numbers to 100 and it still countenanced the bombing of the town, whilst acknowledging the necessity for permission from above to do so. But cold water was about to be poured on the plan from on high. Adding a minute in reply later the same day, SASO wrote:

Ops 1(b)
*I do not agree that such a heavy scale of attack is needed. We do not want
to devastate the town of St Nazaire and kill lots of Frenchmen. The object
is to create a diversion from 2330 hrs to 0400 hrs. For this we want about
twenty Whitleys spaced out to cover the period, hanging around overhead
dropping the occasional bomb. Please show this to the C-in-C.*

R. Saundby
SASO

18/3/42

Worse was to come, and from a greater height, in the shape of the C-in-C, Bomber Command, himself – Air Chief Marshal Sir Arthur 'Bomber' Harris – who added, 'I agree. ATH 19/3'.

This could well be considered a surprising position for a man who earned his soubriquet by his conviction that the war could be won by the bomber alone and his determination to send them 1,000 at a time over Germany. However, other considerations filled his mind at this time, namely to prove his 'firestorm' theory in a raid planned for Lübeck by 200 aircraft on the night following the raid on St Nazaire. The four Wellington squadrons which sent crews to St Nazaire would also send twenty-six crews to Lübeck, six of them flying both raids.

Saundby followed up his cutting minute of 18 March with a memo to the CCO on the 22nd. Referring to CHAR ONE and to further discussions with Willetts, he set out the proposed level of bombing for the three phases as fifteen, ten and ten respectively. This was a far cry from the 100 proposed by Elworthy and derisory compared with the figure of 350 which had been floated early in the planning process, although it is difficult to imagine the effect that so many aircraft flying around over an area measuring no more than one mile long and a quarter mile wide would have.

Saundby's letter contained other notable changes. Not only had the numbers been drastically reduced but the targets had been altered too. Phase one was now to be the docks but, no doubt reflecting Saundby's statement that we did not want to "kill lots of Frenchmen", phase two was to be on the Bassin de Penhoët with three reverting to the docks. In truth, rather than any feelings of Saundby, this was the result of official Cabinet policy, of which he would undoubtedly have been aware, that there was to be no bombing of French civilians.

Also in this letter we begin to see the provisos that would seriously limit the scope of the bombers over St Nazaire. No flares were to be dropped by any of the aircraft and each was to drop their bombs singly. The writing was beginning to appear on the wall for the bombing raid and more was to come. It is no wonder that Lieutenant Colonel Newman was expressing his doubts that the bombing would ever take place. Certainly procedures were to be put in place should that transpire to be the case, but this was more against the weather conditions making it impossible.

Time was now getting short and on the 24th Mountbatten attended a meeting of the chiefs of staff committee at which it was agreed that Operation Chariot should not be undertaken unless the diversionary bombing raid could be carried out. It was a day of fevered activity in which Mountbatten had been briefed by both his military and air advisors. Willetts pointed out that the original plan had been to use all available Whitley aircraft. At that time this numbered seventy, but some had since been transferred to Coastal Command leaving thirty-five now scheduled to take part. With the town out of bounds, Willetts suggested a heavy air raid on the dockyard by thirty aircraft in phase one (0000-0130), a light raid by fifteen aircraft on the dockyard away from the commando activity below in phase two (0130-0330), and a lighter raid by five aircraft over the whole of the dockyard area in phase three (0330-0400). This was an increase to fifty aircraft and Willetts was realistic enough to suggest squeezing this concession out of Bomber Command before putting it to the chiefs of staff.

Brigadier Haydon took this brief to Mountbatten with the plea that he held out for that as a minimum effort. The object was to draw people away from the docks and the heavier the raid the better. The possibility of bombing the town was still being pursued although Willetts had already admitted that "it is doubtful if this change of Cabinet policy can be achieved in the time still available". Although Haydon recommended that they hold to their original request, it was not to be.

There was one further decision to be made. What action was to be taken in the event of a reduced or cancelled bombing attack? Mountbatten consulted with Harris, AOC-in-C Bomber Command, who agreed to draw up a 'bad weather' programme. This would entail part of the bomber force dispersing to southern airfields more likely to be free of fog than their northern bases so that some, at least, of the aircraft would be able to fly. The suggested airfields were Boscombe Down, Exeter, Chivenor and St Eval, but in the event Pershore, in Worcestershire, and Stanton Harcourt, in Oxfordshire were used. It was further agreed that a final decision regarding a reduced or cancelled attack would be taken at 1800 hours on the day of the assault. By that time Chariot Force would have been at sea for more than twenty-eight hours and only seven and a half from their target. In the event of there being less than a full attack the decision to proceed or not would be left to the force commander, Bob Ryder, based on whether or not the flotilla had been sighted. Ryder, however, seemed determined to see the operation through, a determination exceeded only by that of Newman whose commandos had trained for too many actions that were cancelled and they were not going to be denied again.

There were now only two days to go and the next day, the 25th, Bomber Command Operation Order No. 141 was issued. This gave in detail how the outline plan contained in paragraph 46 of CHAR ONE would be put into operation, but since the issue of that outline plan, the existence of the important stricture to all bombing operations over France had made alterations inevitable. The original proposal was that phases one and two would be on the town, phase two being a maximum effort commencing at 0100. However, on 24 March, Willetts sent a memo to the CCO pointing out that "it is evident that the War Cabinet's recent rulings to Bomber Command on the bombing of targets in France are so clear that nothing short of a Cabinet decision could permit Bomber Command to accept the bombing of this town", going on to express his doubt that "this change of Cabinet policy can be achieved in the short time now available".

When the final plan was set out Willetts' suggestions were broadly adopted. The entire raid was to be on areas of the dockyard but with phases one and two on the docks and phase three on a part of the dockyard away from the area of operations on land. There were changes in timing as well, for at 0130 and for an anticipated two hours following, the docks would be teeming with commandos. Thus phase two was to cease at 0120. Also the raid was to start half an hour earlier at 2330 and continue until 0400. These amendments were adopted and set out in paragraph 8 of the Bomber Command Operation Order which also contained a pleasant surprise. In response to the entreaties of Mountbatten, Haydon and Willetts, the number of aircraft employed was now sixty. Although still only thirty-five of these were Whitleys, Bomber Command had added twenty-five Wellingtons from 1 Group and it was these that were to fly from the forward bases.

Plan of Attack[6]

8.   The bombing attack will be divided into three phases:

    (i)   Phase One

                    Target . . . . Target A
                    Time over target 2330–0030
                    Number of aircraft . . . 10 (4 Group)

    (ii)   Phase Two

                    Target . . . . Target A
                    Time over target 0030–0120
                    Number of aircraft . . . 25 (4 Group)

    iii)   Phase Three

                    Target . . . . Target B
                    Time over target . . . . 0120–0400.

---

[6] The identity of Targets A and B would be revealed in the executive order issued on 27 March — see Chapter 7.

There was, though, to be a sting in the tail. To the provisos we have already seen, which would limit the ability of the bombers to operate successfully, was added another which, on the night, would virtually wipe out that ability completely. Whilst allowing the pilots the initiative to attack at the best height to achieve accuracy in the light of the weather conditions which might prevail, the operation order strictly forbade them from flying below 6,000 feet. This was to have the effect of emasculating the entire bomber support plan.

It had been a tortuous process and is set out in the following table which summarises the changes through which the bombing plan progressed:

CHAR ONE 16 March	2330 - 0045 Town	0100 - 0300 Town NOT Docks	0300 - daylight Dock
Saundby 22 March	2359 - 0115 Docks 15 aircraft	0130 - 0300 Bassin de Penhoët 10 aircraft	0300 - 0400 Docks 10 aircraft
Willetts 24 March	0000 - 0130 Dockyard 30 aircraft	0130 - 0330 Dockyard (away from target) 15 aircraft	0330 - 0400 Whole Dockyard 5 aircraft
BC Op Order 141 25 March	2330 - 0030 Docks 10 aircraft	0030 - 0120 Docks 25 aircraft	0120 - 0400 Bassin de Penhoët 25 aircraft

CHAR ONE had not specified the weight or direction of attack – that had been left to the RAF – and it can be seen how this varied right up until 25 March, the day before Chariot Force set sail from Falmouth. What is confusing is the terminology used to identify the targets. 'Town' is used only in CHAR ONE and was dropped in deference to the Cabinet instruction not to bomb civilians, while it also uses 'Dock' in the singular which could be taken to refer to the Normandie Dock itself.

Saundby's plan uses the same terms as the Bomber Command Operation Order, although in an amended sequence, whilst Willetts employs the word 'Dockyard' to describe three quite different targets. In its instruction to switch to the ship-building yards at the northern end of the Bassin de Penhoët for phase three, it is clear that the word 'Docks' in the Bomber Command Operation Order refers to the area of operations of the commandos between the Southern Entrance and Bridge M. (See plan on page 99)

For better or for worse the die was cast, but before we look at the forces that will be entrusted with carrying out the order and the effect the provisos were to have on the raid itself we should look at the factors that, in the light of bombing accuracy pertaining at this time in the war, made them necessary.

Pinpoint-bombing in the early years of the war was largely aspirational and the results of the Butt Report, initiated by Lord Cherwell, the chief scientific officer to the Cabinet, and circulated in August 1941, brought this fact into stark relief. Prior to this, the measure of the success of bombing sorties relied solely on the reports of the crews on their return. They were to be rudely disabused.

By 1941 cameras had been fitted under bombers, designed to take point-of-aim photographs. Those taken in night raids during June and July that year were analysed to produce the report. Of the aircraft recorded as having attacked the target, only one in three bombed within five miles of it. Broken down, the figures showed that over French ports it was two in three, over Germany it was one in four and over the Ruhr, one in ten. Moonlight was a factor, too, for whilst in a full moon the proportion was two in five, in a new moon it was one in fifteen. Even worse, these figures apply only to those planes recorded as having reached the target. If those planes which did not, through navigational error or equipment failure, weather or enemy action, reach the target at all were included, the figure for all sorties was less than one in twenty.

Happily, by early 1942, electronic navigational systems such as GEE and Oboe were coming into use. The first successful raid in which a single plane carried GEE was over Essen on the night of 8/9 March 1942. The first successful mass raid with the equipment was on Cologne on the night of 13/14 March 1942. Several of the planes which flew to Cologne also flew to St Nazaire on 27/28 March in support of Chariot. It seems that electronic assistance had arrived just in time.

It is easy, therefore, to have sympathy with the planners who set the provisos that the bombs should be dropped singly on a separate run and only when the target can be seen. The dockyard area which formed the target for phase one of the bombing support was as small as 1,600 yards long and 400 yards wide and was to be attacked until the very moment the commandos were to storm ashore. There was zero tolerance on the mean point of impact, let alone five miles. Weather conditions on the night would only exacerbate the problem.

CHAPTER 2

BOMBER COMMAND

'I think it is well also for the man in the street to realise
that there is no power on earth that can protect him
from being bombed. Whatever people may tell him, the
bomber will always get through.'

Stanley Baldwin – A Fear for the Future – 1932

Although there had been a powered flight in this country in 1908 by Samuel Cody, it was not until the following year with the crossing of the Channel by Louis Blériot, that excitement began to mount over the potenital of this new development in transport and in warfare. As a military asset it was in the field of reconnaissance that these heavier-than-air machines were first envisaged to have their future, replacing the balloons that had up to that time, been employed for looking over the enemy's fence. Originally unarmed, they flew their missions behind the front lines photographing strategic installations and dispositions, but came the day when the Germans also developed their own capability and flew into our backyard. To combat this intrusion into each other's airspace the pilots began to arm themselves with revolvers and then rifles to shoot down their opposite numbers. These arms were soon replaced with portable Lewis guns and then fixed machine guns firing through the propellers and thus was born the concept of the fighter.

In 1915, a certain lieutenant colonel by the name of Hugh Trenchard, who was to become known as the 'Father of the Royal Air Force', was appointed to command the Royal Flying Corps and he enthusiastically embraced this new development in warfare, pressing for faster, stronger planes with extended range, all based on the thought that improved performance would enable an additional role for the airplane, that of carrying bombs to drop on the enemy. Thus was born the bomber.

With the war virtually static in the trenches and not going anywhere very fast, this new ability to get behind the enemy lines and operate further afield was considered a priceless weapon for attacking military targets. However, between May and July 1917, this extension of the conflict took a sinister turn when German bombers launched attacks on towns in the south-east of England, killing and injuring significant numbers of civilians. It was the effect on the morale of a war-weary public that perhaps most exercised the politicians and they quickly had to review their strategy. Fighters would have to be deployed to oppose the bombers and towns would have to be encircled by anti-aircraft emplacements to protect them.

It was perhaps inevitable that a committee, beloved of politicians everywhere, would be formed to report on this flagrant breach of military convention and so it was, consisting, in reality, of Lloyd George and General Smuts, assisted by advisors from the services. The subsequent report recognised that, even in the current conflict the battle would soon be carried, through air power, well behind the front lines. Certainly it could not have foreseen how the bomber, some twenty years later, would be used in another European war to lay waste whole cities. Needless to say, this was not a realisation that found resonance with the admirals and generals upon whose traditional roles this was intruding. Most far reaching consequence of all, though, was that the report produced by Smuts was the precursor of the Royal Air Force, formed on 1 April 1918. The growth of this force was such that by the end of World War I it boasted an establishment greater than that with which the army had started it.

Having proved beyond doubt its worth, no sooner was the Armistice signed than this fledgling air force was all but dismantled. As with governments before, and certainly since, times of peace would always lead to severe contraction in the budgets of the armed forces. Wars were costly affairs and a population which had suffered great hardship through them was naturally resistant to continued spending on armaments. As far as the RAF was concerned it even had to fight a rear-guard action simply to retain its share of the reduced budget, Trenchard having to use all his guile and experience to keep the force in existence. The burden of his argument was that the air force had ceased to be an adjunct to the army and navy and was now an independent strategic power in its own right, operations with the army or navy being only subsidiary or diversionary, the latter being the role in which Bomber Command would send planes to St Nazaire. The full concept of combined operations was, however, still well in the future.

While these arguments were pursued by the respective arms of the forces, each standing their own corner, the politicians, sensitive both to the fears of the population and to the power of the bomber to cause devastation, turned their minds to the limitation of future targets. In 1923, the Hague Rules of Aerial Warfare were proposed, defining military targets as not only the forces themselves but also the factories and institutions that supplied and sustained them. In the event, the rules were never ratified. A further attempt to restrict the ambit of air warfare was made at Geneva at a disarmament conference under the auspices of the League of Nations. It was not a success, Germany's withdrawal betraying its determination to re-arm.

These failures to find agreement on the subject of aerial bombardment and Germany's transparent position on re-armament brought great benefits to the Royal Air Force cause that no amount of passionate argument by Trenchard could have achieved. The army's proportion of the defence budget had been slowly whittled away until by 1934 it had been halved, while by 1938 that of the RAF had risen to 40%, of which sum priority spending was given to the bomber.

Initially the Royal Air Force had been organised along the same lines as the Luftwaffe, by area, with the formation in 1919 of Northern and Southern Commands and Coastal Area and in April 1920, the amalgamation of Northern and Southern Commands into Inland Area. In a move away from the geographical concept, in 1936 the organisation had been changed to one based on function and four separate commands were created – Fighter, Bomber, Coastal (which we shall meet in the next chapter) and Training.

With the realisation that Germany was planning for war an expansion scheme was approved by the Cabinet in 1934 and as a result of this, shortly after its formation, Bomber Command, initially conceived as a daylight operating force, received their first machines designed to carry out that function. They were the Wellington and the Whitley, both of which would fly on the diversionary raid to St Nazaire, and the Hampden and all were twin-engine monoplanes. Although not the only aircraft developed at this time it was essentially these three which would form the backbone of the bomber offensive as the RAF entered the Second World War.

As early as 1932 the concept of daylight bombing was endowed with a false sense of security when, in a speech in the House of Commons, Prime Minister Baldwin used a phrase that would become a mantra for air operations – "the bomber will always get through". The pernicious worm of this belief was to be painfully discovered for it would infiltrate tactical thought to the highest level, with no less a personage than Arthur Harris, then an air vice-marshal and commander-in-chief, 5 Group, being quoted as saying, "as long as three bombers are in company in daylight, the pilots considered themselves capable of taking on anything".

The early months of the war, despite the evidence of their own experience, gleaned from unescorted sorties against German naval targets, found commanders drawing the wrong conclusions – the bombers did not maintain formation; the flak was too heavy – anything but admit that defence by fighter escort was a pre-requisite of such incursions. Even the proposed solution to combat the flak was flawed as to mount their attacks above the effective range of 10,000 feet made hitting the small target presented by a ship, already difficult, virtually impossible. At that stage of the war bomb aiming was far from a precise science. Some useful alterations were, however, made to the aircraft. Too prone to catch fire when hit, the fuel tanks were now made self-sealing, and the limitation of the rear turret, which would not traverse a full 180°, was addressed by the addition of beam guns.

Following the realisation in 1933 that Germany was re-arming, expansion of the RAF had become essential. Government policy had been centred round the so-called 'Ten-Year Rule', an assessment that no war would be fought in the next ten years. This rule was observed on a rolling year-by-year basis so that each year that passed without the obvious prospect of future war, the ten years was extended another year forward. When the certainty of war in Europe loomed there would not, regrettably, be ten years in which to prepare for it.

The scheme approved by the Cabinet in 1934 was detailed as Expansion Scheme A and included the provision of forty-one bomber squadrons. It was succeeded by seven further schemes, the last being Scheme M in November 1938. Each scheme was approved before its predecessor had been completed and thus they were really updates of the original. The direction of these revisions was not only in numbers but also in machines as the changing nature of conflict became apparent and was manifest in a gradual drift away from light bombers – twenty-five of the forty-one squadrons in Scheme A would be equipped with light bombers while in Scheme M all 85 squadrons proposed would have heavy bombers.

The expansion of the RAF would not be sufficient if confined to aircraft alone and so a parallel programme of extended airfield construction and aircrew training was also implemented. A recruiting poster of the time proclaimed, 'Every new plane needs a pilot'. A building programme of 100 new airfields was set in train in 1935 and continued right up until the outbreak of war. The decimation of the RAF following the Armistice had seen the number of airfields then in existence reduced from 300 to a mere twenty-seven by 1924. Even when war was declared, Bomber Command had only twenty-four airfields from which to operate and none of these had concrete runways. Inclement weather could seriously hamper operations from grass fields, especially since, as we have seen, the trend was for bigger and heavier machines and the expansion schemes therefore included not only the building of the new but also the upgrading of the existing and in respect of accommodation and facilities as well as of runways.

The airfields now under construction were to incorporate much improved design features, both for men and machines. Larger hangars were required for the larger planes and to protect against mass destruction in the event of an air raid dispersal pans were spread at intervals around the perimeter, each to accommodate but one machine. Large civilian firms were contracted to carry out the work which continued apace up to and well after the war had started and at one period in 1942 a new airfield was being commissioned every three days.

That the threat of war was from Germany dictated on a geographical basis the sites on which the airfields should be constructed. They should be within flying time of their intended targets and yet sufficiently removed from the vulnerable south-east to be beyond the range of enemy fighters. The area chosen, therefore, was in the east of central England, mainly in Yorkshire and Lincolnshire but also some in other counties such as Cambridgeshire, Oxfordshire and Nottinghamshire. The bombing raid on St Nazaire on 27/28 March 1942 would be flown by squadrons based, with one exception, in Yorkshire, the exception being in Lincolnshire.

It was an enduring feature of RAF aircrew that all were volunteers and in the early days they had been young men approaching their mid-twenties who lived for flying and could thus indulge their passion. As the war rolled on and losses began to take their toll that average fell to nearer twenty-one and although all were still volunteers their motivation was more of patriotism and a desire to get to grips with the enemy and win the war.

When it came to training new aircrew it soon became apparent, once war was declared, that it could not be carried out in the UK. The airfields were now operational and thus fully occupied and employed. They were also subject to possible bombing attack and the vagaries of the British climate. The solution, encompassed in the British Commonwealth Air Training Plan, signed on 17 December 1939, by the governments of Britain, Canada, Australia and New Zealand, was to give elementary training in the volunteers' home country before sending them to Canada for advanced courses. The great open spaces of Canada were ideal for flying training, especially for navigators, and the weather was ideal. Not least, Canada was far removed from the regular attentions of the Luftwaffe.

Not only did Commonwealth aircrew train in this way, but those of many other countries who were allies in the cause against a common enemy took advantage of the facility. Whole squadrons from the Commonwealth and other countries would fly in the war but individual aircrew of many nationalities would be found amongst the crews of almost every RAF squadron. Operation Chariot would be supported by Australian, Canadian and Polish squadrons.

It was inevitable that those men who would rise to high command in the RAF would have been engaged as soldiers and progressed through transfer to the RFC in World War I and to the RAF on its formation in April 1918. Indeed it was an accusation that was sometimes levelled against them that they still thought like soldiers. A few high-ranking RAF officers had also risen through the Royal Naval Air Service (RNAS).

The first commander-in-chief of Bomber Command, appointed in 1937 and still in post when war broke out in 1939, was Sir Edgar Ludlow-Hewitt. He had been commissioned from Sandhurst into the Royal Irish Regiment and had transferred into the RFC in August 1914. Not an immediately approachable man, but widely respected by his subordinates, he came to Bomber Command after several inter-war staff appointments and had to face the difficult times occasioned by the labile expansion schemes. He was quick to recognise the limitations of daylight bombing and the first to see through the fallacy that 'the bomber will always get through'. The urgent necessity, therefore, was to develop a night-bombing capability, a requirement which was not being addressed.

Posted as inspector general of the RAF in April 1940, Ludlow-Hewitt was succeeded at Bomber Command by Air Marshal Sir Charles Portal, whose high flying credentials marked him for rapid removal to high office and he was appointed chief of the air staff after only six months in post.

Air Marshal Sir Richard Pierse was appointed to succeed Portal, coming from his post as vice-chief of the air staff where he had been responsible for the bomber programme and thus had overseen the introduction of several types of new aircraft. Sadly, Pierse never lived up to his promise and presided over a long series of poor bombing results, for which he was apportioned the blame, culminating in a disastrous raid in poor weather in November 1941 when thirty-seven aircraft were lost. He was eventually posted to South East Asia Command in January 1942.

No permanent successor was immediately appointed and Air Vice-Marshal 'Jack' Baldwin, at that time air office commanding 5 Group stood in as caretaker. Thus we find that during the critical planning stage for Operation Chariot, when the provision of bombers for the diversionary raid was a contentious issue, there would not be a permanent hand on the helm at Bomber Command.

When a permanent replacement for Pierse was appointed on 22 February 1942, a mere five weeks before Chariot, it was none other than Air Chief Marshal Arthur Harris, soon to earn the soubriquet 'Bomber', the man who we have earlier seen expressing his view that bombers could look after themselves. He remained in charge of Bomber Command for the remainder of the war and left himself an uncertain legacy by the policy he single-mindedly pursued of area bombing, believing that to be the only way to win the war. That legacy still excites debate to this day.

At the outbreak of the war Bomber Command consisted of five groups, each flying aircraft in a specific role, either of heavy, medium or light bombers. Of these five groups, only four were in England in September 1939, 1 Group having been deployed to France in the guise of the Advanced Air Striking Force (AASF) in a bid to stem the lightning over-running of that unfortunate country. Flying the rather inadequate Fairey Battle light bomber it had a torrid time and returned to England in June 1940, the army already having been evacuated at Dunkirk. 1 Group was to provide bombers for Operation Chariot.

2 Group was established as a heavy-bomber group at Abingdon in March 1936, and on 3 September 1939 flew the first operational sortie of the war, following that with the first bombing raid of the war the next day. 3 Group was formed at Andover in May 1936 and was a heavy-bomber group as was 4, formed at Mildenhall in April 1937, the other group destined to fly in support of Operation Chariot. The last group formed pre-war was 5, also at Mildenhall, in September 1937.

In order to achieve its metamorphosis into the AASF, the ten squadrons of 1 Group were organised into five wings and in September 1939, they set off for France where they quickly began to accrue losses of both men and machines. It was a miserable time for the crews, for not only were they flying an obsolete aircraft – the Fairey Battle was not unpleasant to fly but it was pitifully slow – conditions on the ground were far from comfortable. The accommodation was in tents and the weather was cold and miserable.

When, in May 1940, the leviathan of the German armed forces carved its way through France and the Low Countries, sweeping before it the proud French army and the British Expeditionary Force, the AASF also felt the full force of the rampant Luftwaffe, to which it had little or no chance of effective reply. Withdrawing from one airfield to another in the face of the furious onslaught, the AASF lost aircraft at an alarming rate until, in June, unable to sustain the fight, it returned to England. Of the ten squadrons that had set out the previous September only four were left – 12, 103, 142 and 150.

These four squadrons would form the basis of a resurrected 1 Group and while they awaited the availability of the new airfields that were being built under the expansion schemes they were dispersed far and wide at other bases. Their ground crews, having been pushed westwards across France from Dunkirk to Brittany, found themselves stranded when the planes departed and had to make their own way home through Brest and St Nazaire. In yet another setback for the group, those leaving through St Nazaire found themselves on the *Lancastria* and several of them, together with all the equipment, were lost when the ship was bombed and sunk by the Luftwaffe.

1 Group was reformed on 22 June 1940 at Hucknall, Nottinghamshire, under Air Commodore J.J. Breen, and to provide it with an area from which to operate they were allocated the northern half of 5 Group's area, being mostly north Lincolnshire but also including parts of Nottinghamshire, with 103 and 150 Squadrons based at Newton, to the east of Nottingham and 12 and 142 at Binbrook. By mid-July they were back on operations with 103 Squadron flying a raid on targets in Holland.

Commencing in October the outdated Battles were gradually phased out as the crews converted to Wellingtons but on the basis of one Wellington for every two Battles as the larger aircraft required double the number of crew. However the group had been boosted by the arrival of four Polish squadrons, 300 and 301 in July and 304 and 305 the following month.

The group now began to fly in earnest the almost daily round of raids that was the lot of the Bomber Force and by January 1942, with their bases now in Lincolnshire and Yorkshire and commanded by Air Vice-Marshal R.D. Oxland, comprised the ten following squadrons, all now flying the Wellington 1C:

12 RAF at Binbrook
101 RAF at Bourn
103 RAF at Elsham Wolds
150 RAF at Snaith
300 (Masovian) at Hemswell
301 (Pomeranian) at Hemswell
304 (Silesian) at Lindholme
305 (Ziemia Wielkopolska) at Lindholme
458 RAAF at Holme-in-Spalding-Moor
460 RAAF at Breighton

Four of these squadrons would send a total of twenty-seven planes to take part in phase three of the Operation Chariot diversionary raid, 103 Squadron (eleven aircraft), 150 (thirteen), 304 (two) and 305 (one).

4 Group had enjoyed a short existence at the end of World War I having been formed on 1 April 1918, from the RNAS, and disbanded on 24 March 1919. With the prospect of another war looming the group was reformed on 1 April 1937, at Mildenhall, its headquarters moving in July of that year to Linton-on-Ouse and in April 1940, to Heslington Hall where it would stay for the remainder of the war. The first air officer commanding the group was Arthur Harris, then an air commodore. On its formation the group would inherit a variety of aircraft all of which, with the exception of the Whitleys of 10 Squadron, were already obsolete.

Once war was declared squadrons from the group were soon operating, with Whitleys from 51 and 58 Squadrons dropping leaflets on Hamburg, Bremen and several cities in the Ruhr. Four weeks later, on 1/2 October, three Whitleys of 10 Squadron would be the first to overfly Berlin. The group would also be the first to fly aircraft on the long and tiring haul over the Alps to attack targets in Italy. It was a measure of the depth to which the 'bomber will always get through' school of thought had infected Bomber Command that 4 was the only group to have received training and experience in night flying, the rest having been trained for daylight operations only.

A further limitation to an effective bomber offensive was the tacit acceptance that the attacking of civilian targets – even factories were considered to be 'private property' – would bring reprisals. As a result, during the first three months of the war, regular leaflet drops were the order of the day, but they did have the merit of providing practical experience of night flying and navigation.

In July 1941, Air Vice-Marshal C.R. Carr succeeded Air Commodore Arthur Coningham who had been appointed two years earlier, as air officer commanding 4 Group. Roddy Carr came from New Zealand and had fought with their army in the trenches before transferring to the RNAS and then joining the RAF on its formation in 1918. At the beginning of the war he had served with the AASF in France. He would stay at 4 Group until February 1945.

By January 1942, the strength and disposition of the squadrons in 4 Group comprised:

10 RAF at Leeming – Whitley V
35 RAF at Leconfield – Halifax I & II
51 RAF at Dishforth – Whitley V
58 RAF at Linton-on-Ouse – Whitley V
76 RAF at Middleton St George – Halifax I & II
77 RAF at Leeming – Whitley V
78 RAF at Middleton St George – Whitley V
98 RAF at Leconfield – Whitley V (non-operational)
102 RAF at Topcliffe – Whitley V
104 RAF at Driffield – Wellington II
138 RAF at Stradishall – Whitley V
405 RCAF at Pocklington – Wellington II

Three of these squadrons were to provide a total of thirty-five aircraft to fly in support of Operation Chariot; 51 Squadron (twelve aircraft), 58 (eleven) and 77 (twelve). The group remained at the forefront of the bomber offensive for the entire duration of the war. It flew a total of 57,407 sorties in the course of which they dropped 200,000 tons of bombs. With such an extensive operational profile losses were correspondingly high with over 1,500 aircraft being lost.

CHAPTER 3

COASTAL COMMAND

The true position in September, 1939 may be briefly
summarized as follows: of the three operational
Commands, one (Coastal) was an acknowledged
Cinderella, weak in numbers and almost entirely
equipped with obsolete aircraft.

John Terraine – *The Right of the Line* – 1985

For an island such as Britain, control of the surrounding seas is of paramount importance
both for the maintenance of trade and the security of the nation. For hundreds of years
this had been a matter for the navy and Britain had 'ruled the waves', not only around
our own coastline but also over the vast oceans of the entire world. However, the gradual
development of the aeroplane in the years between the turn of the century and the First
World War had added a new dimension to the situation in which speed and distance became
less of a constriction and weapons more destructive and easy to deliver.

Necessity being the mother of invention, the First World War had accelerated the rate at
which this new weapon and its power were developed and by 1918 two new branches had
evolved in the ranks of the existing army and navy which in their traditional form had for
so many years maintained our pre-eminent position as a power in the world. These were
the Royal Naval Air Service, founded on 1 July 1914 and whose activities were not only
seaborne but also land-based, and the Royal Flying Corps, founded on 1 April 1912 and at
that time a unit within the army.

However, on 1 April 1918 and with no formal engagement, a forced marriage was
arranged between the RNAS and the RFC to form the Royal Air Force, a consummation which
did not meet with universal approval among the ranks of the RNAS who made strenuous
efforts to retain Admiralty control of those aspects of air power which they felt to be the
true province of the Admiralty. Indeed, those flights of the RNAS which were carrier – rather
than land-based – were formed into 29 Group, a separate entity which became the catalyst
through which the drift back to naval flying would ensue with the formation of the Fleet
Air Arm, firstly in 1924 as the naval branch of the RAF, becoming part of the naval service
in 1937 and finally to direct control by the Admiralty in 1939.

We have seen earlier how the fledgling RAF had been organised by area, one of which
was Coastal. In 1936 this Coastal Area became Coastal Command and after the secondment
of the Fleet Air Arm to the navy in 1937 it took its place as the premier maritime arm of
the Royal Air Force.

The duties apportioned to the new command were very much in line with those of
the Royal Navy in the days before the development of the aeroplane – the maintenance of
trade and the security of the nation. They therefore included the protection of coastal waters
to ensure the free passage of mercantile shipping and offensive action against any hostile

activity that threatened our shores. This would include not only active intervention against enemy ships and planes but also against the submarine, the threat that had nearly lost us the First World War. Its success against the latter can be seen in the figures – of the 727 U-boats destroyed during World War II, 192 were sunk by Coastal Command. Additionally, air power being a new dimension in war, they would also have to protect the ships of the Royal Navy against air attack and could assist them in the spotting and sweeping of mines. In short, it was charged with the prosecution, in close cooperation with the Royal Navy, of all aspects of the war at sea – find the enemy, attack the enemy, protect our shipping.

To nurture and maintain this cooperation it was imperative that the two services worked closely in tandem and to achieve this Area Combined Headquarters were set up where officers from the relevant Naval Command and RAF Group worked side by side. At each of these headquarters an operations room was maintained where the most important feature was a huge wall map, usually of glass, on which could be plotted all the myriad details of actions and movements of planes and ships within the area. An RAF controller and a naval staff officer, together with their respective assistants, worked in shifts around the clock accompanied by a plotter, a navigator and the numerous other trades inseparable from such an operation including communication by telephone, wireless and teleprinter, many of whose operators were members of the WRNS and the WAAF.

Coastal Area Headquarters had moved from London to Lee-on-the-Solent in January 1932 and when it became Coastal Command there was to be little change, all units being controlled from that one location. The waters around the entire coast of the British Isles were divided into three areas, each covered by a group. By far the largest was that of 15 Group which was responsible for all the seas from west of a line running due south from Lyme Regis to the French coast to south of a line running north-west from the tip of the Mull of Kintyre. From north of that line around the coast to a line running a little north of east from Flamborough Head to the Danish coast was the province of 18 Group, while the remaining area, from south of that line to east of the north-south line from Lyme Regis was covered by 16 Group.

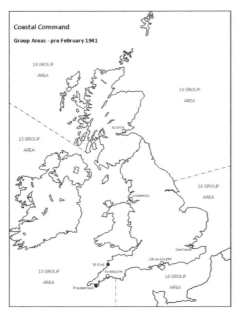

Maps showing the changes made to Coastal Command Group areas in February, 1941. Coastal Command HQ had moved to Lee-on-Solent in January, 1932 and Area Command HQs from there to within their own Areas in 1938 and 1939. In early 1941 Nos. 15 and 18 Groups were reduced in size and a new No. 19 Group formed in the south-west. Although aircraft were drawn in from other bases, the entire Coastal Command effort for Operation Chariot was flown from either St. Eval or Predannack, except that of No. 10 RAAF Squadron who flew from RAF Mount Batten.

In November 1938 the individual Area Command Headquarters moved out of Lee-on-the-Solent to locations within their own areas of responsibility, 16 Group moving to Chatham and 18 Group to Donibristle, close to Rosyth from where, in February 1940 it would move the short distance to Pitreavie Castle. In June 1939, 15 Group moved to Plymouth.

In early 1941 the boundaries of the groups were altered, no doubt to reflect the change of circumstances in the Battle of the Atlantic now that the U-boats had the French ports at their disposal. The boundary running from the Mull of Kintyre was moved north to run north-west from Cape Wrath and the resulting enlarged area split in two by lines drawn east to west across the Irish Sea from Borth to Cahore Point and another running due west from Slyne Head, near Galway, on the west coast of the Irish Republic. The northern of these two new areas would be covered by 15 Group whose Area Command Headquarters moved to Liverpool and the critical south-western part by the newly formed 19 Group based in Plymouth, first at Eggbuckland Fort and then from January 1942, in a huge underground headquarters at Mount Wise. The whole of the Coastal Command support for Operation Chariot would be directed from there and flown from two of its airfields, St Eval and Predannack in the west of Cornwall, although it would be reinforced by aircraft that flew in from other groups.

It is worth noting that all these Area Command Headquarters were established at existing naval bases revealing the importance placed by the authorities on navy/RAF cooperation and thus facilitating the conditions in which it could be operated and developed.

Also represented at Area Command Headquarters, and of prime importance, was a meteorological department which maintained a round-the-clock weather service. The first of the demands on Coastal Command, namely to find the enemy, depended wholly on visibility suitable for reconnaissance, whether it was flown over land or at sea. Whilst this applied to both surfaces, at least on the land targets did not move about. Submarine pens, for example, tended to stay in the same place and could be found by dead reckoning or other navigational aids without sight of land. At sea, where the hunted were mobile it was a very different matter. Another important aspect of the weather was that reconnaissance pilots needed to know that at the end of a long period aloft they would have conditions at their home base suitable for landing and, if necessary, since they would by then often be short of petrol and possibly even damaged, know that a suitable field, clear of cloud, was available nearby. With some Coastal Command sorties exceeding twenty hours, forward knowledge of meteorological conditions was an essential requirement. We shall later see how a change in the weather was to lead to the loss of three Whitleys of the air diversion raid on St Nazaire on their return to their bases. The burden placed on meteorologists and the accuracy of their forecasts was perhaps best displayed in June 1944, when D-Day was postponed for one day in deference to the information and intuition of Group Captain Stagg, who was Eisenhower's meteorological officer.

It is perhaps worth contemplating at this point whether Operation Chariot should have been postponed when flying conditions meant that the constrictions placed on the bombers precluded a successful diversion raid. The difference here is that of which element is most important. For the Normandy landing it was the wind and consequent sea conditions for the Channel crossing that drove the decision whereas at St Nazaire it was the tide, as the window of opportunity in which the water over the dangerous mud banks in the Loire estuary would allow the passage of HMS *Campbeltown* was critical and, if missed, would not occur again for some time. The force commanders for Operation Chariot sailed armed with the discretion to call off the operation if the bombing diversion was not successful but chose, with justification, not to exercise it.

In addition to the Meteorological Section two other units were maintained at Area Command Headquarters in the shape of photographic reconnaissance and air sea rescue. The photographic reconnaissance unit has a chapter of its own, so suffice it here to say that the general rule was for all aircraft of Coastal Command to carry a camera and to photograph anything of interest. In this way much useful intelligence was gathered. Here we shall have a brief look at air sea rescue, some of whose aircraft would be called on to provide support to Operation Chariot by locating the crew of a Whitley who had ditched in the Channel while returning from the diversionary bombing raid.

Trained aircrew are priceless assets and every effort was made to recover downed crews. As with all other aspects of Coastal Command naval and air force cooperation was of the first importance and in order to improve the recovery rate, in January 1941, an officer of air rank was appointed to the new post of director of Sea Rescue Services with a naval captain as his deputy and they were to have officers of both services at each of the four Area Command Headquarters of Coastal Command.

Perhaps the greatest spur to improvement in air-sea rescue had been the disproportionately high number of pilots lost in the Channel during the Battle of Britain. The subsequent organisation of RAF high speed launches, naval auxiliary patrols and army cooperation Lysanders into a coherent force made a significant difference, but it was the fact that responsibility for recovery lay with the unit of the downed aircrew that led to the formation of the directorate in order to coordinate the effort in one body. This improvement in the recovery rate led to the retention of twelve Lysanders on a permanent basis. Even so, during the six months to August 1941, only about one-third of ditched airmen were recovered so in November of that year the decision was made to form four air-sea rescue squadrons. Unfortunately this required robbing other squadrons of the Hudsons with which it was intended these new squadrons were to be equipped.

The value of trained aircrew had not escaped the Germans who made determined efforts to thwart their rescue and WOp/AGs posted to the ASR squadrons soon found themselves attending a lecture on air gunnery, both for their own protection and that of the men in the water. The little Lysanders, not well equipped to protect themselves, would be accompanied on their missions by fighter aircraft, usually Spitfires, who would remain as long as possible over the dinghies to protect them until their occupants were picked up.

It has to be admitted that some responsibility for the low survival rate rested with the airmen themselves who did not always prepare well for a possible ditching. They had to be better equipped with survival gear and to be drilled in its quick deployment, always making sure it was readily to hand. As the war progressed great improvements were made in the equipment that could be dropped to survivors from the air. These included the Thornaby Bag, the Bircham Barrel and the Lindholme Gear.[7] The rate of recovery began to improve and by the end of hostilities over 10,500 personnel had been plucked from the

---

[7] These inventions were all named after the RAF stations where they were developed. The Thornaby Bag and the Bircham Barrel both contained food, water and first aid kits, the Bircham Barrel including distress flares. The more sophisticated Lindholme Gear consisted of five circular containers roped together, the centre one of which contained a dinghy which inflated on impact.

sea. Of these about 5,500 were Allied airmen, 4,500 others, mainly seamen and nearly 300 enemy aircrew.

The ability of Coastal Command to carry out its duties was very much limited by the neglect of naval aviation in the twenty years between the wars and even after the outbreak of war in 1939 the nature of the conflict, originally in the Battle of France and then, following Dunkirk, in the Battle of Britain, resulted in the RAF concentrating their minds and resources on the needs of Fighter and Bomber Commands. Even the First Lord of the Admiralty, Mr A.V. Alexander, was moved to describe Coastal Command as the "Cinderella Service".

At the beginning of the war the mainstays of Coastal Command were the Anson, the Whitley and the Wellington. The Anson was a steady, sturdy workhorse and although manoeuvrable it lacked speed, while the Whitley and the Wellington were conventional bombers. Indeed, it is interesting to note that Bomber Command squadrons equipped with these two aircraft carried out the diversionary bombing raid on St Nazaire. However, they did much sterling service with Coastal Command. The Hudson, an American-built machine, ideally suited for reconnaissance owing to its long range and the wide field of view afforded by its cockpit, was introduced early in the war and as quickly as numbers became available they would be taken up by Coastal Command. The Hudson was also superior in speed to the British-built machines. In 1942 another American-built aircraft, the Liberator, was becoming available. It, too, had a good range and was well armed, both for attack and defence.

Part of the problem with using planes not designed for Coastal Command work was the different operating criteria. A bombing mission would be flown at a fixed altitude over a finite distance, allowing of course for damage and diversion, and along a set course. Reconnaissance over the ocean was exactly the opposite. Altitude could vary from 'on the deck' to just below cloud level, the target could be anywhere and the duration of the sortie was limited only by fuel-carrying capacity. Engines were designed to work at optimum efficiency at a certain altitude and speed and the same engine fitted in one plane could find itself working at much higher or lower revolutions per minute when fitted in another. The problem with lack of range, however, could always be overcome by the use of drop tanks.

As one would expect of a maritime service, Coastal Command also operated flying boats. It is astonishing to realise that the first take-off from water had been as early as 1909, the year of the first flight across the Channel by Louis Blériot. It was achieved by Commander Oliver Schwann in an Avro for which he paid £700 of his own money and to which Vickers had fitted floats. Initially three types of seaplane, all British-built, were deployed – the London, the Stranraer and the Sunderland. The two former did not last long into the war, leaving the Sunderland, often flown by Commonwealth crews, to carry the burden, but later to be joined by the American-built Catalina. Ideal because of its range, a Catalina had flown a twenty-six-hour sortie in the hunt for and destruction of the Bismarck. That a flying boat could land on water, albeit only when sea conditions allowed, also made it indispensable for the rescue of ship-wrecked mariners and downed aircrew.

The critical nature of range was brought into sharp relief following the sinking of HMS Hood on 24 May 1941. When Bismarck had subsequently been damaged by a torpedo fired from a Fairey Swordfish she had signalled her intention to make for St Nazaire for repairs. The operations record book for 217 Squadron at St Eval recorded "a terrific flap going on all evening" of 25 May when Bismarck was reported to be heading their way. All available crews were put on standby waiting for her to come within range and during the next two days aircraft had been pouring into St Eval from other bases for a strike. When it was reported on the morning of the 27th that the navy had sunk the *Bismarck* the visitors departed and St Eval returned to normal, but Pilot Officer Hunter, navigator on a Beaufort of 217 Squadron remembered:

> "The powers-that-be had worked out a wonderful plan to enable us to intercept this ship at sea. The idea was to locate her by means of a normal Radius of Action and then, since she would most likely be beyond our range, we must expect to ditch as we ran out of fuel on our return. To obviate any difficulty, however, there would be high speed launches at the ready."[8]

Two months later Jim Hunter was to be shot down and captured during an attack on the *Scharnhorst* and he spent the rest of the war in captivity.

Coastal Command would maintain an aircraft in the sky during every hour of the entire war and by March 1942 had already marked up some notable achievements. Early in the war its aircraft had successfully conducted the search for the prison ship *Altmark* when she was sighted and photographed on 16 February 1940 by Hudsons who shadowed her until the navy arrived.

Later that year, although the Battle of Britain quite rightly belongs in legend to Fighter Command, Coastal Command did much useful work in conjunction with Bomber Command at that time. Even had the Luftwaffe prevailed the subsequent invasion would have been seaborne and Coastal Command's operational effort lay in attacking shipping in the Channel and in mining the entrances to the harbours in which barges were collecting and from which any invasion force would sail.

Bismarck features large in the story of Operation Chariot. The whole operation had been sparked by her stated intention to make to St Nazaire for repairs, pointing to the importance of that port to the huge German battleships. On 21 May 1941, it had been a Coastal Command reconnaissance aircraft that had started the hunt when it discovered *Bismarck* and *Prinz Eugen* in Dobric fjord, clearly preparing for sea. In the chase that had followed across the vast expanse of the north Atlantic, both before and after the sinking of HMS *Hood*, it was again an aircraft of Coastal Command that had located *Bismarck* when the navy had temporarily lost contact, three Catalinas each flying over twenty hours in the search.

Until the rapid conquest of northern Europe had radically altered the balance of power, the only access for the U-boats to our trade routes in the Atlantic lay through the North Sea and the inhospitable northern waters, access through the Channel having been denied by the Royal Navy, aided by our French allies. Now, not only were the Biscay ports available to the U-boats but RAF airfields were in range of the Luftwaffe. The patrol of the south-west approaches and the Bay of Biscay had become a strategically important role for Coastal Command in the shape of 19 Group.

As if in confirmation of her perceived role as Cinderella, during the first three years of the war the most enduring battle for Coastal Command, together with the Admiralty, was with the RAF and the Air Ministry. The dispute was over the relative importance of the bombing of Germany against the defeat of the U-boat. Not only did our day to day

---

[8] Quoted in *From Coastal Command to Captivity* by W.J. (Jim) Hunter.

requirements of food and supplies depend on the Atlantic convoys but across these turbulent waters would have to pass the men and machines with which to supply and support the eventual launch of the second front.

Surprisingly, Churchill supported Bomber Command – surprisingly because he had openly admitted that the Battle of the Atlantic was the only one he had feared he might lose. Even so, the requirements of the 'ugly sisters' in Fighter and Bomber Commands still took precedence over the "Cinderella Service".

As a result of the insupportable losses occasioned by the determined efforts of the naval hunting groups and Coastal Command, the U-boats were withdrawn from the North Atlantic in 1943. When, in 2013, celebrations took place to recognise the 70th anniversary of that victory, scant mention was made of the role of Coastal Command. It seems even now it still retains its 'Cinderella' image.

In March 1942 the commander-in-chief of Coastal Command was Sir Philip Joubert de la Ferté. Sir Philip had been commissioned from the Royal Military Academy at Woolwich into the Royal Field Artillery but his interest in flying had been stirred when his parents moved to a house adjacent to Brooklands racetrack, which a short time later was developed as an aerodrome. Taking flying lessons at his own expense in 1912, he had attended the Central Flying School the following year and transferred to the Royal Flying Corps with which he served throughout the First World War. On its formation on 1 April 1918 Joubert, then a lieutenant colonel, transferred to the RAF. He held various staff and command posts during the inter-war years until in July 1936, he succeeded Sir Arthur Longmore as commander-in-chief, Coastal Command but after twelve months in the post he was appointed air officer commanding RAF India, the country in which he had been born while his father, an officer in the Indian Medical Service, had been serving there. Returning to England in 1939 he again took up the position of commander-in-chief, Coastal Command which he held until 1943. During the protracted wrangling with the RAF and the Air Ministry Sir Philip had been sufficiently frustrated to write:

> "So far in this war we have had to scrape along . . . it's clearly useless to devote all our resources to maintaining and increasing a bomber offensive to win the war while neglecting the coastal resources which will prevent us losing it."[9]

Air officer commanding 19 Group at its headquarters at Mount Wise, Plymouth, was Air Vice-Marshal Geoffrey Rhodes Bromet. Ideally suited to a position that required close and cordial cooperation with the navy, he had graduated from Britannia Royal Naval College and his early career had been in the Royal Naval Air Service with which he had served in the First World War, taking part in two of its greatest battles, at Gallipoli and on the Somme. In 1917 he had been awarded a DSO for commanding a squadron of the RNAS "with conspicuous gallantry and success. Under his command the squadron developed into a most efficient and formidable fighting force." After being awarded a permanent commission as a major in 1919 he served as Admiralty liaison officer at Headquarters Coastal Area and officer commanding, School of Naval Cooperation and Aerial Navigation and in 1923 attended RAF Staff College. At various times he served as SASO to both Coastal Area and Coastal Command and thus confirmed his suitability for appointment as air officer commanding

---

[9] AIR 15-46 Aircraft Requirements, Jul 1939-Jun 1943. Joubert memo to AM c. Feb 1942. Quoted in *The Cinderella Service*, by Andrew Hendrie.

19 Group. Under his leadership all the arrangements for support of Operation Chariot would be planned and carried out.

True to its proud tradition, Coastal Command would not fail in its support of the forces engaged in Operation Chariot. Eleven squadrons flew forty-three sorties involving nearly 200 aircrew in over 250 hours of flying time to ensure the safety of the flotilla of little ships sailing to and returning from St Nazaire. Eight of their number lost their lives and three their freedom, but no ship or aircraft of the enemy was to bring harm to the Charioteers.

CHAPTER 4

THE MEN FROM THE PRU AND THE WOMEN TOO

"The story of the development and achievements of the twin arts of photographic reconnaissance and photographic interpretation . . . . . .is to me the most fascinating aspect of the last war; a story of British genius at its best . . . ."

Marshal of the Royal Air Force, The Lord Tedder, GCB[10]

Although the evacuation from Dunkirk had ended on 4 June 1940, there were many British units still scrambling to return to England. Now the effort spread westward, even as far as St Nazaire, where thousands of troops were embarking, some on the *Lancastria* which, on 17 June, two days short of its eighteenth birthday, was sunk by dive-bombers, resulting in a heavy and unnumbered loss of life.

That same day a Lockheed aircraft landed at RAF Heston, Middlesex. The pilot, having assured himself of the arrangements for the withdrawal of his own unit from France and having been forced by fog in the Channel to spend a night in Jersey with his co-pilot and an English secretary and her dog to whom he had given a lift, alighted from the plane. As he did so he was handed a letter.

```
                                    Air Ministry, Dept. OA
                                              London SW1

                                            16 June 1940

SECRET

S.5884/S.6.

Sir,

1.  I am commanded by the Air Council to inform you that
they have recently had under review the question of the future
status and organisation of the Photographic Development Unit
and that, after careful consideration, they have reached the
conclusion that this unit, which you have done so much to foster,
should now be regarded as having passed beyond the stage of
```

[10]Foreword to *Evidence in Camera* – Constance Babington-Smith (Chatto & Windus, 1957).

experiment and should take its place as part of the ordinary organisation of the Royal Air Force.

2. It has accordingly been decided that it should be constituted as a unit of the Royal Air Force under the orders of the commander-in-chief, Coastal Command, and should be commanded by a regular serving officer. Wing Commander G.W. Tuttle, DFC, has been appointed.

3. I am to add that the council wish to record how much they are indebted to you for the work you have done and for the great gifts of imagination and inventive thought which you have brought to bear on the development of the technique of photography in the Royal Air Force.

> I am, Sir,
> Your obedient servant,
> Arthur Street

Wing Commander H.L. Cotton, AFC
Royal Air Force Station,
Heston, Middlesex.

Thus did the Royal Air Force rid itself of its 'turbulent priest'. In an act of unpardonable carelessness that can only have rubbed salt into the wound, they had addressed him with the wrong initials and accorded him a decoration which he had not won. Sidney Cotton had committed the cardinal sin of being proved right in the face of official disdain and now his enemies in high places, against whose ridicule he had persevered and succeeded, had exacted their revenge.

It was the French that started it. Ever in the forefront of invention and innovation they were to lead the world in the developments that would revolutionise photographic reconnaissance. Although the gathering of intelligence is as old as war itself, for hundreds of years it involved a man on a hill trying to see what was on the other side. Communication of the intelligence thus gained was either on foot or on horseback and although the popular conception of light cavalry is coloured by the epic Charge of the Light Brigade, it was for the rapid delivery of intelligence on the battlefield for which light cavalry was first formed.

In Paris on 15 October 1783 an event took place which provided the catalyst for the revolution in the gathering of such intelligence when Jean-François-Pilâtre de Rozier made the first ever ascent in a tethered balloon.[11] This was followed a few weeks later by a free flight in which two other Frenchmen travelled a distance of twenty-seven miles. A further year later, in January 1785, Jean-Paul Blanchard crossed the Channel by balloon, although this did not have the same impact on British thinking as would the crossing by powered flight by Blériot in 1909.

The advent of all this activity by French balloonists had been made possible by the experiments on the relative density of hydrogen by a British scientist, Henry Cavendish, in 1776. Even so, the first balloon flight in England had been undertaken in May 1784 by

---

[11] Tethered balloons were still in use in 2014 when the British army employed them in Afghanistan. They were helium filled, double-tethered to guard against breaking away and carried a camera which relayed moving pictures to a command post or vehicle via an optic cable.

an Italian and though a flight by a British army major took place the following month the British remained unimpressed. Not so the French who went on to invent a suitable apparatus for producing hydrogen in the field which enabled them to successfully employ balloons in the war against Austria and Prussia.

The next development, which was to make it possible to counter to some extent the vagaries of wind and weather, was powered flight and again the French led the way when, on 24 September 1852, Maurice Jullien successfully flew in a powered airship. Meanwhile development in England continued to lag behind due to both official scepticism and lack of money and it was not until 1878 that a development unit was set up at Woolwich, a full twenty-six years having elapsed since Jullien's flight.

Now that the man on the hill could choose the location for his 'hill', the next innovation that would influence battlefield intelligence was the development of photography and once again we find the French in the van. It was Daguerre who had pioneered an early form of camera, the Daguerreotype, but it was unwieldy and impractical. Now an Englishman, Fox-Talbot, would make his contribution with the introduction of a more suitable method. Even then it took another Frenchman, Felix Tournachon, a photographer and journalist, in 1858, to be first to apply this new method of producing images to aerial photography. The need to sensitise and develop plates whilst airborne was an early limitation on progress but by 1863 free balloons were in use in England which could not only fly higher but which carried plates that could be developed on landing. Aerial photographic reconnaissance was becoming a reality. The next big step forward was the development of powered machines that were heavier than air when, on 17 December 1903, the Wright brothers got off the ground at Kitty Hawk. In this country the showman Samuel F. Cody had pioneered powered flight and on 16 October 1908 had flown 400 yards but this had failed to impress British officialdom. By 1909, photographs were first being taken from aircraft, with the United States joining France in this field, and in May of that year the British, at last catching on to the potential of powered flight, could boast a home-grown pilot in John Moore-Brabazon, who was to become a giant in the British aircraft industry and in 1942 was created 1st Lord Brabazon of Tara.

Then came Louis Blériot. On 25 July 1909, he had the temerity to fly an aeroplane across the English Channel and thus puncture the insularity of these islands, but although the public imagination was fired and the press were up in arms, official British reaction was one of lethargy and little or no interest was shown.

At the time Blériot flew the Channel the British army (the RAF would not be born until 1918) possessed only one aeroplane, but in 1912 the Royal Flying Corps was formed and training of personnel instituted, not only for pilots but for observers and, tellingly, for aerial photographers. The man on the hill had come a long way and with war seemingly looming on the horizon it was quickly noted that intelligence gathered from air reconnaissance – gun emplacements, troop dispositions, fall of shell – would be vital.

As we have seen earlier, it had not passed notice that the enemy would be similarly exercised and that mastery of the air to carry out this reconnaissance would be vital to ultimate victory. In order to command the skies dogfights broke out between the opposing pilots, firstly using revolvers and later rifles and Lewis guns. When Anton Fokker[12], a Dutchman

---

[12] Anton Herman Gerard Fokker had established aircraft factories in Germany before World War I. In 1922, however, he emigrated to the United States, was naturalised and created the Fokker Aircraft Corporation of America.

born in the East Indies, perfected a method of firing a machine gun through the propeller, enabling head-on attacks, the fighter was born.

The bomber, too, had its inception at this time when Lieutenant Colonel Hugh Trenchard sought stronger machines from which bombs could be dropped on the enemy. When Trenchard correctly divined how vital aerial reconnaissance was to success he appointed the young Second Lieutenant Moore-Brabazon to head up air photography. The taking of photographs could not stand alone and was of no value without interpretation and a great skill was required to pick out the salient points for the planners. For this task Sergeant-Major Victor Laws was appointed and he was soon running courses to train interpreters for the increased number of photographs now requiring attention. Together, Moore-Brabazon and Laws would establish the basic principles of photo intelligence in this country.

In the air, the battles between the opposing pilots were driving development of both aircraft and cameras. The planes had to fly higher and faster, not only to avoid enemy aircraft but also anti-aircraft fire and so cameras were needed to provide readable plates from the increasing altitudes. On the ground, Laws' courses were to result in enough interpreters being available for every front-line squadron to have its own photo-interpretation section.

One of the spin-offs from aerial reconnaissance in World War I had been the great strides forward in the field of map-making. Not only had ground commanders gone into battle with detailed trench maps but in the Middle East, where action had also been seen during World War I, vast tracts of land were now being mapped for the first time. The trench maps were produced from the constant observation from the air that was necessary in the static situation that was trench warfare to not only pin-point artillery positions and troop dispositions but also to watch for signs of reinforcements that might signal an imminent push by the enemy in an attempt to break the stalemate.

On 1 April 1918, the Royal Air Force was formed by the amalgamation of the Royal Flying Corps and the Royal Naval Air Service and in November of that year the war had been won. For the next twenty years the lessons that had made Britain pre-eminent in the field of aerial reconnaissance would be neglected and, where other nations forged ahead, the next conflict, spawned by the terms of the Treaty of Versailles which had ended this one, would find the RAF once again poorly prepared.

Between the wars the rise of Hitler in Germany, his flouting of the provisions of the Treaty of Versailles and his heavy-handed treatment of the German people themselves by his Nazi bullies, did not go unnoticed in England but memories of the decimation of British manhood in World War I left no appetite for further conflict. Happily, officialdom was not entirely idle. Churchill appeared to be a lone voice, crying in the wilderness, but Baldwin, and later Chamberlain, had begun to rebuild the RAF and the production of the Hurricanes and Spitfires that would later dominate our skies had already been commissioned. Furthermore, and obviously unknown to the public, MI6, the Secret Intelligence Service, had turned its professional gaze upon the goings-on in resurgent Germany and it was an initiative by an officer of the SIS, Fred Winterbotham, which would lead to a revolution in RAF photo intelligence. Enter Sidney Cotton, the man who would set up the organisation for photo reconnaissance that would make the RAF pre-eminent in that field.

The organisation within the RAF for photo intelligence at the outbreak of war was not, in modern parlance, 'fit for purpose'. Fortunately, in the shape of Sidney Cotton, the hour was to produce the man. Here was a man with an array of qualities, not all good, that fitted him for the role he was about to play – that of almost single-handedly and certainly single-mindedly putting into place an organisation that made the RAF leader in the field of photo intelligence.

The son of an Australian father of some substance, Cotton had learned to fly with the RNAS in World War I and had later flown bombers with limited success, but had not been found amenable to military discipline, a trait that was to colour his relationship with top brass in his development of photo reconnaissance. His first useful asset, therefore, was his pilot's licence. Between the wars he had followed a variety of occupations but his conviction that he was always right had seen him fall out with all his business partners and even his own father. This stubborn conviction would also define his prickly relationship with the senior RAF officers who would seek to control his activities as he advanced the development of photo intelligence.

A second useful string to his bow was experience gained in Newfoundland where he flew surveys for map-making companies and for locating seals for seal traders. Allied to that was a keen interest in photography and, later on, a business interest in a new film system called Dufaycolor which gave him the opportunity and the excuse to be flying around Europe as the war clouds gathered. Last, and by no means least, he possessed friends whom he would find of great assistance at critical times as his ideas progressed.

In the autumn of 1938 when Cotton's film venture with Dufaycolor looked doomed to failure one of those friends, A.J. Miranda, gave him an introduction to Fred Winterbotham who was working with the Secret Intelligence Service, who thought that Cotton could prove useful and took him on to the SIS payroll. Asked to fly with the French *Deuxième Bureau* Cotton demurred and with Bob Niven, a former RAF pilot, insisted on flying the plane himself. It was a Lockheed 12A supplied by Miranda and was ideal as it was typical of the sort of machine a businessman would use. The French took the photos but did not produce a satisfactory result, and true to form Cotton fell out with them and insisted on having his own aeroplane and adopting his own methods.

The Lockheed was left with the French and a new one provided which Cotton had equipped to his own requirements. He based himself at Heston, an aerodrome that was much used by civilian pilots and flying clubs and would as such lend excellent cover for his flights as business trips in connection with his Dufaycolor interest. He had found that polishing an aeroplane, filing down rivets and removing extraneous equipment would greatly improve the performance and with three cameras fitted – one vertical and two oblique – he could cover a ten-mile-wide strip of land in a single pass. This was an arrangement he had wanted the *Deuxième Bureau* to adopt but they had refused.

With the new Lockheed Cotton and Niven set off on an extensive 'mapping flight' in the Middle East and further flights over Germany 'selling Dufaycolor'. They led a charmed life and rode their luck and in late August 1939 managed to get permission to leave Berlin by the skin of their teeth, photographing the German Fleet on the way.

At the start of World War II there were only seven photo-interpreters in the RAF. Photographs were taken from Blenheim aircraft flying at 10,000 feet and at a speed of 260 mph, another indication that the lessons of World War I had been forgotten. At this speed and altitude the casualty rate for the Blenheims was unacceptably high and as few as 50% brought back useable photographs.

At this stage of the war it was the Admiralty who showed most interest in Cotton's methods – it was he, after all, who had first supplied them with top-class pictures of the German Fleet on the eve of war – but in the event it was the Air Ministry that sent for him. At an inconclusive meeting at which Cotton's methods had been held to be impossible, a further meeting was arranged for the following day. In the interim Cotton and Niven set off to take the 'impossible' photographs and when they produced them at the reconvened meeting the indignant response was such that Cotton, as he had done so often before in his life, walked out. Later called back to the Air Ministry he met Air Chief Marshal Sir Cyril Newhall, chief of the air staff, who agreed to the setting up of the Heston Flight which would operate outside the RAF with Cotton in unfettered control. It came into being on 23 September 1939 and Cotton was commissioned as a squadron leader with the acting rank of wing commander and as the unit grew Wing Commander Geoffrey Tuttle was added to the strength to handle the increasing administrative load.

During his flight around the Middle East with Niven, Cotton had met a pilot officer with the delightfully oxymoronic name of 'Shorty' Longbottom who was later to become a founder pilot of the Heston Flight, but his greatest contribution to photo intelligence at that time was to write an insightful paper on the subject that was submitted to the Air Ministry. Amongst other proposals he argued that the fastest plane available was essential for successful reconnaissance. In real terms, this meant the Spitfire.

With the ongoing developments that were being introduced Cotton picked up on this argument but with Fighter Command having priority no Spitfires were available. A Blenheim was streamlined but it fell short of the performance that Cotton required. The problem was solved following a chance meeting with Air Vice-Marshal Sir Hugh Dowding who was keen to know how Cotton had increased the speed of his Blenheim. Dowding responded by getting two Spitfires made available to the Heston Flight.

Streamlining in accordance with Cotton's principles – the guns, together with all excess weight, were removed and all surfaces highly polished – increased the maximum speed by 10%. The Spitfires were painted a duck-egg green making them virtually invisible against the azure sky (condensation trails would have to be avoided at all costs) and for defence they would have to rely on their height and speed. Auxiliary petrol tanks were fitted, stretching their range to 650 miles, but official scepticism at their ability to take useful photos at a height of 30,000 feet would now have to be countered.

As well as the streamlining of the aircraft it was therefore also necessary to improve the photographic side of the operation. In the early twenties Victor Laws had designed the F8 camera but a smaller and lighter model was required and the Royal Aircraft Establishment at Farnborough came up with the F24. It was three of these that Cotton had wanted the *Deuxième Bureau* to install in their Lockheed and when he was given his own outfit he lost no time in putting them in his own. The F24 had the advantage of fitting into a standard-sized suitcase and could thus be secretly carried on board, protecting Cotton's 'businessman' status. This camera served the RAF well throughout the war and long after.

An initial problem with photography at certain altitudes had been blurring of the image by what was at first thought to be icing, but Cotton identified it as condensation and remedied it by directing warm air from the cockpit over the cameras. The F24 took a 5" x 5" picture which, from 30,000 feet, gave little definition for the interpreters, but help was at hand as another old friend now came to Cotton's aid.

Lemnos Hemming was the managing director of the Aircraft Operating Company which, with its associated company Aerofilms, ran a service for oil exploration and mapping concerns and Hemming possessed a Wild A5 Stereo Plotter. It was a vast machine and required an expert operator, but it could provide eight times magnification. Approached by Cotton, Hemming was able to produce a print, taken from 34,000 feet, on which thirty points of military interest could be identified. Cotton having proved his point to his detractors, negotiations were now put in hand to bring the two companies under RAF control. The move was arranged on 28 March 1940, RAF personnel were gradually introduced and all was completed on 31 May, the new unit becoming known as the Photographic Development Interpretation Unit. Earlier that year, on 17 January the Heston Flight had been renamed the Photographic Development Unit (Interpretation) (PDU [I]).

While all this was going on Cotton had moved his two Spitfires and the Lockheed, together with a mobile photographic printing unit, to France from where it was easier to overfly Germany. Heston worked more for the Admiralty, but in the early months of 1940 they found themselves working increasingly in support of the British Expeditionary Force under Lord Gort. The Heston Flight was expanded with additional aircraft, pilots and support staff, but was often getting caught in the crossfire between the Admiralty and the Air Ministry.

When the Germans broke through in France, a move which could have been anticipated had the reconnaissance photographs taken on the Luxembourg-Belgian border showing tanks massing in the forests not been ignored in London, the unit was pushed south and west and, on 10 May, Cotton hurried back to France. On 9 June they were near Orléans and by the 14th had withdrawn to Poitiers. Eventually they scrambled home by whatever means they could, abandoning and destroying such equipment as they could not take with them.

Sidney Cotton flew back, via Jersey, to Heston where the fateful letter advising him of his dismissal awaited. Difficult he may have been, stubborn and unmanageable certainly, but his legacy was an organisation that would be priceless in its contribution to the winning of the war.

Whatever feelings Cotton may have had about his summary dismissal − and it is difficult not to have some sympathy with the senior RAF officers with whom he had dealt in such a cavalier manner − he can have only been delighted with the choice of his successor. Wing Commander Geoffrey Tuttle had been in charge of the administration for Cotton since the early days, had won a DFC in India and was a qualified aeronautical engineer. At the same time as he was appointed it was decided to remove photo reconnaissance from Fighter Command and place it in Coastal Command under the administration of 16 Group where it would sit comfortably between the sometimes conflicting demands of the Admiralty and the Air Ministry.

With the BEF evicted from France the navy would become the reconnaissance unit's best customer for they desperately needed to know the whereabouts and movements of the German Fleet which could become a useful force for Hitler only if it could break out into the hunting grounds beyond the narrow seas surrounding these islands. Therefore on 1 July, Tuttle decided to disperse his command, which the previous month had become known as the Photographic Reconnaissance Unit (1PRU), in order to cover better the seaborne exits from Germany. With C and D Flights remaining at Heston from where they would cover Denmark, Holland, Belgium, the Channel and parts of France, he sent A Flight to Wick, in the far north of Scotland and B Flight to St Eval, in the far west of Cornwall. With German forces now having reached the west coast of France where they were building U-boat pens and developing Brest as an important base for their capital ships, St Eval would become a busy and important location and provide much, if not all, of the photo intelligence essential for the planning of the raid on St Nazaire. A little later a PRU presence would be established at Leuchars, also in the north of Scotland, but far enough south of Wick to reduce the time taken to transport images south for detailed analysis by a whole day. Each flight of 1PRU consisted of four Spitfires and all flights, both aircrew and ground crew, were rotated between stations every three months to give the men a fresh environment and keep them on the top line.

If you were to ask that mythical being 'the average man in the street' to name a wisteria-clad country house, not far from London, in whose extensive grounds Nissen huts mushroomed and which played an important, top secret role in the field of intelligence in World War II, the chances are that he would answer, if he could answer at all, "Bletchley Park". There was, however, another large mansion answering this description on the Thames near Marlow called Danesfield House. In this fine building, eventually also to be surrounded by Nissen huts, was housed the operation which, while Bletchley handled signals intelligence, dealt with the collection and interpretation of the intelligence provided by aerial photography. In the time-honoured practice of the RAF it was christened RAF Medmenham after the nearby village of that name.

And the women, too? One of the outstanding features of Medmenham, not seen even at Bletchley Park, was the situation regarding women, not only in the numbers involved but in the positions they held and the responsibility they carried. At that time it was the practice for women, on marrying, to leave work for a life of domesticity and the raising of a family. Single women were, therefore, most commonly employed in the routine clerical and non-executive positions where their loss would not be so keenly felt when they left. Not so at Medmenham, where the men worked side by side and where many of the women were in charge of sections with men working under them. Although in the beginning men outnumbered the women, as the war progressed, the pendulum swung. More and more men were posted abroad, particularly after D-Day, and their places at Medmenham were taken by women to the extent that by March 1945, WAAF personnel slightly outnumbered the RAF.

One such section commander and possibly to become one of the best-known was Constance Babington-Smith who had joined the WAAF in 1940 and having served the requisite six months in the ranks was commissioned. Having been an aeronautical journalist in civilian life it was perhaps inevitable that she was posted to Medmenham where she was in due course to head the aircraft section. She and her team would eventually be instrumental in identifying from photographs Hitler's flying-bomb development. Constance was to appear in the iconic wartime film *Target for Tonight* which would also feature an RAF officer, who will briefly touch our story, Group Captain Pickard.

The reasons given for joining the WAAF were many and varied. Ann McKnight-Kauffer, who would serve at St Eval where virtually all of the intelligence for the raid on St Nazaire would be gathered and assessed, had been determined to be in photo intelligence before she even enlisted. Stella Ogle, given the choice of enlisting in the army, navy or air force had chosen the latter as the light blue uniform suited her better. Stella was not the only one to cite the uniform as the reason for joining. Many others joined to escape the stifling social conventions applying to young women at that time and enlistment enabled them to leave home, many for the first time. Others, having already flown the nest to study at university, found themselves in possession of degrees that were particularly apposite to photo intelligence, archaeology, geology and geography foremost among them.

Most high profile, perhaps, among the women of Medmenham was Sarah Churchill, daughter of the prime minister, who was determined and delighted to be doing her bit for the war effort. The men had their celebrities, too, with a young Dirk Bogarde among their number, as well as a young geologist, Glyn Daniel, who would after the war carve out for himself a successful career on television.

In 2014 an anonymous MI6 officer was quoted as saying that the qualities of women included, "emotional intelligence, empathy and the ability to put aside ego and work as a team". There seems little doubt that the women of Medmenham had these qualities in profusion and the whole gamut of photo intelligence was the better for their being there.

As the war progressed, in the latter part of 1940 conditions at Heston became progressively more uncomfortable due to bomb damage so C and D Flights moved to RAF Benson. The PDU(I) at Wembley also suffered and would later move to the new Central Interpretation Unit (CIU) which had been set up at Medmenham, which had been requisitioned in November 1940 and opened for business on 1 April 1941. (What is it with the RAF and All Fools' Day? The RAF itself had come into being on that day in 1918.) The PDU(I) would also be joined at Medmenham by the modelling section which until that time had been housed at the Royal Aircraft Establishment at Farnborough and it formed V Section.

Life at RAF Benson was far removed from Heston Aerodrome which had always been a civilian airfield, set up in 1929 by two pilots who had formed a company called Airwork Limited and in that year had hosted the King's Cup Air Race. It was also the base for the Guards Flying Club and was much used for air displays and races. Its claim to lasting fame, however, would be that it was to Heston that Prime Minister Neville Chamberlain returned from Germany in September 1938 waving his piece of paper and declaring "peace for our time".

It was ten years later, on 1 April 1939 that RAF Benson was opened, construction having begun in 1937. The first two squadrons to be based there were 103 and 150, flying the Fairey Battle, but at the same time as 1PRU moved in they converted to Vickers Wellingtons, planes in which they would fly in the diversionary raid on St Nazaire, but by then operating from Elsham Wolds and Snaith respectively.

Geographically, Benson was ideally suited, being close to Coastal Command Headquarters at Northwood, Middlesex, and handy for London. Proximity to Benson would be a factor in the choice of Danesfield House, now named RAF Medmenham, to become the home for the Central Interpretation Unit. Benson played host to photographic reconnaissance for the remainder of the Second World War.

The establishment at RAF Medmenham was split between men and women in the proportion of roughly three to one, but as we have seen, that ratio would change with time. Cotton had correctly divined that many of the tasks to be undertaken in photo interpretation required the patience of Job and that women were particularly suited in this respect.

Photo interpretation was carried out in three distinct phases. As soon as a reconnaissance flight landed the cameras would be unloaded and the film rushed to be processed, which took about an hour. During this time the pilot would be de-briefed by the intelligence officer, having also been briefed by him before the flight. The prints, when available, would be set out in a mosaic by WAAF plotters who placed them in position on a large trestle table to replicate the flight path of the sortie. This enabled the location of the image to be identified on a map. Prints were also passed to a photo interpreter who, with the assistance of a stereoscope, searched for items of military interest. Both of these tasks were aided by the fact that each photograph taken overlapped its predecessor by about 60% and so two images of each target were produced between which the aircraft had moved forward. The second image, therefore, was slightly offset from the first, allowing an operator skilled in the use of the stereoscope to obtain a three-dimensional effect. Items of immediate interest were sent directly to the organisation which had requested the flight and copies of all photos were sent to Medmenham. This initial procedure at the RAF station was known as 'first phase interpretation' and was expected to be completed within two hours of the plane landing.

On arrival at Medmenham the photos were subjected to much deeper analysis by highly-trained men and women who had, on joining, attended an initial two-week intensive training course which had included, among other disciplines, instruction in the use of a slide-rule by which the size and scale of objects were calculated. Here also was maintained a complete and comprehensive index so that interpreters could cross-reference with previous photos to monitor progress in, for example, the building of rocket sites or U-boat pens and even of the U-boats themselves. This was 'second phase interpretation' and was expected to be completed within twenty-four hours.

Third phase interpretation was the most detailed of all and was carried out by men and women who specialised in particular fields of interest to the military planners – aircraft, shipping, industry, airfields, railways – and these interpreters became amazingly proficient in finding and identifying the almost invisible.

At the Royal Aircraft Establishment at Farnborough model making had been carried out by the camouflage unit and, transferred to the CIU at Medmenham, it had initially been concerned with making models of military equipment and installations rather than complete landscapes and these were used to teach recognition to the newly recruited photo interpreters. The model makers came from a variety of professional backgrounds but their skills were all appropriate to the production of the models required of them – painters, artists, engravers, sculptors – and the landscape models could measure several feet in length and width. Some of their more remarkable and well-known efforts included those for the raid on Bruneval, for the Dam Busters and an extensive series for D-Day.

Built on a hardboard base, the first procedure was to replicate the contours by applying a series of cut-out layers, the whole then being covered with a flexible material such as plastic or rubber that would give a smooth finish. Buildings and features would then be added. Above all, accuracy was essential and photo reconnaissance images were used in close consultation with the photo interpreters.

In late 1941 the model-making section at Medmenham had been tasked with making a model of the docks at St Nazaire. It was given the serial number M139 and Ursula Powys-Lybbe, a WAAF flight officer at Medmenham, was later to write of its provenance:

> "Preparation of the model for the combined operations raid on the port of
> St Nazaire began eight to nine months before the actual attack on 27/28
> March 1942. Four photographic sorties taken during this stage of the planning

produced some perfect vertical prints as well as an oblique sortie. All during the period of construction these were studied stereoscopically and the oblique prints gave information regarding elevation. Measurements based on all the individual buildings and quays were calculated and detailed plans and sections were produced by the wild section for the construction of land form and topographical detail. The scale of the model made it possible to show alterations in ground levels and surface detail up to a height of four feet or more. Objects less than three feet were indicated by surface painting."[13]

The model had in fact been ordered by Lieutenant Commander Gonin, RN, for the earlier plan for a raid in 1941. It was delivered on 15 October and given a 'confidential' classification. A diary note in the files gave it a cover story by suggesting that it was for briefing purposes in the United States. Measuring 57" x 24" it is a monument to the model makers' art and the DNI himself was moved to send a letter of appreciation. The model was to play a prominent part in the planning of and briefing for the raid and before Chariot Force sailed from Falmouth in the afternoon of 26 March every participant had seen it and committed it to memory. In June 1947, it was transferred to the Imperial War Museum where it can still be seen.

In mid-February, Lieutenant Colonel Newman, who was to be the military force commander for Operation Chariot, was summoned to London to meet Brigadier Charles Haydon, commander of the Special Service Brigade, at COHQ in Richmond Terrace. While waiting for Haydon to arrive Newman was handed a rather portly file containing all the intelligence on St Nazaire, which he was invited to read. Then, having been briefed on the raid by Haydon, Newman was locked into a small room where he pored over the reports, photographs and plans that the file contained but, above all, "the beautiful little model of the docks made by the RAF, which he took wholly to his bosom till he had learnt it by heart so well that he could have walked about the docks blindfold".[14]

Commander Ryder, the naval force commander, would not see the model until 26 February. Arriving late at a meeting at COHQ whence he had been summoned from Wilton where he languished as a naval liaison officer, having incurred their Lordships' displeasure through losing his ship, he found a table surrounded by senior officers and dominated by the model of St Nazaire. Following the meeting Ryder and Newman met for the first time and Ryder was constrained to enquire what target they had been talking about. Newman was able to tell him it was St Nazaire and that there was a comprehensive intelligence file and outline plan as well as the splendid model. They had but four weeks to translate all this into action.

On Friday 13 March, Newman left London for Falmouth, Ryder having left a few days earlier. Noting the date and hoping it wasn't an ill omen, on the steps outside COHQ Newman encountered Mountbatten who left him in no doubt about the importance of the operation. With his car full of plans, maps, photographs and the model of the docks he drove by way of Medmenham to collect the latest reconnaissance details from which he found, as he always did, that there was something new to consider. Breaking his journey at Tavistock he spent a restless night guarding his precious cargo in a hotel room with a defective lock.

On the evening of 18 March the model would be centre of attention when Newman

---

[13] *The Eye of Intelligence* – Ursula Powys-Lybbe (William Kimber & Co Ltd., 1983).
[14] Quoted in *The Greatest Raid of All* by C.E. Lucas Phillips.

briefed his officers. Going over in outline the plans for the raid he stressed the importance of becoming totally acquainted with the geography of the port which he described as 'French' but stopped short of naming it. One officer would recognise it immediately, for the previous year Captain Montgomery of the Royal Engineers had, with his good friend Captain Pritchard, drawn up a plan for its destruction. The following morning he went through the process again with the men and thereafter, in the groups in which they would go ashore, they sat around the decks of their troop carrier, *Princess Josephine Charlotte*, discussing their tactics and returning often to the model and the plans until they were totally au fait with their duties. Newman had already briefed each group in detail in his cabin, the model again being present.

It was not until 23 March that the naval force was briefed and they, too, were not told of the destination, the fact that it was St Nazaire not being disclosed to them until after they had sailed. After the war, one of the sailors was to write:

> "We were invited to gather round a table in the centre of the room. Here, we saw, was a large scale model of an undesignated dock area. I studied it carefully, but couldn't make out any distinguishing feature that identified it to me."[15]

One aspect of the raid which the model facilitated for the naval force was the ability to replicate the conditions they knew, following a disastrous dummy raid against Plymouth, would be encountered when approaching their landing points. Sailing into searchlights directed horizontally across the estuary would be extremely difficult and they practised by studying the model at eye level while torches were shone into their eyes. It was to be a foretaste of reality.

We shall become better acquainted with St Eval in the next chapter but here let it just be said that its situation on the north Cornwall coast, between Newquay and Padstow, made it the ideal location for keeping watch on enemy shipping in the western approaches to the Channel and in the many ports along the French coast now occupied by the Germans, from St Malo, through Brest and down almost to the Spanish frontier.

On 1 July 1940, B Flight of 1PRU had been formed at Heston and despatched immediately to St Eval. It consisted of four officers, twenty-five aircraftmen, two Spitfires and a Tiger Moth. Flight Lieutenant Clark and Flying Officers Blatchford, Christie and Craxton made up the flying strength, the first three named arriving at St Eval by air the following day. The importance of St Eval and the area of its responsibility quickly saw the establishment increased and by the end of November its complement of aircraft had increased to five Spitfires, one of which was armed and one in reserve, a Blenheim IV with another in reserve and the Tiger Moth.

On 4 July Assistant Section Officer Anne Dorrien Smith was posted in for administration duties. It was WAAF regulations in those early days of the war that, following enlistment, women had to serve six months in the more mundane and routine tasks historically allotted to them before undergoing specialist training. Such was the case with Anne, who would later become a photo interpreter (PI) at Medmenham. The regulation was dropped later in the war.

---

[15] Taken from *St Nazaire to Shepperton* – Ralph Batteson (Highedge Historical Society, 1996).

On the day Anne Dorrien Smith arrived, B Flight was to fly its first operational sortie with Flying Officer Christie taking photographs of St Nazaire and Nantes and, on the following day off St Malo and the Channel Islands. On the sixth flight Lieutenant Clark was over Brest, a port that was to loom large in the attentions of B Flight as it was such an important dock facility for the German navy, first for the *Hipper* and later *Scharnhorst*, *Gneisenau* and *Prinz Eugen* prior to their dash through the Channel in February 1942. Such was the emphasis on Brest that the pilots coined the expression for their activities as "Brest or bust".

During its first month at St Eval B Flight would operate on twenty-three days, flying a total of thirty-eight sorties of which twenty-eight were successful. These sorties would produce approximately 2,633 exposures, all taken over enemy territory. When Ann McKnight-Kauffer arrived at St Eval as a PI in February 1941, she found only one officer, Flight Lieutenant Wiginton, carrying out that task. In view of the quantity of photographs being taken that complement would appear to be insufficient for purpose but it should be remembered that operational practice for PRU pilots was to switch on their cameras for a straight run over the target, thereby getting several exposures, such as over the sea, which could immediately be discarded. In this way as many as two-thirds needed no attention from the PIs and the remainder, in first phase, only required evidence of any new or altered activity by the enemy. It was therefore reckoned that only two trained PIs were required in a first phase unit.

At first the St Eval PIs were based on the airfield but bombing attacks began towards the end of August 1940 and continued into 1941 when on 25 January a number of enemy aircraft attacked the airfield at dusk, dropping high-explosive bombs, one of which hit a shelter, causing eight fatalities, although not to PRU personnel. As a result of the ongoing raids and increasing danger it was eventually decided to move to accommodation away from the airfield.

By March 1942, the pilots flying reconnaissance sorties out of St Eval were Flight Lieutenants Steventon, Jones and Robinson, Flying Officer Scafe, Pilot Officer Bonnar and Sergeant McLeod. Apart from specific flights requested by planners for the raid their regular sorties took them often over St Nazaire. They would probably never have known, but their contribution to the planning and eventual success of Operation Chariot was inestimable.

While Newman was still in London dealing with plans for the raid from the room that had been put at his disposal at COHQ, 1PRU would provide him with something of a problem, not that he didn't have enough already. On 7 March a set of reconnaissance photographs arrived which clearly showed the heavy defences of St Nazaire and that they included four heavy coastal defence emplacements that had only recently been built.

Newman quickly realised that extra forces would be needed to counter the estimated sixty personnel the Germans would employ to man these new positions. He calculated that two more motor launches and thirty additional commandos would be required and after making urgent representations to the MACO, Brigadier Haydon, he was advised the following day that the launches had been found and he gave immediate orders for the extra troops to be added to those already training for the raid. The men from the PRU had provided another valuable contribution to the planning process.

At 1225 on Wednesday 25 March 1942, Spitfire N311, with Sergeant McLeod at the controls, took off from St Eval, 'objective St Nazaire'. At 1500 he landed back safely with his photographs and the film was hurried to be processed. Following first phase interpretation, in which a nasty development had been identified, copies were rushed by motorcycle despatch rider to Chariot Force assembled in Falmouth while further copies were sent to Medmenham for second and third phase appraisal.

At Falmouth the commandos were on board *Princess Josephine Charlotte* filling the last hours before their coming operation by carrying out the myriad tasks that both prepared them for battle and took their minds off the dangers that lay ahead when, soon after 9 o'clock, Newman was summoned to join Commander Ryder on HMS *Atherstone*, complete with his magnifying glass. On arrival Newman found Ryder looking over the images that had recently arrived from St Eval and he was invited to inspect them. Apart from two tankers under repair in the Normandie Dock it was also possible to see, tied up in the submarine basin not many yards from the building Newman had designated as his headquarters, the five ships of the *Möwe* class which formed the 5th Torpedo Boat Destroyer Flotilla. They were *Seeadler, Falke, Kondor, Jaguar* and *Iltis*.[16] Typically, Newman could only see them as added targets for his commandos but Ryder, as a naval man, was acutely aware of the fire power that these would add to the defence of St Nazaire if still in the basin and the danger they posed to Chariot Force if they put to sea. Ryder later wrote:

> "The result was not without humour, as the enemy had chosen that moment to berth four [sic] torpedo boats alongside the very place Newman had picked as his headquarters. He inquired hopefully how many men were needed to capture them. When asked how many reserves he had got he answered, 'Twelve'. I suggested that he would probably need them all."

The following morning, 26 March, before they sailed, Ryder found time to go ashore and telephone Plymouth to beg additions to his escort. As a result two more Hunt class destroyers, HMS *Cleveland* and HMS *Brocklesby* would be despatched to meet the retiring force as it withdrew from the Loire estuary following the raid.

The force having sailed later that day, all now settled down to the long voyage to St Nazaire. Their first night at sea behind them, at 1240 the next day the German warships entered the equation again when a signal from Plymouth advised Ryder that they had put to sea. Such a superior force, if encountered, had the ability to scupper the whole operation. That no encounter took place was due to intervention from an unexpected source, as we shall later discover.

The collection of the vast amount of data that was so vital to the war effort did not come without exacting a high price and far too many PRU pilots were to lose their lives in action. Flying at the extremes of their range, unarmed and painted a distinctive colour, and with the Germans well aware of their existence, losses were inevitable. Here will be named but three who died in quite contrasting circumstances.

Squadron Leader Alastair Taylor was, as a young pilot officer, one of Cotton's early recruits and three DFCs bore testimony to his great prowess as a reconnaissance pilot. On 4 December 1941, with Sergeant Horsfall as navigator, Taylor flew from RAF Leuchars, on a sortie that took in Trondheim and Bergen, in a Mosquito, a plane recently added to those flown by the PRU. They failed to return and it was some time before a story emerged from Norway that they had been hit over Norway by the Germans' new high-altitude anti-aircraft capability

---

[16] These ships were markedly different from a British MTB and were more akin to a Hunt class destroyer.

and although judged to have been able to crash-land it is thought they had chosen to fly west and crash in the sea to protect the secrets of the equipment they carried.

Destined to die in totally different circumstances was Flight Lieutenant Alistair Gunn, RAFVR. He, too, was on a sortie over Norway, on 5 March 1942, having taken off from Benson, when he was shot down by a fluke round from a Me109 but parachuted safely to ground and was taken prisoner. He was interrogated for three weeks at Dulag Luft as the Germans under-estimated the range of the Spitfire V he had been flying and thought he had flown out of northern Norway. Whilst in Stalag Luft III he took part in the Great Escape. He was well down the list in the lottery for places in the tunnel at about number sixty and his exit was delayed by a fall of sand between 'Piccadilly Circus' and 'Leicester Square'. However, he was one of the seventy-six who got away from the camp and was later recaptured near Gorlitz. Last seen alive on 6 April 1944, Gunn was shot by the Gestapo and cremated at Breslau. The ashes of the escapers were buried at Sagan and in 1948, on the instructions of the Commonwealth War Graves Commission, they were transferred to Poznan Old Garrison Cemetery.

At 0740 on the morning of 28 March 1942, as Ryder and the survivors of the raid made good their escape from the Loire, a Spitfire, R.7044, took off from Wick, on a sortie over Trondheim Fjord. The pilot was Flight Lieutenant Alfred Fane Peers Fane. Before the war, Alfred Fane had been a successful racing driver, entering all the big events of the day at Brooklands, Crystal Palace and Donnington. He had driven in the Mille Miglia and also twice taken part in the Le Mans 24-hour race, on both occasions failing to finish, but in 1937 he had driven a BMW to victory at the Nürburgring.

On the outbreak of war he had joined the RAFVR and spent the early years in photographic intelligence in Bomber Command at High Wycombe where he was remembered as always carrying a loaded revolver, with which he was a crack shot. His experience with Bomber Command would stand him in good stead when he later became a pilot in 1PRU for he would have first-hand knowledge of the requirements for a good photograph.

Fane landed back at Wick at 1332 where the laconic entry in the operations record book, 'Objective: Trondheim. Result: Photos Trondheim', masked the fact that he had returned with a magnificent vertical photograph of the *Tirpitz*, whose crew were no doubt as blissfully unaware of his presence as they were of the fact that the only dry dock on the Atlantic seaboard that could accommodate their ship had that very morning been destroyed by the commandos.

Less than three months later, on 18 July 1942, returning in his Spitfire from a reconnaissance mission over France he crashed near Duxford, Cambridgeshire, and was killed. He is buried in the churchyard of St Nicholas, Hedsor, High Wycombe, yet another of the brave young men who flew solo, unarmed, high and fast to bring in the intelligence that was such a huge factor in the winning of the war, and who made the ultimate sacrifice.

On the day of the raid, 28 March, and in the days following, reconnaissance planes from B Flight, 1PRU, would again overfly St Nazaire and bring back the momentous news of the success of HMS *Campbeltown* and the raiding force in the destruction of the southern caisson and dock installations that would render it inoperable for the remainder of the war. The flight had been continuously associated with Operation Chariot since they made possible the production of the model back in 1941 and until its shining conclusion.

CHAPTER 5

BAY WATCH

The Bay of Biscay is a dangerous stretch of water at any time without the added complications of hostile forces. Following the fall of France the building of Hitler's *Festung Europa* had seen the Atlantic coast of France dotted with U-boat pens at Brest, Lorient, St Nazaire, La Rochelle and Bordeaux making for heavy traffic across the bay as the U-boats sailed to and returned from their patrols against Allied shipping. Now, for a day and a half, the Charioteers would have to make their way across these patrol lines and hope against hope that none of these leviathans of the deep would be encountered. To make them keep their heads down and to attack them should they dare to show themselves, Coastal Command flew numerous anti-submarine sweeps and anti-shipping patrols to ensure the safe passage of Chariot. They did, as we shall see, stumble into one, with unseen consequences that would benefit the raiders.

With the planning and the training now behind them, the pay book wills and those last, difficult letters written, the commandos, never wholly comfortable at sea, as a seasick-ridden trip to the Isles of Scilly had proved, could now but commit themselves to the care of the navy, the vagaries of wind and sea and the Almighty for the thirty-four hours it would take to deliver them to their destiny. Happily they were to be fortunate with the weather for only a light swell disturbed the surface of the sea while a fine haze drifted by, borne on a light easterly breeze, and over all shone a warm spring sun.

The flotilla of little ships had sailed from Falmouth in the early afternoon of 26 March, to be followed at 1400 by the escorting destroyers and HMS *Campbeltown*. There was no point in giving prying eyes ashore a pointer that this was a joint venture. Above them, backwards and forwards at low altitude, flew a lone Hurricane from 247 Squadron, based at nearby Predannack. Many eyes followed it wistfully for this iconic symbol of the indomitable spirit of the nation would, for many, be their last link with home.

At sunset the Hurricane, with one last pass over the little fleet, climbed steeply away to return to its base, no doubt ignorant of the great purpose of the force over which he had so diligently watched.

On MGB 314 Ryder watched it depart and speculated on the thoughts of the pilot. Had he wondered why he had orders not to fly above 100 feet? Was he worried about the developing haze that might make hazardous his own return to base? He would certainly not have known that several of those over whom he had watched were on their last voyage. Ryder surely reflected the mood of many when he wrote in 1947:

> "To the pilot this was the end of his spell of duty and in fifteen minutes he would be back in the security of his base. To those below the departing machine represented the last visible link with the homeland they had left six hours before. Much lay ahead and even the least imaginative of the company present, alone with his thoughts, must have speculated on his future."

Standing on the deck of the *Campbeltown*, Lieutenant Corran Purdon, yet to achieve his twenty-first birthday – he would 'celebrate' it as a prisoner of war walking the barbed wire compound at Westertimke with Donald Roy, a fellow commando – watched it with some foreboding. Would he live to see England again? If not, he could think of no finer parting memory of England and the thought, coupled with the knowledge of the task which had been entrusted to him in St Nazaire and the opportunity he had been given to carry the fight to the enemy, filled him with an enormous pride. Corran would not see England again until 1945 when he returned home after the liberation of Colditz whence he had gravitated after an unsuccessful escape attempt.

Another young commando officer on *Campbeltown*, Lieutenant Stuart Chant, also noted the presence of the Hurricane and he, too, would see home again but, badly wounded on the run in to the target, it would be as a 'Grand Blessé' and repatriation on medical grounds late in 1943, arriving in England on the *Drottningholm*, a Swedish ship known affectionately to the returning English servicemen as the 'Trotting Home'.

After the force had formed up off Falmouth Ryder, for the hours of daylight, adopted Cruising Order No. 1, a broad arrowhead formation, with *Atherstone* towing MGB 314, *Tynedale* and *Campbeltown* towing MTB 74 providing the shaft and the two columns of motor launches spread out in echelon on either side, about two cables apart. In this guise they replicated a normal anti-submarine sweep against the chance appearance of a Luftwaffe reconnaissance aircraft.

As the dark cloak of night spread over the force to cover their progress the night cruising order was adopted by drawing in the wings to form two lines astern, either side of the destroyers, and closing up to one cable apart. Speed was increased as that same dark cloak would mask the phosphorescence of their wake and would enable them to slow down again come the dawn.

The force had altered course at point A to a little west of due south to clear the minefields off Ushant, and they were now alone but the departure of the Hurricane had not meant abandonment by the RAF. As they sailed away into the darkness of their first night at sea preparations were afoot in England for planes to fly watch and ward over them that night and the following day as they approached the estuary of the Loire.

```
Four Whitleys commencing sweep 2100/26 following
longitude on 48N. 6W. 6.46W. 7.33W. and 08.20W
thence coming 165 to 44.30N. thence 270 for 18
miles and thence 345° to datum line and base.

Another Whitley commencing sweep 45.15N 01.30W at
2330/26 thence down coast to Spanish territorial
waters and thence to base.
```

Signal to Ryder at Falmouth – 1315/26

Between Newquay and Padstow, a short distance inland from the high cliffs of north Cornwall that stand as England's bulwark against the unremitting force of the waves and weather of the north Atlantic, stands the church of St Eval. This lovely building nudges the boundary of the flat and derelict plateau that was once RAF St Eval, one of the busiest bases of World War II. From its elevated runways, during the years 1939-1945, would fly no less than forty-two RAF squadrons and ten of the RNAS not to mention our American allies. Seven of these RAF squadrons would fly in support of Operation Chariot. It would also be home to a flight of the photo reconnaissance unit that flew regular sorties over the Biscay ports and brought back invaluable intelligence, much of which was used by the Chariot planners. Following the raid a damaged Beaufighter based at Predannack would use it for an emergency landing on return from the fray.

In the inter-war years of the burgeoning threat from the rise of Nazism in Germany it was erroneously thought that the danger to these isles would come from the east but with the rapid collapse and occupation of France and the extension of the Atlantic wall to the Biscay ports the long arm of Cornwall, that reaches out to where the Channel and the Atlantic meet, would be of increased strategic importance. That expectation of attack from the east had seen the planners, with some justification, concentrate on fighter and bomber aircraft but with the formation of Coastal Command the need for reconnaissance planes was realised and in 1937 a search was made for suitable sites for new bases.

The identification of St Eval for development was a controversial and unpopular decision for it meant the total destruction of a village and farming community and, it was initially thought, the church. However, work started in 1938 on clearing the area and it was no easy task, for the numerous small fields were delineated by what the Cornishman calls a 'hedge' and is, in fact, a high, wide, stone-built, earth-filled bank topped with impenetrable growth. The houses and several farms were demolished and some roads disappeared completely. Happily, the church was saved and stands to this day.

The value of this stark and isolated tower had long been recognised as an aid to navigation, for the wool merchants of Bristol who sailed this coast had donated funds towards its construction and although the airfield endured numerous air raids, particularly in 1940 when in August it was bombed four times in six days, on a later raid the NAAFI was hit and Lord Haw Haw boasted of its priority as a target and predicted its imminent destruction, the Germans never bombed the church. It was certainly a beacon of relief to many an RAF crew, perhaps wrestling with a damaged aircraft, on return from a sortie.

On 6 April 1941 a particularly gallant attack was launched from St Eval on the *Gneisenau* which had been in dry dock in Brest but was reported to have moved out into the harbour. Six Beauforts took off to launch a strike, but only two reached the target. Of these, the plane flown by Flying Officer Kenneth Campbell made a near perfect attack with his torpedo from fifty feet and close range. The ship was damaged below the water line but the Beaufort was immediately shot down. Campbell was awarded a posthumous Victoria Cross.

Another notable success for a St Eval-based plane was in the summer of 1942 when a Lancaster of 61 Squadron, detached from Rutland, became the first in RAF Bomber Command to bring back a photograph showing the irrefutable proof of their sinking of a U-boat at sea.

As the strategic importance of St Eval became clear further airfields were established in the county. St Eval gained a satellite field at St Mawgan while a new field was built at Nancekuke, named RAF Portreath, which was provided with its own satellites at Predannack and Trevellas. Of RAF Predannack we shall be hearing more.

502 (Bomber) Squadron RAF had been formed at Aldergrove, Northern Ireland, in May 1925, as a heavy-bomber squadron and took the name 'Ulster' in December of that year, adopting the red hand of Ulster as its badge. Re-designated as a day-bomber squadron in 1935, it flew a variety of aircraft until, in November 1938, it was transferred to Coastal Command and converted to Avro Ansons in January 1939.

When war broke out in September of that year the squadron was used to fly patrols in the Irish Sea and over the Atlantic off the Irish coast. Changing aircraft again the squadron converted to Armstrong Whitworth Whitleys in October 1940 and in November 1941 it was claimed to be the first squadron of Coastal Command to sink a U-boat, although later information cast some doubt on that claim.

In January 1942, after a year at Limavady, the squadron officially moved, via RAF Docking, in Norfolk, where it set up a maintenance facility, to RAF St Eval from where we shall see it fly in support of the raid on St Nazaire.

612 (County of Aberdeen) Squadron was formed as an auxiliary squadron in June 1937, at RAF Dyce, near Aberdeen, from where it took its name. Initially used on army cooperation duties, in December 1937 it assumed a general reconnaissance role flying Hawker Hectors. In July 1939 they converted again, this time to the Avro Anson, which better suited their role, carrying as it did a four-man crew and boasting a much greater range.

Yet another conversion in November 1940 brought them the Armstrong Whitworth Whitley, which they flew until November 1942, when a final conversion saw them take on the Vickers Wellington which they operated until their disbandment on 9 July 1945. The squadron pursued the usual multiple tasks of a Coastal Command unit by flying anti-submarine patrols, convoy escorts and anti-invasion patrols off the Scottish coast and, following the conversion to Whitleys, the increased range allowed them to mount attacks on the Bismarck and the Prinz Eugen in Bergen harbour in May and June 1941, but without any success.

Moving from Dyce to Wick in April 1941, the following December it moved again, this time to Reykjavik where it stayed until August 1942 flying anti-submarine patrols over the mid-Atlantic. During this time in Iceland it would maintain a detachment at RAF St Eval from where it would, in common with 502, fly to support the raid on St Nazaire.

These two squadrons were equipped with the Armstrong Whitworth Whitley GR Mark VII. We shall meet the Whitley V later, but suffice it to say here that the General Reconnaissance Mark VII variant had extra fuel tanks fitted in the bomb bay and fuselage which extended its range to 2,300 miles, which was ideal for the service with Coastal Command for which it was designed, and it also carried air-to-surface vessel (ASV) radar, which required a row of four dorsal radar masts and the addition of a sixth crew member.

On 26 March, the operations record book for 612 Squadron records, "Pilot Officer Bow confirmed in the rank of pilot officer and promoted to the rank of flying officer Substantive w.e.f. 23.1.42". William Desmond Stuart Bow, a Cambridge languages graduate, was not to enjoy his elevation for long as he was that evening to fly one of the four Whitleys about which Ryder had received advice at Falmouth shortly before he had sailed. It was, sadly, a sortie from which he would not return.

The four Whitleys were to carry out an anti-submarine sweep of the Bay of Biscay, from a datum line of 48°N and spread out at intervals from 06°00' W to 08°20'W. They were to fly a course of 165° until reaching 44°30'N then fly due west for eighteen miles before turning on to a reciprocal course of 345° to return to the datum line from where they would fly back to base. The aircraft were to be on the datum line to commence the sweep at 2100 hours on 26 March. All the crews had received verbal instructions regarding S/E[17] contacts which applied, "north of 46 degrees N. (repeat) north of 46 degrees N. only". Friendly forces in the shape of Chariot Force were, after all, sailing below.

---

[17] Special equipment — an oblique reference to radar, at that time top secret.

The weather was fair and there had been a slight mist but there was no low cloud and only a light wind from the north-east as the group took off in succession from shortly before 1900 and turned south for their start points. The two aircraft from 502 Squadron, YG-C and YG-F, flew the two inside sweeps and Sergeant Donnai in YG-C landed back at St Eval at 0238 the following morning having nothing to report after an uneventful sortie. Likewise, Pilot Officer Endicott in YG-F, landing shortly after, had nothing to report except that he had experienced considerable S/E interference. Was this, perhaps, due to the electrical storm about which we shall shortly learn the sad consequences?

Completing the group were two aircraft from 612 Squadron, part of a detachment to St Eval from their home base at Reykjavik. These two, WL-U and WL-X, flew the outside sweeps and after a flight from which he, too, had nothing to report, WL-U landed safely back at St Eval. Nothing more was ever heard of Flying Officer Bow and his crew in WL-X.

On a farm at Kermorvan on the northern tip of the Crozon peninsula, across the Goulet de Brest that led to the harbour itself, between 0530 and 0600 on the morning of 27 March the noise of an aeroplane was heard followed by an explosion. It was still dark and there was a little fog. Adrien Clorennec, one of the first to reach the crash site later described how the plane had circled above for between five and ten minutes and he had thought the pilot was seeking a suitable strip of land on which to make a forced-landing. Although captained by Desmond Bow it is reported that Douglas Stein was flying the aircraft, which was already on fire when suddenly it fell to earth, coming to rest against a grass bank and catching fire. It had been armed with six 240-lb depth charges but these may well have been jettisoned earlier. However, there was nothing anyone could do and no hope of any survivors. German soldiers were soon on the scene and while they stood in front of the wreckage they allowed a member of the Péchonière family to take a photograph.

The International Committee of the Red Cross had informed the Air Ministry in 1942 that the crew had perished and had forwarded a German *Totenliste* naming five of the crew and giving the sixth as unknown; it was not until after the war that the location of the crash was established. On the Sunday, two days after the crash, at 0800, the bodies of the crew had been laid to rest with full military honours in a communal grave in the local cemetery at Roscanvel. The Germans mounted a guard of honour consisting of an officer and twenty-seven men, a minute's silence was observed and a volley fired over the grave. A large wooden cross was erected bearing the inscription: Here lie six English airmen, fallen on 27 March 1942.

In 1946, at the behest of a local resident, Louis Thomas, the council of Roscanvel gave the airmen a re-burial and in 1947, when the War Graves Commission came to identify the bodies, three traditional headstones were erected bearing the names and details of the crew.

Flying Officer W.D.S. Bow, RAFVR
Sergeant L.K. Newman, RAF
Flying Officer J.W.G. Potter, RAFVR
Pilot Officer D.M. Stein, RAFVR
Sergeant H.M. Tookey, RAFVR
Sergeant D.A. Young, RAFVR

In the operations room at St Eval mounting concern at the lack of contact from WL-X was lightened when a call was received at their 2 D/F from RAF Leuchars to say an aircraft was calling them. Although 2 D/F immediately attempted to raise WL-X on the radio they were not successful and received no reply. Another RDF station, that of 10 Group, had also reported an aircraft, thought to be WL-X as it was off Bolt Head at about the time the aircraft was expected to have been in that position, but the plot had faded out near the French coast.

The squadron commander at St Eval was of the opinion that the crew were disorientated for at 1500 on the 26th, almost four hours before the crews had taken off on their anti-submarine sweep, a signal was sent from the Air Ministry warning of an imminent magnetic storm, but having been given no priority it was not received at St Eval until 0254 on the 27th. It was surmised that this storm may have affected the compass and W/T apparatus on WL-X and the crew wrongly thought themselves to be over the Bristol Channel when, in fact, they were south of Bolt Head on the south coast of Devon. Plotting a course south of east which they estimated would give them a landfall in Cornwall and return to St Eval, they crossed instead the English Channel and the landfall they made, far from being England, home and safety, was the Crozon peninsula in Brittany.

Twenty minutes before the others, the fifth Whitley about which Ryder had been advised, YG-P, piloted by Flight Sergeant Pope, took off from St Eval for a patrol that would take him down almost to Spain. He was charged with patrolling from a point off the French coast at 45°15'N, 01°30'W southward to the limit of Spanish territorial waters. This required an almost complete traverse of the Bay of Biscay, closer to the coast than any of the anti-submarine sweeps already flown.

Their orders were to attack any suitable targets except fishing craft, but shipping over 1,500 tons was to be reported by wireless telegraphy when clear of the French coast, while S/E contacts north of 46°N were subject to special instructions which had been passed verbally. This would prevent them from attacking the Chariot Force below, making its steady progress to St Nazaire. They carried a bomb load of two 500-lb MC, and maximum number of 250-lb GP, all set to 3-second delay. Their flight yielded only the sighting of fishing boats and no shipping as detailed to attack and they landed back at St Eval at 0345 on the morning of the 27th.

The night wore on and the sailors went calmly about their tasks, happy to be at sea where they felt so much more at home. They were now aware of their destination for, unlike the commandos, they had not been briefed until their officers had opened their sealed orders once at sea. The off-watch sailors turned in, as did the commandos for whom the calm sea had eased their anxiety about seasickness. Even so, sleep did not come easy for "the thrill of the moment was upon them" and thoughts of the impending action brought mixed emotions.

An hour before midnight the force arrived at Point B, almost due west of Ushant, and the course was altered to port to a little east of due south. They would maintain this course until 0700 the following morning when they would arrive at Point C and turn east towards their goal.

The dawn, when it came, brought disappointment for the light mist that had so suited their purpose the previous evening had dispersed and Ryder was presented with a bright sun, cloudless sky and unlimited visibility. With the coming of the light the force again adopted the anti-submarine arrowhead formation and at Point C, with 160 miles to go, they set a course of 112°. Five minutes later the disappointment of the dawn was followed by potential disaster with the sighting of a U-boat, U-593, seven and a half miles on the port beam.

Ryder despatched *Tynedale* to investigate and followed himself in *Atherstone*. An inconclusive action followed in which *Tynedale* opened fire too early and the U-boat dived, re-surfaced and dived again. *Tynedale* and *Atherstone* carried out an unsuccessful square search for two hours after which Ryder abandoned the hunt, taking the precaution of setting off on a false course to the south-west and re-joining the main force by way of a wide sweep. It was not until a little before 1400 hours that the U-boat eventually deemed it safe to surface after several hours below. U-593 had indeed seen the force but was misled by its course and later signalled, "Three destroyers 10 MTBs 46° 52'N, 5° 48'W. Course West".

Even as Kapitänleutnant Gerd Kelbling, the captain of U-593, was sending his message to Group Command West, a Spitfire of B Flight, 1 PRU, was getting airborne from St Eval. The pilot, Flight Lieutenant Robinson, had instructions to take photographs of locations from Bordeaux to St Nazaire. Earlier in the day Pilot Officer Bonnar had been sent on a photo-reconnaissance flight to Bordeaux but had returned with a "nil result due to weather". Robinson therefore crossed the French coast at Morlaix, flew on over Lorient, St Nazaire and Nantes, and took photographs of all of these towns. Returning over St Nazaire, he again photographed the port.

Two days earlier, on the 25th, also flying from St Eval, Sergeant McLeod had overflown St Nazaire and taken the photographs which had been made urgently available to Ryder and Newman at Falmouth. Now, on the 27th, Robinson also found the torpedo boats, in fact five in number, and they were on the move.

Ryder had already received a signal from C-in-C Plymouth that the German squadron had moved thirty miles upstream to Nantes where, whilst berthed, they would pose little threat to Chariot. Ships at sea, though, were an entirely different matter. Robinson reported that, at 1510 hours, he had "sighted and photographed five T/Bs – steering westward along Loire – line astern – off Painboeuff [sic]". Forty minutes later he reported the "same vessels seen almost stationary to seaward side of St Nazaire Harbour – photographed". The enemy ships were now parked in the middle of the fairway.

Help, however, was to come, albeit unwittingly, from the hand of Gerd Kelbling. His message, when received by German Command Group West at 1420, caused them to think that the British force was withdrawing after laying mines, and an attack on the coast was not suspected.[18] Their reaction had been to order the 5th Torpedo Boat Destroyer Flotilla to carry out mine reconnaissance that night. Thus, as Ryder led his force over the shoals to St Nazaire, the German ships were leaving along the deep Charpentiers Channel under the lee of the north shore and ne'er the twain did meet.

Now re-united as a single entity the force resumed its progress towards Point D, the next milestone on their journey. Here another diversion exercised their attention. Around 1130 they found themselves approaching a cluster of fishing boats, of which the Bay of Biscay

---

[18] Many years after the war Gerd Kelbling met with Bill Green, the officer who had navigated Chariot Force over the shoals of the Loire estuary, to whom he confirmed that, although his message had been received, the German High Command had a ruling that signals received from U-boat captains early in their first command should be disregarded since they might be unreliable.

boasted an abundance. Two particularly stood apart from the others and Ryder, fearful of a planned rendezvous with the U-boat and of the trawlers carrying radios, ordered them to be boarded. Finding none, and assured that the others did not carry them either, Ryder spared them but nevertheless sank the two which had been boarded after first removing their crews who were taken to England and later joined the Free French Forces. The flotilla continued through Point D where they adjusted their course a little to the east and set off towards Point E, from which they would launch their attack. It was a few minutes after midday on 27 March.

```
To   : SO  10th A/S Striking Force¹⁹
       TYNEDALE.
         (R) Admiralty.
            CCO
From: C-in-C Plymouth

       Weather. Wind E to S.E. Force 2 to 3. Coastal haze
       possible extending well to seaward.
       (2) 4 Whitleys commence sweep at 1400 27th between
       006° W and 008° 20'W from 048° N course 154° to
       045° N and return.

       (3) 4 Sunderlands commence sweep at 2130 27th
       between 006° 40'W and 009° 32'W. course 140° to
       044° N and return.
                 = 1127/27
```

At precisely the moment Ryder was sinking the fishing vessels, back at St Eval the aircraft were setting off down the runway for the second anti-submarine sweep of the Bay of Biscay. Taking off towards the land, two Whitleys of 502 Squadron, piloted by Flying Officer Hill in YG-N and Flying Officer Cotton in YG-K, banked towards the sea and set course for the start of their patrol on the datum line of 48°N. Closely following them were two Whitleys of 612 Squadron, WL-U and WL-L, who were also to commence patrols from the same datum line. The four aircraft would start their sweeps spread out from 08°20'W to 06°00'W in a repeat of those sweeps that had been flown overnight, flying 165° course down to 45°N, turning west for eighteen miles before returning on a course of 345° to the datum line and thence return to base at St Eval. Having drawn the most westerly patrols it was, perhaps, not surprising that the two aircraft of 502 Squadron produced no result, Flying Officer Hill reporting "patrol without incident" and Flying Officer Cotton a "negative response".

---

[19] As a cover for the collection in Falmouth of the various craft that would sail on Operation Chariot, Ryder had called it the 10th Anti-Submarine Striking Force.

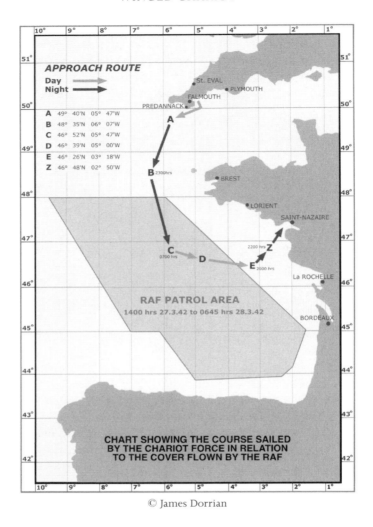

APPROACH ROUTE

Day
Night

A   49° 40'N   05° 47'W
B   48° 35'N   06° 07'W
C   46° 52'N   05° 47'W
D   46° 39'N   05° 00'W
E   46° 26'N   03° 18'W
Z   46° 48'N   02° 50'W

RAF PATROL AREA
1400 hrs 27.3.42 to 0645 hrs 28.3.42

CHART SHOWING THE COURSE SAILED
BY THE CHARIOT FORCE IN RELATION
TO THE COVER FLOWN BY THE RAF

© James Dorrian

Patrolling closer to the coast than their colleagues from 502, although WL-U of 612 Squadron also made no report, closest to land of all, WL-L encountered, following an S/E contact eight miles to starboard, four large trawlers sailing due north and, about five miles astern of them, two larger vessels, bows pointing east and apparently hove to. A further contact at 1805 hours, eight miles ahead, proved to be a Whitley on a course of 330°, a course that would take him back to England.

Some seven and a half hours after the first Whitley had lifted off from St Eval, the long-range Whitley YG-P, now piloted by Warrant Officer Bell, set off to repeat the anti-shipping patrol flown the previous night by Flight Sergeant Pope. Having received the same briefing and the special verbal instructions they made the long haul across the Bay of Biscay to their start point at 45°15'N, 01°30'W, sighting only fishing vessels as they went, and left them unmolested in accordance with their orders.

However, at 2212 hours their progress across the Bay was interrupted by a much more serious contact seventeen miles ahead in position 46°32'N, 03°48'W and eight minutes later they sighted four destroyers and two motor vessels sailing due south at ten knots.

This being within their 'special instructions' area they took immediate evasive action and radioed for instructions. It was not until 2330 hours, an hour and ten minutes later, that they received a signal to attack and during this time they had continued with their patrol, again encountering only fishing vessels. On receipt of the signal, although they searched diligently, the enemy force was not sighted again and aircraft YG-P returned to St Eval, landing at 0545 hours on Saturday 28 March, after a long and exhausting sortie. The report of these four destroyers was relayed to HMS *Atherstone* and received at 2306. By this time HMS *Campbeltown* and the flotilla of little ships had set off from Point Z leaving the escorting Hunts to patrol overnight off the estuary. The sighting put the enemy destroyers forty miles to the westward and steaming south so Lieutenant Commander Jenks saw no point in trying to find Ryder to pass this information to him.

Down below, Chariot Force sailed serenely on at a steady twelve knots, no doubt unaware of the anti-submarine sweeps that had been flown above them to keep them out of danger. At 2000 hours, as Whitley YG-K was landing at St Eval, they reached Point E and turned north-east, the course that would take them to their target. They were now in the formation in which they would make their attack. Their next marker was Point Z, at 46 °48'N, 02 °50'W, and here they were to meet HM Submarine *Sturgeon* which had been sent ahead to give them a navigation fix. It was at this time that the last Whitley airborne, Warrant Officer Bell, in YG-P was in contact with the four destroyers and two motor vessels at 46 °32'N, 03 °48'W, which were crossing their track some 75 miles behind them. Meanwhile, during the hour before the force had reached Point Z, yet another group of aircraft had arrived to patrol the bay.

In a sheltered arm of Plymouth Sound, called Cattewater, plans were afoot in 1916 to open a Royal Naval Air Service seaplane base and RNAS Cattewater duly opened in February 1917. Seaplane trials had taken place here as early as 1913 but sustained development of the base did not take place until after 1 April 1918, when, with the birth of the Royal Air Force, it became RAF Cattewater and two large hangars were built, together with slipways.

Completed as World War I finished, the base then saw little activity but starting in 1923 it was rebuilt and extended and it re-opened in 1928, when it was re-named RAF Mount Batten after the castle that crowned the nearby promontory. Here, too, were developed air-sea rescue launches and on these, in the 1930s, was employed T.E. Lawrence, seeking anonymity in the guise of Aircraftman Shaw.

When the fall of France brought the Germans to Brittany, RAF Mount Batten became in range of Luftwaffe bombers and suffered several raids and although, in 1940, the earliest of these caused little damage, a heavier raid in November destroyed two Sunderlands, one in a hangar and one on the water. With the war effort intensifying and with regular bombing raids on Plymouth a balloon barrage was raised and the Sound became ever more congested so the then resident squadron, 10 (RAAF), moved to Pembroke Dock in May 1941, from where it would return in January 1942.

10 (RAAF) Squadron was the only Australian squadron to serve continuously throughout World War II. Having been formed at Point Cook, in Victoria, on 1 July 1939, later that month a small group of both aircrew and ground crew flew to England to train on the Short Sunderland aircraft with which the squadron was to be equipped. These aircraft were to be flown to Australia on completion of training but events overtook them and when war was

declared the Australian government offered to retain the squadron in Britain.

Based initially in Pembroke Dock, to where sufficient extra personnel were flown to bring it up to full strength, 10 (RAAF) Squadron was engaged in the usual round of anti-submarine patrols, convoy escorts and air-sea rescues that was the staple diet of a Coastal Command squadron and they patrolled particularly the Biscay ports to intercept U-boats setting out on Atlantic forays. However, in April 1940 the majority of the squadron moved to RAF Mount Batten while the remainder went as a detachment to Oban until April the following year and in May 1941, for reasons we have already seen, it returned to Pembroke Dock. In January 1942 it was back at RAF Mount Batten from where it flew in support of the raid on St Nazaire.

The Short S.25 Sunderland was unusual among the aircraft in our story in that it grew out of a design for a civilian passenger aircraft. The Short S.23 Empire flying boat had been the flagship of Imperial Airways and the forerunner of the extensive air routes that now criss-cross the globe. Extensively re-designed for military use it became one of the most powerful and widely employed flying boats of the war and, later, converted for civil use, continued to carry passengers until 1974. The prototype had first flown in 1937.

The early Sunderlands were not too effective as anti-submarine aircraft but excelled at air-sea rescue and performed valiantly in the military evacuation of Crete. However, the crews developed their skills and armament was increased while a more effective depth charge replaced the anti-submarine bomb which had not been suitable for purpose. What it lacked in weight of fire it made up for in number and so bristled with guns that the Germans were reputed to refer to it as the 'Flying Porcupine'.

The Mark III as flown by 10 (RAAF) Squadron became the definitive version. With a crew varying between nine and eleven – two pilots, radio operator, navigator, engineer and bomb aimer and gunners varying between three and five – its range was 1,780 miles at a cruising speed of 178 mph with a maximum of 210 mph. It was powered by four Bristol Pegasus XVIII engines. The defensive armament was 16 x .303 and 2 x 0.5 Browning machine guns and it carried a veritable arsenal of weaponry, both offensive and defensive – bombs, mines and depth charges and flares, sea markers and smoke floats. All in all the Short S.25 Sunderland was a formidable fighting machine.

Starting at ten-minute intervals at 1910 hours on 27 March four Sunderlands of 10 (RAAF) Squadron had set off for the datum line of 48°N from which, like the Whitleys before them, they would carry out their patrols. It would take two hours flying time to get there.

Commencing his patrol at 2130 hours Flying Officer Miedecke, in RB-R was faced with a long traverse of the bay on a south-easterly course that would take him to the limit of Spanish territorial waters, the furthest south that any of the aircraft would fly. Turning west they then flew a short leg before turning on to a north-westerly bearing on a track parallel to their original and returning to the datum line, where they arrived at 0640 hours on the morning of 28 March. They had obtained numerous S/E contacts throughout but all had proved to be fishing vessels. During the course of the patrol they had received instructions to land at Pembroke Dock but they requested and were granted permission to return to Mount Batten, where they became waterborne at 0845 hours.

Flying his patrol eastward of Miedecke was Flight Lieutenant Stokes in RB-W and after an hour contact was made with a large but unseen vessel estimated to be a merchant vessel or tanker of some 10,000 tons. They dropped two flares but owing to the poor visibility they were ineffective, and with the aircraft turning it was impossible to determine the vessel's course. Descending to 400 feet and no further contact being made after twenty minutes searching, they resumed their patrol, flying south-east to latitude 44°30'N before turning east for a short leg and then setting course north-east towards the datum line. However, at 0030 hours, it became apparent that they were desperately short of fuel and they abandoned the patrol and set course for base. Four hours later, while flying between Lizard Point and Plymouth, they received a message to land at Pembroke Dock. They became waterborne there at 0600 hours but it had been a close run thing. Both port engines had failed owing to lack of fuel and they had to force-land on the flare path. The starboard tanks contained a mere fifteen gallons of fuel.

Eastward of Stokes' patrol was that of Flight Lieutenant Marks in RB-U, who flew a much more convoluted course than his fellow pilots in which he covered most of the area defined by 45°N, 05°W, 46°N and 03°W. His S/E showed contacts with several fishing vessels and other vessels but poor visibility prevented identification. The aircraft returned safely to Pembroke Dock where it became waterborne at 0745 hours.

The most easterly patrol was flown by Flying Officer Pockley in RB-B. Crossing the datum line at 2130 hours he traversed the entire bay to a point on latitude 44°N, 02°20'W where he encountered two Spanish motor vessels. Flying a short leg to the west and then north-east to complete his patrol, he crossed the datum line again at 0335 hours, not a moment too soon as at 0350 he had to report to base that his S/E had become unserviceable, which would have seriously curtailed his capability to search the waters below.

The operation to sweep the Bay of Biscay had been a considerable undertaking made more difficult by the weather conditions. All the Australian crews had reported haze and sea fog while cloud was stated to be 10/10ths from 1,000-2,000 feet and 8/10ths at 3,000 but above that visibility was good. The efforts, therefore, of the RAF and RAAF crews were highly commendable. The first aircraft had left St Eval in the early evening of 26 March as the Chariot Force were turning south at Point A and watching their covering Hurricane depart for home. The last had landed at RAF Mount Batten at 0845 hours on the morning of 28 March when the action in the dockyard at St Nazaire was long over and the survivors were at sea making their tortured way home. For a period of forty hours, sweeps and searches had been flown unseen over their heads to provide them with freedom from interference.

CHAPTER 6

OF BOMBERS AND BASES

The Romans came to Yorkshire long before the Royal Air Force. Julius Caesar first arrived in England in 55BC with 10,000 men but with a storm making it impossible for his reserves to follow, he withdrew. Arriving again in 54BC with a force nearly three times as large he defeated the British north of the Thames. However, having come, seen and conquered, in September he had to return to Gaul to deal with problems there and the Romans again left Britain.

It was 100 years before they ventured back and subdued the British tribes, among them the Iceni and their Queen Boudicca, whose image would become the symbol of Operation Chariot. After having established London, they set off north to Lincoln and York, laying out behind them the ribbon of Ermine Street. Pushing ever further north where they were to construct Hadrian's Wall, they then built, from York to Catterick and beyond, the road they called Dere Street.

Nearly 1,900 years later, with another European power threatening these islands, three airfields hugging this stretch of road would become part of the huge operation that would eventually overcome that threat and restore peace to Europe. These three airfields were Linton-on-Ouse, Leeming and Dishforth and each of them was home to a squadron that would fly in the diversionary raid on St Nazaire.

RAF Linton-on-Ouse was one of the rash of new stations that were developed in the mid-1930s when it became clear that war was inevitable. Started in 1936 it was built as a two-bomber base and was situated near the village of the same name in the Vale of York, nine miles north-west of the city, a location that was not entirely ideal as the flat and damp land was prone to produce mist which tended to develop into fog. It boasted one runway of 6,000 feet and two of 4,200, with five hangars and dispersals for thirty-six heavy bombers.

Although Linton-on-Ouse opened in May 1937 it was not until April 1938 that its inaugural squadrons, 51 and 58, arrived, both equipped with Whitley bombers. Both squadrons would fly in support of the raid on St Nazaire although by then 51 Squadron would be flying out of Dishforth.

When war was declared on 3 September 1939, 51 and 58 squadrons were the first RAF units to overfly Germany when ten aircraft were despatched on the night of 3rd/4th to drop propaganda leaflets, described by aircrew as "free toilet paper", over the Ruhr. The sortie was far from an unqualified success with three of the aircraft having to land in France on the return flight in order to refuel. It was indeed fortunate that such vital lessons could be learned on a 'soft' operation with no opposition and also that landing in France was still a safe option.

The considerable contribution made by Linton-on-Ouse-based bombers in the air attacks on Germany did not go unnoticed by the Luftwaffe and retribution was exacted on 12 May 1941, when a heavy air raid caused extensive damage to the buildings and killed five personnel, including the station commander, Group Captain Frederick Gallaway, OBE. He was succeeded by the appropriately named Group Captain J.R. Whitley who took part in a 76 Squadron raid on Frankfurt, although expressly forbidden to do so. Shot down by a Bf 110 he bailed out successfully and with the civilian clothes and escape kit he habitually carried he evaded capture and was passed down the Comet Line to Spain. Returning to Linton he was awarded a DSO.

These early years at Linton-on-Ouse saw two of the most successful and accomplished pilots of WWII flying with its squadrons. Leonard Cheshire served with 102 and 35 Squadrons until August 1942, when he joined 76 Squadron as its commanding officer. After serving as station commander at RAF Marston Moor from March to November 1943 he took command of the famous 617 (Dambusters) Squadron where he cemented his reputation and following which he was awarded a Victoria Cross for displaying "the courage and determination of an exceptional leader" in four years of fighting. He already held three DSOs and a DFC.

J. B. 'Willie' Tait commanded 51, 35 and 78 Squadrons and was one of the most highly-decorated pilots of the war, amassing four DSOs and two DFCs, with two Mentions in Despatches for good measure. In an interesting footnote to our story it was Willie Tait who, on his third attempt, sank the *Tirpitz*, the ship whose denial to the Atlantic was held up as the *raison d'être* of Operation Chariot.

Having succeeded Cheshire as commanding officer of 617 Squadron in July 1944, Tait led his first attack on the *Tirpitz* the following September. With the ship lying in Kaafjord, out of range for bombers based in the British Isles, the raid was mounted from Russia and with smoke obscuring the target it was not a complete success but enough damage was caused to render the ship unseaworthy. In order to use it as a gun platform and thus utilise its heavy armament the Germans now moved it to Tromsø, ironically now in range from Lossiemouth from which base Tait launched his second attack, but this time cloud obscured the target. In a 'third time lucky' raid, on 12 November 1944, three direct hits with 'Tallboy' bombs, developed by Barnes Wallis, left the ship capsized. The *Tirpitz* would now never threaten the Atlantic convoy routes, whether or not the Normandie Dock was available to it. Tait was recommended for a Victoria Cross, like Cheshire, for sustained gallantry over a long period, but it was denied him and he received instead the third bar to his DSO.

Nine miles north of Linton-on-Ouse along Dere Street, long since having become known as the Great North Road, was RAF Dishforth; another base which had been built during the great expansion of the mid-1930s. It too was named after a nearby village and was a grass field of some 200 acres. Development was completed in 1936 and it opened in September of that year. Comprising runways of 6,000, 4,200 and 3,800 feet, five hangars and dispersals for thirty-six heavy bombers it adjoined the main road which formed its western perimeter although the airfield actually straddled the road in the early years of the war after hard-standings were built in a field on the western side of it. Traffic would have to be stopped to allow aircraft to cross. The runways were still grass in 1942 and were not concreted until the second half of 1943 while the then resident Canadian squadron moved temporarily to Linton.

The base was originally populated by two squadrons who moved up from Boscombe Down in Wiltshire, 10 Squadron arriving in January 1937, and 78 Squadron the following month. Having flown in with Heyfords both squadrons, during the next six months, would convert to Whitleys. Dishforth's war began on 8 September 1939 when 10 Squadron sent eight Whitleys on a leaflet drop over Germany, a mission which, unlike 51 and 58 Squadrons from Linton a few days earlier, they would accomplish without incident. Had lessons been learned already?

Towards the end of the year an exchange of squadrons took place which saw 78 move to Linton while 51 moved to Dishforth from where they would fly on the diversionary raid on St Nazaire. 78 Squadron would return in 1940 when 10 Squadron moved up the road to Leeming.

A further twelve miles north of Dishforth and also skirting the Great North Road was RAF Leeming which had been an airfield for some years in use by civilian aviation before, at the end of 1938, somewhat later than the other two great expansion airfields we have seen a few miles to the south, more land was acquired. The base was completed by the summer of 1940 and we have already seen that the first resident squadron, 10, arrived from Dishforth in July.

By Christmas, 1940, three squadrons, 10, 102 and 35 would have passed through Leeming but it was not until September 1941 that 77 arrived. From here it would take its part in the diversionary raid on St Nazaire and would stay until it moved to Chivenor on 6 May 1942.

The base commander at Leeming in March 1942 was Group Captain Strang Graham who had the distinction of being decorated as a soldier in the Great War and as an airman in World War II. In 1918, as a temporary lieutenant in the Royal Highlanders, he had received a Military Cross for conspicuous gallantry and devotion to duty in a night attack, although wounded. Transferring to the Royal Flying Corps he had been a founder member of the Royal Air Force on 1 April 1918 and after a short spell on the retired list was granted a permanent commission as a flying officer on 24 October 1919. On Valentine's Day 1928 he survived a flying accident on the North-West Frontier when his plane, an Airco DC 9A, had dived into the ground from 100 feet.

Posted in January 1942 to command RAF Leeming he had left to become base commander at Cottesmore in January 1943. In March that year a serious accident occurred there, the story of which is best told in the words of the London Gazette for 9 July 1943.

"Group Captain Strang Graham, M.C., Royal Air Force.

In March 1943 a Wellington aircraft overshot when landing and crashed into another aircraft. The impact carried both aircraft against a hangar, where they burst into flames. Group Captain Graham was on the scene immediately. Disregarding the danger from exploding ammunition, petrol tanks and oxygen bottles, and although he was aware that one of the aircraft carried a 250-lb bomb, he led the rescue party in extricating three members of the crew from the blazing aircraft. Group Captain Graham then led the fire-fighting party in an endeavour to save the burning hangar. He was attacking the fire, which had spread to the offices of the hangar, when the bomb on the aircraft, less than eight feet away, exploded. With his face badly cut by splintered glass and flying debris, and bleeding profusely, he was persuaded to go to the station sick quarters, where he made light of his injuries and inspired others who had been injured by the explosion. After receiving first aid treatment, he returned to the scene of the accident and directed operations until the fire had been subdued."

Group Captain Graham was awarded the George Medal.

These three airfields all formed part of 4 Group within Bomber Command and a squadron from each of them would provide a total of thirty-five of the sixty-two aircraft that would fly in the diversionary raid on 27/28 March. They would be flying the Whitley V and we shall see later how the raid developed, but let us first look at the bomber itself.

The Armstrong Whitworth Whitley was designed by John Lloyd in 1934 in response to the issue of Specification B3/34 for a twin-engine night bomber and it had its maiden flight in March 1936. The early Marks had Armstrong Siddeley engines but they were not reliable and for Marks IV and V Rolls-Royce Merlins, the engine that gave the Spitfire its iconic sound, were introduced. The plane was named after a suburb of Coventry where Armstrong Whitworth had a plant.

There was a crew of five, the pilot and the second pilot/navigator sitting side by side in the cockpit with the latter having a revolving seat to enable him to access the chart table behind him. At the rear of the cockpit sat the wireless operator. The bomb aimer in the front turret had a .303 Vickers K machine gun for aircraft defence and the tail gunner manned a turret containing 4 x .303 Brownings.

Together with the Hampden and the Wellington the Whitley, although it was already obsolete at the beginning of the war, bore the brunt of the British bomber offensive in the early years of the conflict. The drawback of a twin-engine plane was that failure in one engine left it unable to maintain altitude and so as a front-line bomber it did not survive the introduction of the big four-engine planes later in the war. Nevertheless, the Whitley scored a number of notable 'firsts'. It was the first to overfly Germany, dropping leaflets on the night of 3/4 September 1939 and in May 1940 it was also the first to bomb Germany. Its extensive range of 1,650 miles allowed it to be the first to bomb Italy after that country had entered the war, although severe icing proved a problem crossing the Alps, a problem that would recur in other operations. This long-range capability would make it ideal for its role in Coastal Command after its transfer in 1942, when it became the first plane to sink a submarine.

Twenty-one miles due south of York was RAF Snaith, one of a number of airfields that were not named after the nearest village. Although it was first planned during the expansion period in the mid-1930s a decision was not made while alternative sites were under consideration. When the site was eventually decided upon it was felt that to name it after the nearby village of Pollington would invite confusion with Pocklington some miles away and it was thus named Snaith. Construction at Snaith was started in 1940 and by 1941 it was ready to receive its first squadron. Stretching between the A545 in the north and the lane from Great Hock to Pollington in the south, three intersecting concrete runways were laid out and these were extended in the summer of 1941 to measure 6,000, 4,200 and 3,300 feet. Three hangars were built together with the usual thirty-six dispersals for heavy bombers.

Snaith had a very short life but an important one for it was used as a main bomber force field for the remainder of the war and the RAF abandoned the base in 1946. During this period only three squadrons were based there, the first being 150 Squadron, who would fly on the St Nazaire raid and who were replaced in October 1942 by 51 Squadron, another 'raid' squadron. 51 would fly from Snaith until April 1945. A total of 205 aircraft were lost on operations from Snaith, fifty-seven from 150 and 148 from 51.

A further thirty miles south from York an airfield was built, beginning in 1938 and again as part of the expansion scheme, on a large expanse of Hatfield Moor and was named Hatfield Woodhouse, but this was shortly changed to Lindholme to avoid confusion with Hatfield aerodrome in Hertfordshire. Because of the nature of the land, which was virtually a peat bog, and the constrictions of the site, caused mainly by the Hatfield Moor Drain, only two runways were built but one was of full bomber length of 6,000 feet, the other being 4,200. It would be later in 1942 before they were concreted. The familiar establishment of five large hangars and dispersals for thirty-six heavy bombers were constructed. It was here that the Lindholme Gear mentioned earlier was invented by the then-station commander Group Captain Waring as an aid to be dropped to ditched airmen to increase their chances of survival.

Lindholme was a 5 Group station until June 1941, when it was transferred to 1 Group and to effect the change its two resident squadrons swapped bases with two Polish squadrons, 304 (Silesian) Squadron and 305 (Ziemia Weilkopolska) Squadron, from Syerston. Both would fly aircraft to St Nazaire.

Base commander in March 1942 was Group Captain A.P. Davidson. Appointed to Lindholme in August 1941 he was clearly chosen for his Polish connections. On 5 September 1939 he had been despatched to Warsaw as air attaché and was also a member of a committee in London which, in talks with delegates from Poland in a vain attempt to stem the tide of the invasion, launched without warning by the Germans on 1 September, had sought ways to supply that beleaguered country with Fairey Battles, Spitfires and Hurricanes, but before the supplies could reach them they had been overrun by the Germans. Also, from June 1940, Group Captain Davidson had been officer commanding RAF Bramcote, the home of the Polish Battle OTU. A more appropriate posting, therefore, is hard to imagine.

For our sixth bomber base we have to travel east into Lincolnshire, to Elsham Wolds. Not only was this the sole 'raid' station not in Yorkshire it was also the only one with its roots in World War I. The east coast of England was regularly overflown by Zeppelins making night raids on the Midlands and to counter this threat, in December 1916 a defensive line of three airfields was formed between Lincoln and Hull, all manned by 33 Squadron, with A Flight at RAF Scampton, B Flight at RAF Kirton-in-Lindsey and C Flight at Elsham Wolds. Between the wars, however, the field was returned to agriculture.

During the expansion programme of the 1930s, when eyes were cast around for new bases, former World War I airfields naturally came under consideration, and Elsham Wolds was chosen, but the re-development took place on a more suitable site close by.

The land on which Elsham Wolds was built was the flat and somewhat featureless landscape so typical of the East Anglian countryside. Originally equipped with the usual three runways, of 6,000, 4,800 and 4,200 feet, it was short of the infrastructure seen on the other bases in that it only had three hangars and dispersals for twenty-seven aircraft, although later increased to thirty-six. Three further hangars were added in 1944.

First to move in was 103 Squadron, arriving in July 1941 and it would stay there until the end of the war, flying more operational sorties than any other 1 Group squadron and consequently suffering its highest losses, 198 out of a total of 248 on operations from Elsham Wolds. Another 1 Group record was established when the squadron sent thirty aircraft on a single raid. Like Snaith, Elsham Wolds did not long survive the war. Flying there ceased late in 1945 and the following year the RAF abandoned the field and all its facilities and the site reverted to agricultural use.

The base commander in March 1942 was Group Captain Hugh Constantine who, when appointed in June 1941, became one of the youngest station commanders in Bomber Command. He had started his career as a fighter pilot flying in Siskins and in 1928 had escaped death when he had crashed into the sea some 200 yards offshore. However, he was saved by the prompt actions of two RAF personnel who both received the BEM for their gallantry. The incident did not dampen his enthusiasm for flying and he often went on operations with 103 Squadron although it was unusual for an officer of his rank to do so. A sociable man with a great sense of humour, he was popular with all ranks.

The aircraft in which squadrons from these three 1 Group airfields would fly on the diversionary raid was the Wellington 1C. Built by Vickers-Armstrong it was their response to the issue, in 1932, of Specification B9/32 by the Air Ministry and they produced it as a twin-engine, long-range, medium bomber.

Barnes Wallis, inspired by his work on airships, had developed a new geodesic design which had already been used on the Wellesley, a single-engine light bomber, named, like the Wellington, after the Iron Duke. The framework was of an aluminium alloy and resembled a honeycomb. With timber screwed to the metal it was then covered with Irish linen and given several coats of dope. The result was an immensely strong construction that could take quite serious damage and still leave the aircraft a viable unit capable of getting home when other planes would have been lost.

The Wellington also represented a huge advance in both payload and armament. It could carry a 4,500-lb bomb load, more than three times that carried by the Heyford which it superseded, and it boasted eight .303 machine guns in three positions, two in the nose turret, two in the beam position and four in the tail turret, giving it excellent all round defence. Powered by two Bristol Hercules XI engines, each of 1,500 hp, it had an economical cruising speed of 165 mph, was capable of a maximum of 234 mph and could carry a full bomb load over a range of 1,055 miles.

The Wellington 1C operated with a crew of six, consisting of a pilot, a radio operator, a navigator/bomb aimer, an observer/gunner, a waist gunner and a tail gunner. It was the longest serving of the three medium bombers with which the RAF entered the war but, like the Whitley, it would not survive the advent of the big four-engine machines such as the Lancaster, but it continued to give sterling service throughout the war both in the Middle East and with Coastal Command.

Having looked at the home bases of the squadrons flying the diversionary raid there are others to be visited. Apart from the airfields at which several aircraft, for various reasons, landed on their return, there are two from which they flew.

Bases from which the Bomber Forces will operate.

7. In order to minimise the risk of the whole bomber force being unable to take part in the operation owing to weather conditions at home bases preventing aircraft from taking off, all aircraft of 1 Group will operate from advanced bases in south-west England, and all aircraft of 4 Group will operate from home bases. 1 Group are to make the necessary arrangements with the appropriate commands and groups in south-west England for accommodation and

```
facilities. BOSCOMBE DOWN, EXETER, CHIVENOR and ST EVAL
are the most suitable bases for this purpose.
```

Extract from Bomber Command Operation Order No. 141

In the event none of the suggested stations was used, the squadrons instead opting for Pershore and Stanton Harcourt. Although these were much closer to their home bases and further from the target than the south-west fields, it is as well to remember that the decision to use advanced bases was not on considerations of fuel consumption but of weather conditions. All the aircraft set off successfully but ironically it was the adverse weather over the target that was to blight their operation, having been advised at briefing that it would be clear. The importance of accurate meteorological forecasts for air operations cannot be overstated.

A flying facility had existed at Pershore since 1934 when it was the home of the Worcestershire Flying School, but it was requisitioned soon after the outbreak of war. Developed during 1940 and opened in February 1941, it became a base for 23 Operational Training Unit working up crews on Wellingtons and was attacked several times by the Luftwaffe. Used as a base by 103 Squadron and one aircraft of the Polish 305 Squadron, it had three runways, the longest being 6,000 feet.

Stanton Harcourt is a village a few miles to the west of Oxford which became the site of an airfield of the same name in World War II. It was very much a 'hostilities only' field, commencing flying on 3 September 1940 and closing down soon after the war ended. It was a satellite field for RAF Abingdon and, like Pershore, home to an Operational Training Unit, in this case 10, training Whitley crews for night flying. Halifax aircraft also operated from there. The station had its claims to fame as the base from which the 'La Pallice Raid' was launched against the *Scharnhorst* and from which Churchill flew to the Casablanca Conference in 1943. It also had the doubtful distinction of having been attacked by the Luftwaffe whilst still under construction when nine civilian workers had been killed. Thirteen Wellingtons of 150 Squadron and two of the Polish 304 Squadron would fly from Stanton Harcourt to St Nazaire.

CHAPTER 7

THE BEST LAID SCHEMES

The best laid schemes o' Mice an' Men,
Gang aft agley,
An' lea'e us nought but grief an' pain,
For promis'd joy!

Robert Burns – *To A Mouse*

The speed at which the little ships carrying the commandos into battle and that of the aircraft that would arrive over the target two hours before the troops landed were so disparate that Chariot Force had been at sea for over twenty-four hours before the first stirrings of movement among the bomber squadrons detailed to support them. Even then, that movement was restricted to the positioning of the Wellingtons of 1 Group to their forward bases. It would be 1730 on the 27th before the first aircraft took off for the diversionary raid.

Earlier that day, Wing Commander Elworthy, as director of operations at Bomber Command, had issued to Headquarters 1 and 4 Groups, the executive order for Chariot. This would also give definition to Targets A and B:

EXECUTIVE	CHARIOT	TONIGHT	27/28 MARCH	
Target "A"	IS CC,55 "A".	TARGET "B"	IS NORTHERN	
END	OF	BASSIN DE	PENHOËT	IN
CC.55A.	EXACT DETAILS	OF TARGET	WILL BE	
PASSED BY	INTELLIGENCE.			

The Bomber Command operation order had required that all aircraft of 1 Group operate from bases in the south-west in order to guard against the possibility of the whole Bomber Force being grounded by adverse weather (see page 75-76). Helpfully, the order had suggested Boscombe Down, Exeter, Chivenor and St Eval as being the most suitable for the purpose. Almost perversely, the squadrons chose airfields closer to home, as we have seen. No matter, for apart from the few who failed to do so for mechanical reasons, all aircraft were able to get airborne and play their part, as we shall see. However, it would first be appropriate to consider the 'reception committee' that lay in wait at Fortress St Nazaire.

The progress of the German army across Belgium, Holland and France was one of headlong conquest. Crossing the borders on 10 May 1940, by 14 June they had occupied Paris and forced the evacuation of a large part of the British Expeditionary Force through Dunkirk. Now charged by Hitler with capturing the vital Atlantic ports, and driving the remnants of the BEF before them, they moved ever westward eventually reaching St Nazaire on the

22nd of that month. They did not stop long. In the time-honoured practice of the German forces, St Nazaire, being a naval base, would be defended by naval troops. By the end of the month the army had departed and the Kriegsmarine had quickly moved in.

The Germans built five U-boat bases on the Atlantic coast of western France, at Brest, Lorient, St Nazaire, La Rochelle and Bordeaux. Of these, by virtue of the added asset of the great Normandie Dock, St Nazaire would become the most heavily defended port on the whole of the Atlantic Wall. This would be achieved by the disposition of a naval artillery battalion, Marine-Artillerie-Abteilung 280 (MAA.280) and an anti-aircraft regiment 22. Marine-Flak-Regiment (22.MFR). There would also be extensive flak installations in the area of the docks.

MAA.280 deployed twenty-four guns of various calibres for use against naval targets and as such, although it came into action against Chariot Force as it sailed up the estuary, it is not part of this story. However, it should be noted that it also deployed, for the defence of its own installations, fourteen anti-aircraft guns of 7.5-cm calibre that could be used to bolster any action by the flak regiment.

Commanding 22.MFR was Kapitän-sur-Zee Karl-Conrad Mecke, an experienced and dedicated officer who had been born in Bremen on 30 December 1894. Appointed to command the regiment on its formation in St Nazaire in November 1941 he had been promoted to Kapitän-sur-Zee on 1 March 1942. It would be Mecke who first suspected the purpose of the air diversionary raid, having defended St Nazaire on many occasions before, but never against such an unusual pattern of bombing. However, his injunction to his troops to "beware landings" was in anticipation of paratroopers rather than a landing from the sea. When the regiment was reformed as V.Marineflakbrigade in April 1943, he was appointed as its commander. Transferred in August that year to the Russian theatre he forged a reputation as a brave and fearless officer, particularly in ground-attack missions against Soviet tanks. He was captured by the Russians on 21 September 1944 and it would be September 1955 before he was released to return to Germany. A holder of the Iron

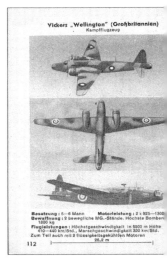

Photos: Luc Braeuer Collection)

Pages from the Recognition Handbook issued to German flak gunners. Wellington KJ-N was being flown over St. Nazaire on 28 March 1942 by Squadron Leader Seymour-Price. If they had shot him down the gunners would have had every reason to be impressed with the attention to detail o those who compiled the book

Cross, both 2nd and 1st Class, he was awarded the Knight's Cross of the Iron Cross in April 1942, in recognition of his service as commander of 22.MFR. Mecke died in Kiel on 26 May 1982, aged eighty-seven.

The 22.MFR comprised three flak battalions, 703, 705 and 809. Each battalion had seven batteries, one of which was a searchlight battery. Each battery operated four 10.5-cm flak guns with the exception of 2/MaFla 703, which had six, and 2/MaFla 705, which had three. Other variations were 5/MaFla 703 and 5/MaFla 809 whose guns were of 12.8-cm calibre. The regiment therefore commanded a formidable firepower.

The searchlight battery of each battalion consisted of about fifteen searchlights under the command of a junior officer. Not all of these searchlights were mounted in the same place but were scattered about the countryside in groups of three or four. Each commanded by an NCO and served by a dozen soldiers; these groups were placed three to five kilometres apart to enable them to follow attacking aircraft across the whole of the area that was the responsibility of the battalion.

The majority of the batteries within the three battalions operated the 10.5-cm C/32 or C/33 (where C = *Constructuksjahr* – year of design) which were capable of firing fifteen to eighteen rounds per minute to a maximum height of 37,400 feet. With an all-round traverse it had a maximum elevation of 85° giving it the ability to command a large area of sky. That only two batteries operated the larger 12.8-cm gun was a matter of availability as it was not in production until 1942. Also having all-round traverse, but with a slightly higher elevation capability of 88° and a maximum ceiling of 48,500 feet, it was considered one of the most effective heavy anti-aircraft guns of its time. The three flak battalions encircled St Nazaire, 703 to the west, 705 to the north-east and 809 across the estuary around St Brevin.

In addition to 22.MFR dispersed around the countryside, the immediate area around the U-boat pens also boasted an array of light flak consisting of thirteen 20-mm flak guns, two of 37 mm and four of 40 mm. These were supported by four 60-cm searchlights. These guns had a dual-purpose capability and whilst not so effective as those of 22.MFR, they added a useful amount of defensive fire. They were, however, to prove a big problem to the motor launches and commandos as they sailed up the estuary. Many were mounted on buildings and there were particularly dangerous quadruple mountings on the Frigo building and the customs building but being high on their mountings, with a minimum depression of only -3°, their effectiveness against ground targets was somewhat limited. Also in the dockyard, close to the northern winding hut, were two flak towers, visited later that night by Micky Burn, who found them unoccupied.

All in all, the town of St Nazaire and the surrounding area possessed the wherewithal to form a most effective reception committee for the aircraft who were due to spend an uncomfortable and frustrating five and a half hours in their airspace. Many of the aircrews would later describe the flak as having been heavy and accurate and although no plane was brought down, several were damaged, contributing to problems on the homeward flight. In the event, it would be the dual-purpose guns around the docks which would cause most distress to the attacking force.

The thistle on the badge of 77 Squadron commemorates its formation in Scotland in October 1916. It spent World War I on home defence duties, both in actions against enemy airships and in cooperation with anti-invasion forces on the ground until being disbanded in 1919. Reformed as a bomber unit in June 1937, it would spend the early months of the war bombarding enemy cities with propaganda leaflets. It was not until the spring of 1940 that it took up a serious bombing role. Flying the Hawker Audax on reformation it converted to Wellesleys in November 1937 and a year later to the Whitley III. In September 1939 it upgraded to the Whitley V and in September 1941 found itself stationed at RAF Leeming from where it would lead the diversionary bombing raid on St Nazaire.

In March 1942 the officer commanding was a man who later in the war would make his name in the field of target-marking, developed to remedy the shortcomings of the bomber offensive which have been mentioned in Chapter 4. Donald Clifford Tyndall Bennett was born in Queensland, Australia. He began flying training as a cadet in the Royal Australian Air Force in 1930 and the following year accepted a short-service commission in the RAF. Subsequently spending time in flying boats, where his commanding officer was Arthur Harris, in 1935 he transferred to the RAAF Reserve and embarked on a career in civil aviation. In 1940, as flying superintendent of Atlantic Ferry Organisation, he would personally lead the first flight of Hudsons, an aircraft which we shall meet later, to make the crossing from America.

Although he constantly took part in operations, Bennett did not fly to St Nazaire on 28 March and the following month was moved to become the commanding officer of 10 Squadron. That same month, during an attack on the *Tirpitz*, a theme that runs through our story, he was shot down over Norway and, evading capture, made his way to Sweden. Although interned, he was soon released and by 4 June was back in command of his squadron. However, when 10 Squadron was posted to the Middle East, Bennett did not go with them, having been summoned to HQ Bomber Command by the AOC-in-C, his former CO Arthur Harris. Bennett's forte had always been navigation. Indeed, in cooperation with his wife, he had written *The Complete Air Navigator* (1935), an essential textbook that remained in print for over thirty years. Now he was to form and command Pathfinder Force which would revolutionise the accuracy and therefore the effectiveness of the bomber offensive. After he retired, in the rank of air vice-marshal, he would always be remembered by the soubriquet 'Pathfinder' Bennett.

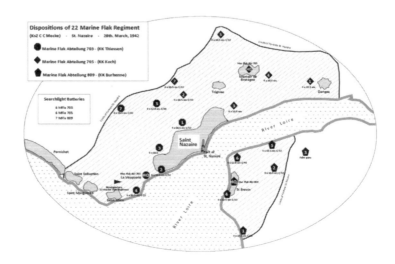

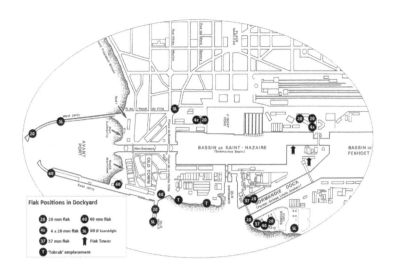

Flak Positions in Dockyard

- (20) 20 mm flak
- (40) 40 mm flak
- (4x) 4 x 20 mm flak
- (SL) 60 Ø Searchlight
- (37) 37 mm flak
- ↑ Flak Tower
- (T) 'Tobruk' emplacement

There had been great excitement at RAF Leeming on 25 March 1942, for the base had been visited by His Majesty King George and Queen Elizabeth, accompanied by the appropriate brass and local luminaries. That evening, for the crews, it was back to business as usual as nine Whitleys of 77 Squadron were detailed to attack the dock area at St Nazaire. As they crossed the Channel there was a slight haze but no cloud and the same conditions prevailed over the target. All pilots were able to identify the estuary of the Loire, the dock area, the coast to the south-west and the river to the north without difficulty.

The aircraft encountered moderate to intense flak from the north and west of the port and across the estuary, the areas where we have seen the disposition of Mecke's 22. Marine Flak Regiment, with light flak also coming from the port area itself. A few searchlights formed cones in the sky but did not succeed in holding any of the aircraft. Over the period of an hour the bomb loads of 1 x 1,000-lb, 3 x 500-lb and 2 x 250-lb bombs were dropped, all in one stick by every aircraft except one who made two runs over the target. All the aircraft returned safely to base. Two nights later eight of these crews would return to St Nazaire, but the conditions and the results would be much different.

The nine Whitleys that flew on the 25/26 March were part of a raid by twenty-seven aircraft which also included one from 51 Squadron, nine from 58 and one from 150. The two aircraft from 51 and 150, together with five of those from 58 would return on the night of 27th/28th, meaning that a quarter of the aircraft destined for the diversionary raid had bombed St Nazaire only two nights earlier. There was only one casualty on the operation when a Wellington of 12 Squadron was shot down. Two of the crew survived and one of them was the rear gunner Sergeant Currie, RAAF.

The first ten aircraft of 77 Squadron to lift off from RAF Leeming on the night of 27 March were briefed to carry out phase one of the attack which was to bomb Target A between 2330 and 0030. Their orders were specific:

> Flares not to be dropped over target in any circumstances.
> No incendiary bombs to be carried.
> A/c to attack from heights best calculated to achieve accuracy under existing weather conditions but should not come below 6,000 ft.
> Bombs to be dropped singly on separate runs.
> No cameras are to be carried.
> A/c must on no account be late off target.
> The target must be definitely identified before attacking and bombs must not be dropped in the sea.

The aircraft were to carry 4 x 500-lb and 4 x 250-lb bombs and in addition each carried two packages of nickels (leaflets) for dropping over France. With a flight time of two hours to the target the first aircraft took off at 1930 and by 2005 all ten were airborne. Setting course over Cottesmore Light and Abingdon, they crossed the coast at Bognor Regis, made landfall at Pointe Barfleur and then flew on to St Nazaire. The conditions they found were in stark contrast to those of two nights earlier. On the flight out they encountered 10/10ths stratocumulus with tops up to 3,500 feet and further altocumulus with tops from 11,000 feet and isolated tops at 14,000 feet. Although this thinned towards the French coast no crew could make pinpoint landfall.

Once over France the cloud thickened again to 10/10ths with its base at 5,000 feet and the crews experienced severe icing conditions. No pilot could positively identify any feature of the target area. Mindful of their orders and having circled over the dock area for fifty minutes the decision was taken to return to base, jettisoning their bombs safely over the sea on the way.

Not all the time spent over the target was comfortable for the crews. Sergeant Silva, in KN-H, Flight Sergeant Affleck in KN-C and Sergeant Fisher in KN-A all encountered accurate heavy flak, with Fisher also reporting searchlights although he found them to be ineffective. By contrast, Sergeant Smith in KN-E merely recorded "some flak" while Sergeant Morgan in KN-M, Pilot Officer Sanderson in KN-K and Sergeant Veal in KN-O found "no flak or searchlights". Squadron Leader Seymour-Price was alone in sighting the enemy when he was tracked from astern by a Ju88, but it did not attack.

The disappointed crews had to console themselves by dropping their parcels of nickels, three around Rennes, two over St Nazaire and two over other locations. So home they went, enduring without incident some light flak over Nantes and a few searchlights and slight light and slight heavy flak over Rennes, but for one crew disaster lay in wait.

The dales of Yorkshire were an area of outstanding beauty long before being designated as such and given the status of a national park by a government anxious to protect them from development and exploitation. A large area of high land divided into several flat-topped moors by the deep dales through which ran the rivers that gave them their names – Wharfdale, Nidderdale, Coverdale and many others. In September, in the golden glow of a southbound sun that lights the purple heather carpeting the moors to the horizon, the dales are as close to paradise on earth as man could wish to be. In the dark of a March night, sprinkled with snow and cloaked by cloud they are a hostile environment into which no man would willingly venture. During WWII they would become the graveyard of many an aircraft whose crew, tired, possibly disorientated and often short of fuel, were vainly seeking the sanctuary of their base. In such circumstances did Whitley KN-G of 77 Squadron come to grief on these forbidding uplands, a crash in which the observer would lose his life. Before the night was out they would also claim two Whitleys of 51 Squadron, happily without further fatalities.

Pilot Officer James Harrison, RNZAF, was a farmer, born in Hastings, Hawkes Bay, New Zealand, who had enlisted in November 1940. His crew comprised Sergeant Douglas Colledge, RAFVR (observer), Sergeant W.P. Louthood, RCAF (wireless operator), and Flight Sergeant Michael Fuller, RAF, and Sergeant Andrew Waddell, RNZAF, (air gunners). Taking off at 1932 hours, the second aircraft of the squadron to be airborne, they had endured the fruitless circling of the target before setting course to return to base, jettisoning their bombs on the way. Nearing base they found that the weather conditions had changed. They were in cloud and the wind, now from the east, had taken them too far west. Assuming they were over the Vale of York and descending to determine their position, the aircraft flew into the ground near Arnagill Crags to the north of Kirkby Malzeard Moor and close to the Roundhill and Leighton Reservoirs. It was 0400 hours on the morning of 28 March. A fire soon broke out and the aircraft was destroyed. They were ten miles as the crow flies from Leeming and safety.

Pilot Officer Harrison sustained serious head injuries, a crushed foot and a broken arm and collapsed, but not before dragging his unconscious wireless operator, Sergeant Louthood, from the wreck. Returning to operational flying after five months in hospital and rising to the rank of squadron leader he survived the war, having been decorated with a DSO and a DFC. Flight Sergeant Fuller had sustained a fractured femur, lacerations and concussion and was eventually taken to Harrogate Hospital. Recovered from his injuries he resumed active service but was killed while flying with 35 Squadron in the Pathfinder Force on 26 May 1943, when his aircraft was shot down over Dusseldorf. The other air gunner, Sergeant Waddell, emerged relatively unscathed from the wreck and was able to make his way off the moor to alert the rescue services. He and Sergeant Louthood both survived the war. Sadly, Sergeant Douglas Murton Colledge, the observer, had not survived the impact. He was buried in the churchyard of St John the Baptist, Leeming. Aged 25 and unmarried, he was the only son of Harry Colledge, a cabinet maker, and his wife, the former Maud May Murton.

Flying BE2s and BE12s, 51 Squadron was formed in May 1916 and like 77 Squadron, was a home defence unit. Based at Thetford, in Norfolk, it spent the war on patrols against the Zeppelins that flew in over the east coast to bomb targets in the Midlands. Disbanded in June 1919, it was reformed in March 1937, flying Virginias and Ansons, which it replaced in February 1938, with the Whitley II. The squadron would fly on the first night of the war on a sortie to drop leaflets over Germany. Working its way through the Marks, by May 1940, it had converted to the Whitley V and was stationed at Dishforth.

The King and Queen had also visited Dishforth on the morning of 25 March and had watched a demonstration of paratroopers dropping from aircraft of 51 Squadron. Later that day Pilot Officer Birch and his crew were part of a raid on St Nazaire by twenty-seven aircraft, a sortie to which we have already referred. They were able to drop their bombs from 15,000 feet in clear visibility with no opposition, but two nights later they would return in vastly different conditions.

The officer commanding 51 Squadron did not fly with his crews to St Nazaire on 28 March. Percy Pickard, then a wing commander and known affectionately as 'Pick', was possibly the most well-known bomber pilot of World War II, not because of his decorations, although he had an impressive array – he was the first RAF officer of WWII to receive a DSO and two bars – but because of his appearance in the iconic wartime propaganda film *Target for Tonight*, in which he portrayed the captain of Wellington F-Freddie.

'Pick' Pickard will also be remembered for his part in two highly successful raids. Operation Biting was the action in February 1942, at Bruneval, on the north coast of France, when the squadron dropped paratroopers, the first time it had been done in the war, to discover the secrets of German radar. The second, Operation Jericho, was the breaching in February 1944, of the walls of Amiens prison at the behest of the French to free Resistance prisoners who were shortly to be executed.

Between these operations, Pickard had been much involved in sorties to support the Special Operations Executive by landing agents and supplies in Occupied France, in which he became proficient in the low-level flying which would be required for the Amiens prison raid. In the closing stages of that operation he was jumped by a FW190 and he crashed close by. Originally posted as missing, it was not until September that confirmation came that he had been killed in action.

In addition to his three DSOs, Pickard had been awarded a DFC in 1940 and following his death the French government lobbied for him to be awarded a posthumous Victoria Cross but it was not to be granted. He and his navigator, Flight Lieutenant Bill Broadley, DSO, DFC, DFM, are buried in St Pierre Cemetery a short distance from Amiens prison on the road to Albert.

Forming part of phase two of the bombing programme in support of Chariot, 51 Squadron provided twelve of the aircraft which, together with eleven from 58 Squadron and two from 77 Squadron, which we have already met, would complete the phase. The first aircraft of 51 Squadron, Sergeant Hughes in MH-H, took off at 2012 on 27 March and would be followed at regular intervals by the rest of the squadron until, by 2037, all twelve were airborne. Their briefing had been attended by two members of COHQ, Captain Hughes-Hallett, RN, the naval assistant and Group Captain Willetts, the air assistant. The group captain would fly in MH-A, the last aircraft to take off, captained by Pilot Officer Monro.

The brief for phase two was to take over the bombing of the docks from the phase one aircraft when they left for home at 0030 and to continue until 0120, thus finishing ten minutes before the time HMS *Campbeltown* was due to ram the southern caisson and the commandos to storm ashore from their launches. They were to operate under the same strictures as 77 Squadron who had preceded them, arriving over the target only to find the thick cloud that made their task impossible. They were greeted by moderate heavy flak by the German gunners who had now been at their posts for two hours.

Brian Nation was born in New Zealand in 1918, but moved to England in the 1930s and joined the RAF before the outbreak of war, dreaming of flying aeroplanes. In the event he was posted to Balloon Command, which had been formed at Stanmore Park in 1938, and it was only by his own persistence that he assumed flying duties. As a rear gunner with 51 Squadron he was to take part in two of the great raids of World War II, those at Bruneval and St Nazaire.

On 27/28 February 1942, Operation Biting took place to raid the German radar installation above the cliffs at Bruneval on the north coast of France and to bring back parts of the equipment for analysis by British scientists. Selected to drop parachutists for the raid, 51 Squadron, not having carried out such a task before, endured a period of intense training.

Sergeant Nation's aircraft, piloted by Sergeant Gray, was late over the dropping zone, having lost sight of the coast in low cloud when leaving Fécamp, but a second approach was successful and the paratroopers were dropped. From his grandstand seat in the rear turret – whilst the view was good, it was also the most exposed and dangerous position in the aircraft – Nation watched the parachutes open and noted many discarded parachutes on the ground. Although some light flak was encountered, the aircraft returned safely to base.

A month to the day later, again in the rear turret, Brian flew on Operation Chariot to St Nazaire, but this time with Pilot Officer Monro and his crew in MH-A. They were carrying Group Captain Willetts, who had been closely involved in the planning of the operation, as a special observer. They flew the plotted course out over Selsey Bill and found the target impossible to identify, as had all the other pilots, and Nation remembered it as one of the most boring operations that he flew, with the monotony of just going round and round:

> ".... as I said, the weather was lousy, pouring with rain, low cloud and visibility not too good. Yes, there was some flak, as I recall not as heavy as we experienced on raids over Germany. As to night fighters, with the weather and the flak they would not normally be around. Away from the target area again I personally did not see any...."[20]

Brian Nation eventually realised his dream of flying aeroplanes when he was posted to an initial training wing for flying training. He was commissioned as a pilot officer on 24 September 1944 and remained in the RAF following the war, eventually retiring in 1961 in the rank of flight lieutenant. He died in Weymouth in 2015 aged ninety-seven.

The experience of the other crews being the same there was nothing for it but to return to base, taking their bombs with them, as instructed. The exception was Pilot Officer Helme in MH-E who reported attacking the docks from 5,400 feet at 0115 with 4 x 500-lb GP and 3 x 250-lb bombs before leaving for his base, where he landed safely. He was one of the few pilots in the whole of the diversionary raid to get his bombs away over the docks.

At 0025 hours on the morning of 28 March an aircraft was plotted by Fighter Control Headquarters of 10 Group at Rudloe Manor, RAF Box. It was flying north-east in the vicinity of Alderney and although the plotters had been briefed that aircraft would be returning from operations that night, this one was an hour earlier than expected. Three minutes later the military liaison officer reported that the aircraft was showing a broad IFF (identification friend or foe) and had broadcast an SOS. The call sign given, BC9/S, enabled it to be identified as Whitley MH-S of 51 Squadron.

At 0052 a fix had been transmitted to MH-S which it acknowledged but at 0109 it asked for a 'P' priority fix which was given, placing the aircraft fifteen miles north-east of Alderney. Notwithstanding the SOS which it had broadcast, it was clear to the watching

---

[20] Brian Nation in a letter to James Dorrian, 27 October 1995. Quoted by permission of Sue Pendry.

plotters that MH-S was in trouble as for the next fifty minutes it steered an unsteady course until at 0200 the contact faded. Its position was twenty-five miles from Portland Bill on a bearing of 225°. Damaged by flak, Sergeant Gray, the pilot, had abandoned the skies above St Nazaire and set a course for an attempt to get his damaged aircraft home. Now, unable to stay airborne any longer, in a feat of extraordinary flying in the dark of the March night, he successfully put the aircraft down in the Channel and the crew were able to scramble clear.

Away from the stricken aircraft and happy to be still alive, although somewhat uncomfortable in their little dinghy, the crew of Whitley MH-S settled down to await the dawn. Sunrise was at 0700 and it would not start to get light until 0548, the beginning of nautical twilight. They had been fortunate to escape the aircraft for the comparative safety of their dinghy and to have avoided a soaking in the choppy waters of the Channel where the temperature for that time of the year would not reach 9°C. Although they had several hours ahead of them their spirits would have been lifted by the knowledge that their position was known and therefore that help would be on the way in the shape of the highly efficient air-sea rescue organisation that operated for just such as them and that as soon as practical an aircraft would be out looking for them.

Back at Rudloe Manor a check was made, at 0743, on aircraft landings and it was discovered that MH-S had still not landed. Bomber Command, however, had originally reported it as having done so but Fighter Control pursued the matter by trying to find out at which station it had touched down and it became clear that the Whitley was still missing. Within a quarter of an hour, now that the facts were known, a staff officer ordered that a search be made by a Lysander, with a Spitfire escort, commencing at the last recorded position of the Whitley, while 19 Group were also asked to despatch marine craft.

The RAF station at Harrowbeer was officially opened on 15 August 1941, although plans to build an airfield there were first mooted in the late 1930s when expansion schemes were in train all over the country in response to the burgeoning threats from Europe. Located on the south-western edge of what is now the Dartmoor National Park it was originally planned to operate from grass runways, but experience at other stations pointed it towards tarmac and it is somewhat ironic that the vast quantity of hard-core required was provided from the rubble of bomb-damaged Plymouth, the very city that the airfield had been conceived to protect.

We have briefly met the air-sea rescue service in Chapter 3 and the help that it now gave to the downed Whitley crew would be provided by 276 ASR Squadron which had been formed at Harrowbeer on Trafalgar Day, 1941. It was equipped with Spitfire, Defiant, Anson, Walrus and Lysander aircraft and had detached flights at Portreath in Cornwall, Warmwell in Dorset and at Fairwood Common (now Swansea Airport). With such extensive cover of the Western Approaches it is not surprising that it was instrumental in saving over 200 people from a watery grave. The value of the recovery of such a number of trained personnel was inestimable.

The Westland Lysander, named after the legendary Spartan general, although first flying in June 1936, was not introduced into service until two years later when it was deployed as an army cooperation aircraft. Several squadrons were sent to France in late 1939 and early 1940 to assist the British Expeditionary Force in this role, but when the German army swept through the Netherlands and Belgium they had to be more aggressive and were used as spotters and light bombers. Sadly, though, their performance was not robust enough to enable them to compete with the might of the Luftwaffe and they suffered grievous losses. Withdrawn from France at the time of Dunkirk they had, during May and June 1940, lost fully two-thirds of the aircraft deployed. Even so, flying from England, the survivors continued to supply troops gallantly holding out in France, especially in the defence of Calais, the tenacity of which, although condemning many troops to spend the next five years as prisoners of war, helped secure the evacuation of the majority of the BEF. Judged by RAF hierarchy to be unsuitable for the purpose they withdrew from their army cooperation role and embarked on a new life of air-sea rescue missions, fourteen squadrons and flights being formed for this function in 1940 and 1941.

Happily, the attributes that had made the Lysander so unsuitable for combat made it ideal for its new role and additionally, with Europe now under occupation, the insertion and extraction of agents and supplies for Resistance groups who continued the fight in a clandestine organisation that was to harry the invader until final liberation. With a crew of two – a pilot and an observer – its low minimum airspeed was suited to search missions and to circling above dinghies in the water and its ability to take off in 275 yards and land in 350 made it ideal for the difficult and diverse landing grounds set up by the French Resistance. Although lightly armed, in its ASR role it usually flew with a fighter escort for the protection, not only of itself, but also the aircrew it was helping to rescue. The Lysander had a maximum speed of 229 miles per hour and a ceiling of 10,000 feet and with full tanks and at an economical cruising speed of 150 miles per hour it had a range of 500 miles, or a little over three hours.

On the runway at Harrowbeer, at 0820 on the morning of 28 March 1942, Lysander AQ-L of B Flight, 276 ASR Squadron, piloted by Sergeant Skellon and with Sergeant Douglas as his observer, lifted off and set course for the point of search which had been given as twenty miles due south of Lyme Regis. It was not a good morning for flying as hazy 10/10ths cloud at 2,000 feet made for poor visibility. However, at 0922, immediately on reaching the point given, the dinghy was sighted and Sergeant Skellon orbited above it until forced by shortage of fuel to make for Exeter. As he set off he would have been reassured to see, five miles north of the dinghy, the group of marine craft which had been sent to their aid.

Although Sergeant Skellon had left the scene the five airmen were not forsaken, but they must have had mixed feelings as they watched the Lysander depart. They had no cause for worry as, had they but known it, responsibility for their welfare had been assumed by another Lysander of 276 ASR Squadron, flying out of RAF Warmwell, which had been ordered to join the search.

Two years before the outbreak of World War II, when facilities were sought for an armament practice range, covetous RAF eyes lighted on the Chesil Bank, that long arm of pebbles that stretches the eighteen miles from the Isle of Portland to Bridport. Trapped on the landward side is a sheltered lagoon known as the Fleet and here it was decided to establish the range, a facility which, later in the war, would be used to test Barnes Wallis' bouncing bomb used against the dams in the Ruhr. In the face of strong local opposition, land was acquired four miles east of Dorchester on which to build the airfield that would service the range and construction commenced. It was still in progress when RAF Woodsford officially opened on 1 May 1937, and continued through 1938 (in which year the station name was changed to RAF Warmwell, after a nearby village, to avoid confusion with RAF Woodford, near Manchester) and on again into 1939. The airfield played a significant role in the Battle of Britain and in the defence of the Portland Naval Base where, during one attack on HMS *Foylebank* on 4 July 1940, Acting Leading Seaman Jack Mantle was to win the only VC awarded for action in mainland Britain.

A Flight of 276 ASR Squadron had arrived at Warmwell on 21 October 1941, the same day that the squadron had been formed at Harrowbeer, and was equipped with the same array of aircraft. At 0947 on 28 March, about the time Sergeant Skellon in AQ-L was setting off for Exeter, Sergeant Smith, with Sergeant Elder as his observer, took off to assume watch and ward over the crew of MH-S adrift in Lyme Bay. They rendezvoused with their escorting Spitfires over Weymouth soon after 1000 and set a course of 260° from Portland which would take them to the dinghy, which they sighted at 1015 in the position given. Having dropped two smoke floats to leeward of the dinghy, which was drifting rapidly in a choppy sea, Sergeant Smith then flew to a convoy that he had sighted ten miles away to the south-south-east and, attracting the attention of the leading vessel, which was a minesweeper, pennant number FY.529, led it and three others of the convoy to the dinghy, circling above it until 1055, at which time the minesweeper took the survivors on board. As Sergeants Smith and Elder left the scene, with their mission accomplished, to return to Warmwell, Sergeants Skellon and Douglas, now refuelled, were leaving Exeter for their base at Harrowbeer.

HMS *Neil Smith* (FY 529) was one of a number of minesweeping trawlers, of no specific class, which had been taken into the service of the Royal Navy. With a displacement of 275 tons she had been built by Smiths Dock Company Limited at South Bank-on-Tees and launched in July 1917. Taken over by the Admiralty in August 1939 she was under the command of her skipper Benjamin Barnet, RNR, until taken over on 21 December 1940 by Temporary Sub-Lieutenant Jack Hoffman, RNVR.

Taking the crew of the Whitley on board, at 1115 Hoffman was able to signal the success of the rescue and the relieved airmen were taken to Lyme Regis where they were put ashore at 1435, little the worse for wear. Another successful operation had been carried out and five precious aircrew had been recovered to carry on the struggle for eventual victory. They were Sergeant Gray (pilot), Sergeant Whitworth (second pilot). Pilot Officer Orchard (observer) and Sergeants Shine and Humphrys (wireless operators/air gunners).

Sergeant Donald Bray, the pilot of MH-U, had been the third aircraft of 51 Squadron to take off. Airborne at 2024 they had made for the target but had been unable to locate it. Sergeant Harold Reeder, a wireless operator/air gunner, recorded in his log that they had searched for three-quarters of an hour at 7,000 feet without success, during which time they had been hit several times. Returning with the bomb load to base they found themselves off course, probably having drifted due to a change in the wind when at 0510 they crashed into Ilkley Moor, near Cowper's Cross, about two miles south of the town of Ilkley.

Catching fire on impact, the aircraft was destroyed but although all the crew escaped, all were injured. Sergeant Bray, RAFVR, Pilot Officer P.D. Smith, RAF, (observer), and Pilot Officer John Duncan, RAFVR, (air gunner) were injured seriously enough to be admitted to hospitals in Ilkley and Harrogate, but it had been 0930 before they had been rescued. Donald Bray was later commissioned and survived the war. John Duncan, promoted flying officer, was killed a year later when shot down over Holland. Sergeant George Whyte (WOp/AG) had escaped lightly from this crash but the moors had not yet finished with him. Flying in a Halifax with 51 Squadron on 21 January 1943 he was involved in another crash on these forbidding uplands. This time it was on Hoar Side Moor, four miles WNW of Hebden Bridge and a mere fourteen miles from Cowper's Cross where MH-U had crashed the previous March. This time, however, Sergeant Whyte did not survive. He lies buried in the War Graves Plot in the cemetery at Selby.

The high moors of the dales would also claim aircraft MH-V. It was piloted by Flight Sergeant Ernest Clow, RNZAF, with, as second pilot, Pilot Officer Arthur Scott. Unusually, the aircraft was carrying a crew of six, the other members being the observer, Sergeant Richard Ryder, RAFVR, the rear gunner Sergeant R.H. Craven and two wireless operators/air gunners, Sergeant Sandy Mackay, RAF, and Sergeant William Jones. The problems with the unexpected weather conditions they found over England were exacerbated by the failure of their wireless set, leaving them with no means of contact by which to alert others to their plight.

Believing that he had worked out their position the observer gave a course of 035° which would take them east of north to their base. The pilot, however, misunderstood this and steered 350°, taking them 45° off track to the west. Thinking they must be flying away from high ground instead of towards it, they descended through the cloud and at 0525 flew into high ground at Great Whernside on Conistone Moor, three miles east of Kettlewell. Seeing the ground at the last moment the pilot pulled up the nose to lessen the impact and in doing so saved the crew from serious injury. Even so, the two pilots and the observer were catapulted out of the aircraft into the deep snow that covered the moor that night. The other three airmen would endure an uncomfortable time in the wreckage until they were released eleven hours later. The tail of the aircraft had broken off and jack-knifed to lie against the cockpit, trapping Sergeant Craven upside down in his turret, while the WOp/AGs were trapped in the fuselage.

The most seriously injured were Sergeant Mackay and the rear gunner, Sergeant Craven. Taken to hospital with serious head injuries it would be a year before Sandy Mackay was discharged and he was never passed fit enough to fly again. The pilot, Ernie Clow, a native of New Plymouth, New Zealand, went on to fly with 138 Squadron and almost a year to the day later his Halifax was damaged over Holland. He successfully put it down in the Ijsselmeer and he spent the rest of the war as a POW, initially for some time in hospital. The observer, Richard Ryder, was still flying with 51 Squadron when they were sent on attachment to Coastal Command. Taking off from Chivenor on 6 September 1942 for an anti-submarine patrol off the Isles of Scilly the aircraft was never heard of again. Sergeant Ryder is commemorated on the Runnymede Memorial. The tally of losses among the bomber squadrons who flew to St Nazaire is now complete, but there were still many sorties to be flown in phase two and phase three and we will now see how they fared.

58 Squadron was formed in Northumberland as part of 36 Home Defence Squadron, becoming a separate unit in June 1917. It was mobilised the following December as a night-bombing squadron and from February to September 1918 operated on the Western Front attacking a wide range of targets. Unlike many World War I squadrons it was not disbanded at the end of the war, but in 1919 moved to Egypt, some of the pilots flying their machines there from France.

Re-designated in February 1920, as 70 Squadron, 58 reformed in England as a heavy-bomber squadron. In 1925 the officer commanding was Squadron Leader A.T. Harris and during his tenure one of his flight commanders was Flight Lieutenant Robert Saundby. Both of these officers would reach high rank in the RAF and we have seen them in a prominent role in the planning stages of the air side of Operation Chariot in Chapter 1.

When war broke out in 1939 the squadron was flying Whitley IIIs from Linton-on-Ouse, Yorkshire, and, in common with 51 Squadron, was dropping leaflets over Germany on the first night of the war. After a short spell with Coastal Command it returned to Yorkshire from where, having converted to the Whitley V, it would play its part in the raid on St Nazaire. It was a very experienced unit, having flown on the first big raid on Germany, the first raid on Italy and the first raid on Berlin, all in 1940. The squadron had flown nine aircraft in the successful raid on St Nazaire on the night of 25/26 March 1942, by twenty-seven aircraft and of these nine, five would return to the port on 27/28.

The first aircraft away on 27 March was Squadron Leader Harvey in GE-Z at 2020 and the last was Squadron Leader Lawson in GE-D at 2108, spanning the same period during which 51 were leaving Dishforth. The route out was over Northampton, crossing the south coast at Bridport before making landfall at Pléneuf and thence to the target. All aircraft were to carry 4 x 500-lb and 4 x 250-lb GP bombs, but were not to carry cameras, flares or incendiaries. However, fourteen packets of nickels were included to be dropped over France during the sortie. Bombs were to be dropped singly and on separate runs over the target.

Squadron Leader Harvey found 10/10ths cloud in three layers and was unable to definitely pin-point the target. He reported the cloud layers to be at 2/4,000 feet, 6/7,000 feet and 9/10,000 feet. Nevertheless he remained over the docks from 0001 until 0120, from 0050 being under accurate, heavy flak. He eventually returned to base, taking all his bombs with him.

All the crews were to find the same conditions. Pilot Officer Stoney in GE-L stayed over the target area but could find no breaks in the cloud. Pilot Officer MacKenzie in GE-V spent an hour and twenty-two minutes searching, being fired on the whole time. Both these captains took their bombs back to base. Flight Sergeant Hayward in GE-P and Sergeant Small in GE-R both found cloud at 17,000 feet and experienced severe icing, Small enduring the added complication of his air speed indicator being out of action. Pilot Officer Wilson in GE-A reported the same layers of cloud and inability to pin-point the target as had Squadron Leader Harvey, but dutifully remained over the target for the prescribed period, all the while experiencing flak at 7,000 feet.

The later pilots were to have no better fortune. Sergeant Alcock in GE-G spent an hour over the target without a sight of it and Pilot Officer Mason in GE-J likewise failed to find a break in the cloud. Flight Sergeant Parsons in GE-E found it impossible to locate the target and returned to base, jettisoning his 4 x 250-lb bombs in the sea twenty-five miles south of Guernsey. Squadron Leader Lawson, probably the most experienced of the squadron's pilots, also had to return without dropping his bombs.

Squadron Leader Harry Reginald Lawson had started at the bottom. On 23 October 1925 he had enlisted in the RAF, serving in the ranks as aircraftman 2nd class, and was posted to the RAF Depot as an aircraft hand undergoing training for carpenter. Progressing up the ranks, in December 1930 he was posted to 2 Flying Training School as a pilot/carpenter-rigger and on 2 June 1931, became a sergeant pilot. A year to the day he was promoted flight sergeant. During the next eight years he had several postings, including at both Central and 2 Flying Schools. On 1 April 1940, he was granted an emergency commission as a probationary pilot officer, a rank that was confirmed after a year.

Harry Lawson's tour with 58 Squadron was sandwiched between postings as an instructor at 10 and 1 Operational Training Units. Retiring as a wing commander in January 1954, with a DFC, AFC and three Mentions in Despatches, his service record contained over fifty postings and appointments and included service in Iraq, the Mediterranean, the Middle East and at Luqa. He settled in St Mawgan, Cornwall, across the valley from St Eval, the airfield from which he had flown with 58 Squadron. He died there in February 1977.

Two of the squadron's twelve aircraft detailed for the sortie failed to take any part. Flight Lieutenant Earp, in GE-T, found his clutch disengaging, no starboard high speed supercharger and then no low speed. He reluctantly returned to Linton, landing at 0001, just as Squadron Leader Harvey had started his fruitless circling of the docks at St Nazaire. Even more unfortunate was Flight Sergeant Scrivens, in GE-U, who did not even get off the ground as his tail wheel burst while taxiing for take-off.

There are two more aircraft to record in phase two and they were from 77 Squadron. Squadron Leader Pryde, in KN-Q, and Flight Sergeant Lord, in KN-Y, had taken off from Leeming at 2039 and 2044 respectively. They, too, were unable to bomb in the prevailing conditions and although they encountered no flak or searchlights they did experience severe icing conditions. They set course for base where they landed safely, having jettisoned their bombs on the way.[21]

When the last aircraft of the Whitley squadrons had left for home, phases one and two, the targeting of docks, had come to an end. The commando assault on the docks below was due to start at 0130 and at the end of a thirty-four-hour sail from Falmouth, HMS *Campbeltown* would ram the southern caisson a mere four minutes late.

If this narrative has been repetitive and monotonous it can only be a reflection of the experience of the crews themselves. On any other sortie they could well have bombed through the clouds on dead reckoning, but given the operational constraints they were reduced to fruitless circling and inevitable frustration. It is a small wonder that collisions did not occur. It may well have helped if they had known the nature of the operation below from which they were expected to draw the attention of the defenders.

The dock area that formed Target A was a small enough target at the best of times. Certainly in respect of the accuracy of bombing that pertained at the time an area approximately 400 x 1,600 yards would present a difficult enough target in the best of weather conditions. Now it was alive with commandos going about their mission of demolition and the bomber effort would switch to the northern part of the Penhoët Basin, notably free, not only of friendly forces, but also of the French civilians among whom Churchill was determined to avoid casualties. These sorties against Target B were to be flown by twenty-seven Wellington 1C aircraft drawn from four squadrons of 1 Group.

103 Squadron was formed on 1 September 1917 at Beaulieu, in Hampshire, and in May 1918 was sent to the Western Front where it flew daylight bombing and reconnaissance

---

[21] It is to be hoped that some of the co-ordinates for the jettisoning of bombs as given in the squadron operations record books are in error as one is on Cranborne Chase, in Dorset, and the other just outside Buckingham.

operations for the remainder of the war. Like many other WWI squadrons it was disbanded in the latter half of 1919. Reformed at Andover in August 1936 as a light-bomber squadron it flew Hawker Hinds until July 1938, when it converted to a more advanced monoplane bomber, the Fairey Battle. In a reprise of its WWI service, it was again deployed to France, proceeding there on the day before war was declared. There it would sustain serious losses operating with the AASF. As it was driven ahead of the rapidly advancing German forces it flew from six different airfields in nine and a half months until finally quitting France on 16 June 1940, and relocating to Abingdon. From a one-time strength of thirty-one aircraft, by early June but sixteen were left. Of those sixteen, only eight escaped back to England. In October 1940 the squadron converted to the Wellington and in July 1941 moved to Elsham Wolds, in Lincolnshire, where it would remain for the rest of the war, at the conclusion of which it disbanded.

Commanding officer of the squadron in March, 1942, was Wing Commander Joscelyne du Boulay. Born in Burma on New Year's Day, 1913, he was the son of a major in the Border Regiment. With his father back in England he was later educated at Wellington College and then entered Cranwell as a cadet. An exceptional student, his logbook noted that he had qualified to fly solo in the shortest possible time. Commissioned as a pilot officer in December 1932 he was promoted flight lieutenant in June 1934, and on his first posting, to Afghanistan, he crashed his aircraft while flying a patrol in the Khyber Pass. During World War II he flew Wellingtons and earned a DFC and by June 1941 he was an acting wing commander. Then, on 9 March 1942, he was posted from 21 OTU to command 103 Squadron at Elsham Wolds, although he did not fly to St Nazaire. Towards the end of the war, as a group captain, he was at Supreme Headquarters Allied Expeditionary Force on Eisenhower's staff and was present at the signing of the German capitulation on 7 May 1945.

Twelve aircraft from the squadron were detailed to take part in the bombing of Target B and at midday on 27 March 1942, they flew to their advance base at Pershore, Worcestershire, where they were briefed at 1515. No cameras were to be carried and no photo flashes, flares or lights were to be shown. If the target was not identified the bomb load of 5 x 500-lb GP bombs was to be brought back. They were destined to have no greater success than their colleagues at Target A.

Charged to cause maximum destruction to the docks at St Nazaire the first aircraft lifted off at 2220 and by 2313 eleven crews were airborne, the twelfth, captained by Pilot Officer Martin in PM-G being left behind with engine trouble. The route from Pershore took them over the coast at Bridport and they made landfall at Bréhat before proceeding over Belle Isle to the target where they found the same impossible weather conditions as had prevailed all night. The sortie was to be the now familiar catalogue of frustration and failure. The crews found a few searchlights operating and got the impression that the gun crews were firing the light flak that they encountered along the beams. Pilot Officer Brookes flying PM-B spent twenty-eight minutes searching and returned to Elsham Wolds, as did Flight Lieutenant Gillespie in PM-H who spent an hour in the target area. Back in England the deteriorating weather was to spread the returning aircraft around the country. Pilot Officer Smith in PM-K tried for twenty minutes to find a gap in the clouds and returned to England, landing at Tattenhill. Squadron Leader Holford in PM-Q returned to Pershore, Sergeant Staniland in PM-U, suffering with wireless failure, to Middle Wallop and Pilot Officer Tett landed PM-D at Colerne. All had been unable to locate the target.

This sorry procession continued and Pilot Officer Gorman, PM-L, Flight Lieutenant

Saxelby, PM-Z, Flight Sergeant Bray, PM-O, and Sergeant Lewis, PM-X, similarly failed to find an opportunity to attack and took their bombs safely back to Elsham Wolds. The one successful exception was Squadron Leader Godfrey flying PM-C, who managed to drop his bombs on one end of the Penhoët Basin through a gap in the clouds. Once again, though, a squadron sortie to support the raid below had failed to achieve its object.

The subsequent experiences of the crews of 103 Squadron would be typical of those of any other squadron. There were those who would survive the war, some unscathed, some wounded and some after enduring the grimness of a prisoner of war camp. Then there were those, far too many, who would make the ultimate sacrifice.

Such was the rate of losses among bomber crews that, before three months were out, three of the captains who flew to St Nazaire had been killed in action. On 12 April Flight Lieutenant R. Gillespie was lost, together with Sergeant G.B. Fairhurst and Flight Sergeant D. Campbell. On 25 April Flight Sergeant C.L. Bray, RCAF, and fellow crew members Sergeants D.W. Musgrove, A.F. Blencowe and S.H. Harle were killed. Squadron Leader Oliver Godfrey, DFC, having by then been promoted wing commander, was killed in action over Holland on 23 June with crew member Pilot Officer A.C.R. Downward. All these men took part in the raid on St Nazaire. Oliver Godfrey is buried in Wierhuizen Protestant Cemetery, De Marne, the Netherlands and Duncan Campbell is buried in Flushing Northern Cemetery while all the others are commemorated on the Memorial at Runnymede.

Few who witnessed the arrival of David Holford at Barnetby station in October 1941 would have believed that this young officer, still looking like the schoolboy he had been only a few short years before, would in two years be recognised as one of the finest pilots in Bomber Command. Having joined the RAF aged 17, in 1938, by March 1940 he was a qualified Wellington bomber pilot and he honed his skills flying second pilot on eleven sorties, six of them with Percy Pickard.

Posted to 103 Squadron on 12 February 1942 he was one of only two of the squadron's pilots who flew against the German battle-cruisers *Scharnhorst* and *Gneisenau* in their dash up the Channel. The other pilot, Squadron Leader Cross, was shot down and rescued from the water by German sailors. He would later be shot by the Gestapo as one of the Great Escapers. In the poor visibility Holford was able to put his bombs close to the ships and was awarded a DSO to go with the DFC he had been awarded earlier in the war.

On 16 December 1943 and now commanding 100 Squadron as the youngest wing commander in the RAF he put himself down to fly on a raid on Berlin on what became known as Black Friday. To the twenty-five aircraft that were lost over Berlin were added thirty-three that crashed in fog-bound England on return to their bases. Holford's aircraft was damaged by a night fighter on the way out but he pressed on to the target, only to be attacked again on the way back. With the airfield fog-bound he held off while other, less experienced pilots tried to land. Eventually running out of fuel he hit rising ground and was thrown out of the aircraft into the deep snow, where he was found by his wireless operator who wrapped him in a parachute against the bitter cold. When ambulances finally arrived he was dead. His last thoughts were for his crew. "The crew.... Are the crew alright?"

Flight Lieutenant Clive Saxelby was to be thrice lucky. A New Zealander, he was by any standard a most able captain, fearless and determined. One night over Karlsruhe a British incendiary bomb fell into his engine nacelle and started a fire. Switching off the petrol, he ran the engine dry and switched it off. Then, jettisoning his bombs, he set course for home. Later in the flight he successfully restarted the engine and flew safely back to his base where he landed on one wheel, the other having been burnt out. On another occasion, after bombing Cologne, he was attacked by a night fighter. The citation for his DFC tells the story:

> "His second pilot was killed and the rear gunner wounded. The rear turret of the aircraft was shattered, the fuselage near the astro hatch set on fire and the hydraulics were damaged, causing the undercarriage and bomb doors to fall down. The aircraft went out of control. Although he was choked by fumes, Flight Lieutenant Saxelby skilfully regained control at 6,000 feet. He was again attacked at this height but, descending to 300 feet, he succeeded in evading the attacker. He courageously flew the damaged aircraft back to this country where he made an excellent crash-landing at an aerodrome without further injury to his crew."

This incident bears testimony, not only to the skill of an extraordinary pilot, but also to the designer of the aircraft that it could still be flown in such a condition. His third flirtation with death came during the Great Escape from Stalag Luft III. Clive Saxelby was still flying with 103 Squadron when he was eventually shot down during a raid on Duisburg on the night of 7/8 September 1942 and he became a prisoner of war. At the bottom of the exit shaft and next but one to leave, shots were heard as the Germans became aware of the break-out. Turning and scurrying on his hands and knees back along the tunnel to the entrance, expecting to be shot from behind at any moment, he managed to avoid discovery. He had been but a few minutes from leaving the tunnel which would have eventually resulted in almost certain death at the hands of the Gestapo.

The history of 150 Squadron has a distinct international flavour to it. It had been formed in Salonika, Macedonia, as a fighter squadron on 1 April 1918, the birthday of the RAF itself, and it operated in Macedonia and Turkey for the remainder of WWI before being disbanded in 1919. Reformed in England in 1938, the squadron had been sent to North Africa in December 1942 and took part in the campaigns in Tunisia, Sicily and Italy. Having moved to Italy it was disbanded there in October 1944.

Between its reformation in 1938 and its despatch to North Africa in 1942 the squadron followed a remarkably similar path to that of 103 Squadron. Based at Benson flying the Fairey Battle it found itself deployed to France on 2 September 1939 to operate with the AASF. Like 103 they were driven from one airfield to another, taking heavy losses as they went. On 15 June 1940 they left France for Abingdon, shortly moving to Stradishall and then on to Newton where, in October 1940 they converted to the Wellington 1C.[22] In July 1941 they moved yet again, this time to Snaith.

It was left to 150 Squadron to bring down the curtain on what had been a most frustrating night for the squadrons involved. Thirteen of the squadron's aircraft had been standing by at two hours' notice from 0900 and later in the day flew the one and a quarter hour trip to their advance base at Stanton Harcourt for the raid on St Nazaire. Each aircraft carried 5 x 500-lb bombs and took on 650 gallons of petrol at Stanton Harcourt and at their briefing it was made perfectly clear to the crews that they were not to release their bombs unless

---

[22] In November 1941 the squadron started conversion to the Liberator. However, after five Liberators had been delivered in early 1942 they were removed and 150 continued to fly the Wellingtons.

they could clearly pin-point the target, their main task being to occupy the defences.

The first aircraft away was flown by Wing Commander Mellor at 0005 on the 28th followed at intervals of five minutes by the rest of the crews. The route was over Sywell, crossing the Channel from Bridport to Pleubain and on to the target. Layers of cloud covered most of the route out and extremely adverse weather accompanied the flight. Over the target, however, some of the crews were able, through gaps in the cloud, to see fires burning and the flashes of gunfire, which they took to bear witness to the action below. Through one of these breaks the crew of one Wellington reported having identified the target and dropped two of their bombs.

Another pilot, Sergeant Law, who had flown in the raid on 25/26 March as a 'fresher' found a marked difference in the conditions. On that raid St Nazaire was in perfect visibility and he dropped his bombs, bursts being observed between docks 1 and 4. Now, on 27th/28th, he was one of seven crews who would be unable to locate the target altogether.

The squadron's operation order 67, detailing arrangements for the raid on 28 March had listed alternative and last resort targets as 'nil'. Nevertheless, four crews attacked flak positions at St Brieuc while another, captained by Flight Sergeant Stirling, bombed the aerodrome at Lannion. It was conveniently illuminated by the customary Chance light[23] and the men had the satisfaction of seeing detonations all along the runway. The crews encountered severe icing on the way back to base and some of those who still retained their bombs were obliged to jettison them in the Channel. No serious opposition had been encountered and all the aircraft returned to base without incident.

Pilot Officer Powell would not long survive the dangers that were the lot of the bomber pilot, night after night taking the fight to the enemy. On the night of 2 April 1942, a mere six days after the Chariot operation he had flown in his Wellington to attack the Matford Works at Poissy, near Paris. It was a perilous mission, for bombers had attacked the same target, unsuccessfully, the previous night and this time the defences were prepared. Powell's aircraft was soon hit and caught fire, plummeting from the sky into a wood, where a large explosion was heard and the burning fuel set fire to the wood itself.

It seemed that no-one could have lived through such a crash, but a young French boy, venturing into the wood, heard faint cries for help. The tail section of the aircraft had broken off and lay apart from the fuselage and there, struggling to extricate himself, although badly wounded, was the tail gunner, Sergeant Maltby. Chris Maltby had not flown to St Nazaire but had been spare gunner for the Paris raid and at the last moment had replaced a sick Canadian.

The boy helped Maltby out of the wrecked turret and was turning to look, in vain, for other survivors when more villagers arrived. Making a rough stretcher they carried the badly wounded airman to a nearby house and began to tend his wounds, but they were so severe that the arrival of the local Feldgendarmerie left the rescuers with no alternative but to hand him in, knowing he would then get the care and treatment he so desperately needed.

Thus perished not only Pilot Officer Powell, but also his wireless operator, Sergeant Barton, and front gunner, Sergeant Shepherd, who had both flown with him to St Nazaire. That was not all, though, for flying with them that night as pilot was the station commander at Snaith, Group Captain Webb. Eric Webb had been born in Ireland in 1905 and had won the Sword of Honour when passing out of Cranwell in 1925. He was posted to Snaith as

---

[23] Aerodromes often had a number of powerful moveable floodlights to aid night landing. Among those used by the RAF were floodlights manufactured by Chance Bros.

station commander in September 1941. The crew, which also included the navigator, Flight Sergeant Sykes, now lie in a collective grave in the cemetery at Les Gonards at Versailles.

Maltby was taken to a hospital in St Germain and in order, no doubt, to discomfort him and to stir up the antagonism of the French civilian population, the Germans placed him in a ward containing children, some of whom had been injured in previous air raids. What happened next, had such an act been known when planning the diversionary raid on St Nazaire, might have changed Churchill's mind about the chance bombing of French civilians. Instead of being the target of anger and retribution from the patients, the children gave him their chocolate ration, so wrong-footing the Germans that the following day he was moved to a hospital in Paris.

Polish forces in exile made an enormous contribution to the Allied effort in World War II. Not least of that effort was the manning of four bomber squadrons, 300, 301, 304 and 305 (302 and 303 were fighter squadrons). Two of these squadrons would supply aircraft for the diversionary raid. 304 (Silesian) and 305 (Ziemia Weilkopolska) Squadrons were formed a week apart at Bramcote, Warwickshire, in August 1940 and led a parallel existence until they eventually went their separate ways when 304 joined Coastal Command. Originally equipped with Fairey Battles they converted to Wellingtons in November 1940 and the following month moved to Syerston. In July they moved again, this time to Lindholme where they stayed until mid-1942.

The weather at Lindholme on 27 March was fair at first, but became cloudy during the morning and during the afternoon, in accordance with Bomber Command instructions, two aircraft from each squadron flew to forward bases for the operation against St Nazaire, those from 304 to Stanton Harcourt to fly with 150 Squadron and those from 305 to Pershore to fly with 103, although one of the latter would be cancelled on reaching the advance base.

Sergeant Engel of 305 Squadron had left Lindholme just after 1600 for Pershore and later that night flew among the crews of 103 Squadron. Carrying 5 x 500-lb bombs he found the cloud layers still banked high above the docks. The weather, also, was bad and visibility poor and after circling for over twenty-five minutes he returned to Pershore, taking his bombs with him and landing safely at 0439.

Flying Officers Figuera and Skarsynski of 304 Squadron had flown to Stanton Harcourt where they joined the thirteen Wellingtons of 150 Squadron which had flown there from Snaith. At 0005 the first crews of 150 had set off, followed at regular intervals by the others and the Polish crews joined in at 0120 and 0130 respectively. They found the same impossible conditions and Figuera reported visibility down to a thousand yards. Skarsynski, also unable to bomb the docks and unwilling to waste the sortie, attacked as an alternative target a flak installation at Vannes. He had the satisfaction of seeing his bombs burst and the fire from the battery ceased. By 0615 both crews were safely on the tarmac at Lindholme, Figuera having deposited his bombs in the Channel.

When the last of the aircraft of 150 Squadron had touched down at Snaith at 0725 on 28 March only the crew of the ditched Whitley V of 51 Squadron were unaccounted for as they sat in their dinghy in Lyme Bay awaiting rescue. It had been a most unsatisfactory and disappointing night. Only three of the sixty-two aircraft that had comprised the operation to draw attention away from the little flotilla carrying the commandos on their raid, had managed to drop any of their bombs, with effect unknown. However, it is impossible to blame

THE COMMANDERS

Above left: Vice-Admiral The Lord Louis Mountbatten, chief of Combined Operations. (IWM IB 122)
Above right: Admiral of the Fleet Sir Charles Forbes, C-in-C Plymouth, flag officer responsible for launching Operation Chariot. (© World History Archive/fotoLibra)

Above left: Commander Robert Ryder, naval force commander. (IWM HU 1916)
Above right: Lieutenant Colonel Charles Newman, military force commander. (IWM HU 16542)

ROYAL AIR FORCE PLANNERS

Above left: Air Marshal Arthur Harris, AOC-in-C Bomber Command. (IWM CH 13020)
Above right: Air Vice-Marshal Robert Saundby, senior air staff officer, Bomber Command.
(IWM CH 14544)

Above left: Air Vice-Marshal Geoffrey Bromet, AOC 19 Group, Coastal Command. (IWM
CH 7025)
Above right: Group Captain A.H. Willetts, air advisor Combined Operations. (US Air Force
Academy)

RAF MEDMENHAM

Above left: A man from the PRU, commanding officer Wing Commander Geoffrey Tuttle, DFC. (Crown Copyright – courtesy of Medmenham Collection)
Above right: Tirpitz in Tromsø fjord on 28 March 1942 unaware of the raid on St Nazaire. (Crown Copyright – courtesy of Medmenham Collection)

Left: Constance Babington-Smith, head of the aircraft section, RAF Medmenham. (Crown Copyright – courtesy of Medmenham Collection)
Right: Ann McKnight-Kauffer, photo interpreter at St Eval. (Crown Copyright – courtesy of Medmenham Collection)
Below: The model of the dockyard at St Nazaire made by the model section at Medmenham. (Crown Copyright – courtesy of Medmenham Collection)

THE VALUE OF
AERIAL RECONNAISSANCE

Above: Vertical shot of St Nazaire taken on 25 March 1942. The five boats of the 5th Torpedo Boat Destroyer Flotilla (1) can be seen tied up alongside in the submarine basin. (IWM C2351)

Below: On 27 March 1942 the torpedo boats (1-5) can be seen moored in the estuary having returned from a brief visit to Nantes. The sixth boat is the *Sperrbrecher Botilla Russ.* (NCAP/ncap.org.uk)

RAF ST EVAL

Above: A vertical shot of the airfield at St Eval on which has been marked the field system that was destroyed when the base was constructed. (IWM HU 92963)

Left: The crew of a Whitley of 502 Squadron debriefing at St Eval after a twelve-hour anti-submarine patrol. (IWM CH 7056)

Bottom left: St Eval church, the only remaining building of the village, now a centre of pilgrimage for those who served on the station. (Lajla Johansson)

AIRCRAFT OF COASTAL COMMAND

Above: Lockheed Hudsons of 233 Squadron who flew searches from RAF St Eval, here seen over Northern Ireland while based at Aldergrove. (IWM CH 2841)
Below: Bristol Blenheim Mk VIFs of 254 Squadron who flew their searches from Predannack, also seen here over Northern Ireland. (IWM CH 2992)

10 SQUADRON RAAF

Above: Short Sunderland Mk III, RB-Z, W4004. This aircraft patrolled the Bay of Biscay on 26 and 28 March but not on the 27th. (IWM CH 5548A)

Left: A navigator plots a change of course at his spacious navigator's position. (IWM CH 420)

Bottom left: The galley where meals were prepared for the large crew on the long sorties of which this aircraft was capable. (IWM CH 418)

These two pictures betray the origin of the aircraft as the S23 Empire Flying Boat, built to carry passengers for Imperial Airways.

THE LOSS OF WHITLEY Z6964

Above: The crash site with the remains of the aircraft guarded by German soldiers. (Péchonière family collection)
Left from top to bottom: Flying Officer William Desmond Stuart Bow, captain of the aircraft. (Lang family collection); The graves as laid out by the War Graves Commission in 1947. (Arnaud Théron); The graves following the re-interment by the municipal council in 1946. (Marcel Burel)

the crews, who had been dealt a very poor hand. That a conspiracy of climatic conditions and operational constraints had combined to make the diversionary raid impossible was no fault of theirs.

CHAPTER 8

FIRE DOWN BELOW

'Nothing more exactly resembled a scene from the
Inferno. The very river itself was on fire....while
in the night beyond, seemingly suspended in the air,
there blazed a sea of burning petrol which had spread
outwards and outwards from each burning ship....'

Recollection by Major Bill Copland,
Second-in-Command, 2 Commando[24]

We last saw Chariot Force having passed through Point E, formed up in battle order and proceeding at 12 knots to their next and last reference position. This was the important Point Z at 46°48'N, 02°50'W and here they would rendezvous with the submarine HMS Sturgeon which had been sent ahead to act as a navigational check. Due to approach on an approximate course of 045° and arrive at 2230 hours the commandos watched in wonderment as, dead on time and dead on track, a red light flashing the Morse letter M from Sturgeon's conning tower appeared in the middle of the ocean wastes, seemingly beckoning them forward.

The mysteries of navigation at sea were unknown to the land-based commandos but not to Lieutenant Bill Green, RN, who, having got them thus far, was now faced with the daunting task of guiding the flotilla over the dangerous shallow waters that barely covered the mud banks of the Loire estuary. His success in doing so was hailed by the professional Loire pilots as "unparalleled in the history of the port".

Filing past the partly-submerged submarine in their two columns and boosted by the stentorian expressions of good luck from her captain, Lieutenant Commander Mervyn Wingfield, RN, the force now had three hours to sail before their audacious enterprise would reach its climax. There would be little sleep now. The commandos cleaned and re-cleaned their weapons, the sailors, never more at home than when at sea, busied themselves around their craft. As they sailed away the two Hunt class destroyers, HMS Atherstone and HMS Tynedale, that had escorted them from Falmouth left to set up their patrol line off the estuary to await the survivors the following morning. An hour later Lieutenant Tibbits, RN, would activate the delayed-action fuses in the charge in Campbeltown's bows. The targets in the dockyard fell into three groups, those around the Old Town to the south of the Old Mole and Bridge D (Group 1), those between the Old Mole and Bridge M (Group 2) and those relating to targets associated with the Normandie Dock itself (Group 3) and including the biggest prize of all, the southern caisson.

---

[24] Quoted in The Greatest Raid of All – C.E. Lucas Phillips, 1958.

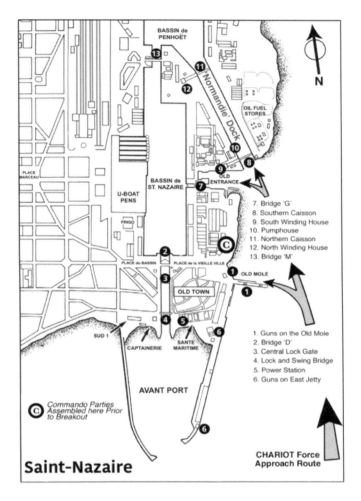

7. Bridge 'G'
8. Southern Caisson
9. South Winding House
10. Pumphouse
11. Northern Caisson
12. North Winding House
13. Bridge 'M'

1. Guns on the Old Mole
2. Bridge 'D'
3. Central Lock Gate
4. Lock and Swing Bridge
5. Power Station
6. Guns on East Jetty

CHARIOT Force
Approach Route

Commando Parties
Assembled here Prior
to Breakout

Saint-Nazaire

© James Dorrian

Each group had its own landing place; Group 1 at the Old Mole, Group 2 at the Old Entrance while the commandos for Group 3 would land from *Campbeltown* directly on to the caisson itself by means of scaling ladders.

The flotilla was led by the gunboat MGB 314 carrying Commander Ryder, Lieutenant Colonel Newman and their headquarters parties. On either hand, and slightly astern, were two torpedo-carrying MLs, those of Boyd and Irwin, with no troops and a roving commission. Following these three little craft came HMS *Campbeltown*, commanded by Lieutenant Commander Beattie, and carrying not only commandos but also an explosive charge, consisting of twenty-four Mark VII depth charges, in the bows. Stretching out astern of *Campbeltown* were the two columns of MLs, the port column to attack the Group 1 targets and the starboard column to attack those of Group 2. Bringing up the rear was the spare ML 298 of Sub-Lieutenant Nock RNVR with no troops and last, but by no means least, sailed the MTB 74 of Sub-Lieutenant Micky Wynn RNVR, one of the most unusual craft in the Royal Navy.

The troops for the assault were trained in three separate disciplines. The first troops ashore would be assault troops to silence the formidable defences that would greet them. These would be followed by the demolition parties, generally five strong and each with a specific target and each accompanied by the third type, protection parties, for the heavy loads carried by the demolitionists allowed them only small arms for personal protection. The assault and protection parties were provided by 2 Commando while 1, 2, 3, 4, 5, 6, 9 and 12 Commandos provided the troops for demolition duties.

An hour after *Sturgeon* had slipped below the surface of the bay to withdraw southward before resuming its normal patrol and the Chariot Force had sailed away on their final leg to the target, those on deck began to see and hear the unmistakeable signs of the bombers mounting their diversionary raid. On ML 457, in the port column and destined for the Old Mole, Second Lieutenant Bill 'Tiger' Watson, ever the pragmatist, had decided that sleep was the best option, probably one of the few to do so, and had therefore missed the rendezvous with the submarine. When at last he came on deck, "I could see several miles ahead that the air raid had already begun," he remembered. "Searchlights criss-crossed a sky spangled by flak bursts. We were now in the estuary and moving steadily forward. It was time to get ready."

On *Campbeltown*, Stuart Chant "could see the glow of searchlights and, shortly afterwards, the sound of aircraft", indicating that the RAF had arrived to distract the enemy. His mind went back to England. "I remember thinking that the scene was no different from the air

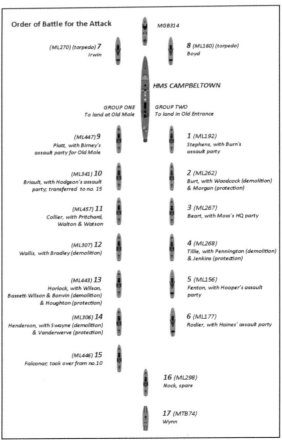

Order of Battle for the Attack

MGB314

(ML270) (torpedo) **7**
Irwin

8 (ML160) (torpedo)
Boyd

HMS CAMPBELTOWN

GROUP ONE
To land at Old Mole

GROUP TWO
To land in Old Entrance

(ML447) **9**
Platt, with Birney's
assault party for Old Mole

1 (ML192)
Stephens, with Burn's
assault party

(ML341) **10**
Briault, with Hodgson's assault
party; transferred to no. 15

2 (ML262)
Burt, with Woodcock (demolition)
& Morgan (protection)

(ML457) **11**
Collier, with Pritchard,
Walton & Watson

3 (ML267)
Beart, with Moss's HQ party

(ML307) **12**
Wallis, with Bradley (demolition)

4 (ML268)
Tillie, with Pennington (demolition)
& Jenkins (protection)

(ML443) **13**
Horlock, with Wilson,
Bassett-Wilson & Bonvin (demolition)
& Houghton (protection)

5 (ML156)
Fenton, with Hooper's assault
party

(ML306) **14**
Henderson, with Swayne (demolition)
& Vanderwerve (protection)

6 (ML177)
Rodier, with Haines' assault party

(ML446) **15**
Falconar; took over from no.10

16 (ML298)
Nock, spare

17 (MTB74)
Wynn

raids we had been witness to since 1940. But this time there was a difference: we wanted this air raid and we wanted it to continue until we arrived right in the middle of it."

Bringing up the rear of the port column, in ML 306, Ordinary Seaman Ralph Batteson was to recall:

"At 1130 in the distance, and growing gradually louder, we heard the familiar drone of engines. The British bombers had arrived, again right on time. Far ahead of us, the German searchlights which had been playing on the water now thankfully turned their dazzling beams skyward and the enemy opened up with their anti-aircraft batteries. I heard the exploding crunch of distant bombs and the dull crashing answer of the German guns. Thus far, everything seemed to be going to plan."

It was a little while later that Ryder, in the van in MGB 314, noted that the RAF was about its business:

"From about midnight gun flashes were seen in the distance to the northeast. Half an hour later, while still 12 miles off the port, it was obvious that heavy air activity was in progress. Gun flashes could be seen over a wide arc, together with a considerable amount of flak. We were unable to ascertain if our air attack was progressing satisfactorily or not, but there seemed no reason to have doubts on that score and the presence of our aircraft greatly encouraged us."

Ryder, however, and he was not alone in this, identified a serious problem for he was well aware of the restrictions that Churchill had imposed on the air raid:

"The weather, for our purpose, was perfect. The sky was completely overcast with low cloud; indeed, it was at times misty with a light drizzle, while the full moon above the clouds prevented the night from being too dark."

As has been seen in the previous chapter the weather, whilst ideal for the approach of the seaborne force brought with it severe disadvantages. What was sauce for the goose did not at all suit the gander. All too soon the raiders would reap the bitter harvest.

Ashore in his control post at St Marc, close by the chateau he had made his headquarters, Kapitän-sur-Zee Mecke was also aware of the presence of the British bombers. He had been warned by a radar station at 2320 and had brought his battalions to a state of readiness. Ten minutes later, exactly on schedule, the bombing runs had started and with the searchlights probing the poor visibility, the guns opened fire. Mecke had been through all this before. On the night of 7/8 March seventeen aircraft had bombed St Nazaire and on 25/26 March a force of twenty-seven aircraft had bombed the port and one Wellington had been lost, although not to enemy action. Tonight, though, something was different, something was missing. There were no bombs.

"I was surprised when the English aircraft came —they dropped no bombs and I said to my officers, 'There is devilry going on'."

Indeed there was. The 'devilry' planned by combined operations was to attract the attention of the enemy away from the force sailing up the estuary, but confined within the strait-jacket of their restrictive orders, only a few bombs had been dropped and now, far from diverting attention from the river, they had pointed to it.

"I hurried up to the outlook and I saw the shadows of seventeen vessels going
at high speed in the direction of St Nazaire."

A phone call to the harbour commander confirmed that no German craft were expected that night. It was 0118 and although the guns had now ceased firing, Mecke ordered his men to stay alert.[25]

The approaching raiders and the forces manning the air defences of St Nazaire were not the only ones to be aware of the aircraft overhead. In St Nazaire itself the inhabitants, sleeping peacefully in their beds, were awakened by the air raid siren but remained blissfully unaware of the action which was about to descend on the town. For one family, however, the air raid was to have disastrous consequences. Such bombing raids were a feature of their lives – had not there been one on the town only two nights earlier? – and so the sound of the alarm on 27 March came as no surprise.

M. and Mme. Ollivier, in their house on the Chemins des Ecuries de la Ville,[26] on hearing the siren, immediately rose and dressed to be ready for any emergency, but left their two young daughters asleep. The sound of the circling planes could clearly be heard above the noise of the anti-aircraft fire and, although they noted no bombs were falling, they took the precaution of settling themselves in the safest part of the house.

Close by, in the Rue Commandant Gaté, other residents were woken by the air raid and also noted that although the aircraft had been circling for an hour or more, no bombs had been dropped. Hélène Bouveyron, living with her parents in a lane off the main road, left her house and ventured into the garden to find out what was going on but the whistling of a shell overhead left her terrified and she rushed indoors and returned to bed. André Jehan, living at number 98 with his parents, was looking out of his window when a shell whistled past.

At the Olliviers' house there was a sudden violent explosion above their heads and they were deluged with debris and dust. M. Ollivier had serious injuries to his head and chest and Mme. Ollivier found her left arm hanging useless by her side. Rescued by neighbours, she was taken to hospital where her left arm was amputated but for her husband there was no hope and he succumbed to his injuries. The two little girls both survived the impact and were later taken in by neighbours. M. Ollivier is commemorated on the Commando Memorial on the seafront at St Nazaire.

The circling bombers had dropped a few bombs, but the damage at the Olliviers' house was not caused by one of them. No doubt aware that other residents had witnessed its

---

[25] Mecke was speaking thirty-two years later in a film made by Mickey Burn for BBC television. We shall learn later that the contemporary German records show there was no suspicion of a landing from the sea.

[26] Now called Rue d'Arsonval.

passing, the next day the Germans were forced to admit that it was indeed a stray shell from the anti-aircraft battery at Le Pointeau, on the east bank of the Loire, which was responsible. Indeed, a second shell had landed in the garden but did not explode.

Out in the estuary *Campbeltown* had by now crossed the dangerous shoals and although she had grounded twice she had driven herself free. By such margins do great enterprises stand or fall. The bombing schedule required the first wave to target the dockyard from 2330 until 0120, but by 0100 many of the bombers had left and the guns were falling silent. It was a situation that did not escape the notice of those out in the river who had previously recorded their arrival.

Stuart Chant recalled that "the noise of the aircraft continued, but then seemed to get less" and that shortly afterwards "the noise of the planes died away altogether and the searchlights were dimmed". Tiger Watson also recorded that "the air raid seemed to have petered out and the searchlights were switching out one by one. This boded no good". Ralph Batteson also felt keenly this sense of foreboding:

> "After the noise of the gunfire and exploding bombs there was a terrible stillness as the searchlights were switched off and the German batteries fell silent. Would they now turn their guns on us?"

He did not have long to wait for an answer. At 0120 Mecke gave the order to "beware landing" and two minutes later the scene was illuminated by the powerful searchlights, now pointing out across the water. In MGB 314 Ryder attempted to prolong the bluff with spurious messages in German which for a short time confused the defenders and some of the lights were switched off but a desultory fire broke out which further false signals failed to halt.

There now occurred on *Campbeltown* an incident that was to cause no little discomfort to those who had to land from her deck after she had rammed the dock. Having successfully crossed the mud banks and passed the dangerous heavy battery at Fort de l'Ève they had approached to within a mile of their target. The time was 0128 and Ryder had finally exhausted the tricks he had carried up his sleeve from Falmouth. The Germans were to be deceived no longer and the eerie silence was shattered by a furious outburst of fire from every gun which the enemy could bring to bear.

Standing in front of the bridge superstructure, but protected by a screen that had been erected for that purpose, Major Bill Copland, Newman's 2 i/c, was taken aback by the weight of fire now descending on *Campbeltown*. The German flag at her masthead had already been replaced by a White Ensign and the eight Oerlikons on their bandstands being already in action, Copland now gave the order to the crew of the twelve-pounder and the two mortars ahead of him to open fire, not in the accepted manner, but with a somewhat unmilitary cry of "let her go!".

Almost immediately, and certainly before the crews could get their second rounds away, there was a tremendous explosion accompanied by smoke and flying debris. Copland, who attributed it to a large coastal shell, probably 4", recalled that it seemed to come from beneath his feet and when all had settled down again he saw that, although the mortars and their crews were intact the men manning the twelve-pounder had completely disappeared. Beattie, however, on the bridge, attributed it to a large Thermite bomb.

It is possible to speculate that one of our aircraft, lingering above in a desperate attempt to carry out its mission, scored an own goal. Certainly the British were the only ones in the sky over St Nazaire that night. However, it is more likely that it was a German shell for phosphorus shells were in use by both sides at that time and contemporary wisdom suggests that such extensive damage could not have been caused by a British incendiary bomb. Whatever the true cause at least two commandos fell into the burning hole, one having phosphorus burns on his uniform the other having his trousers catch fire and, after removing them, playing his part in the raid in his underpants.

Directly in front of Copland's position had appeared a yawning, smoking chasm "about two-thirds of the width of the deck". The missile also penetrated the chief petty officers' mess, setting it on fire, but a Fire Control Party soon had the blaze under control. What was of more serious concern, however, was its proximity to the charge which Tibbits had cleverly placed immediately abaft the twelve-pounder and which, later that same morning, was to bring the operation to its dazzling climax.

Six minutes to go. It was 0128 and no longer could the subterfuge be sustained. On *Campbeltown* Beattie had earlier ordered the German flag to be struck and the British Battle Ensign broken out, a necessary pre-requisite for opening fire, and had increased speed. Initially mistaking the eastern arm of the Southern Entrance for the Old Mole, he quickly corrected his error and with a withering fire now being brought down by both sides he rammed the southern caisson at 20 knots. The bows of the old destroyer crumpled back thirty feet and rode up over the caisson, leaving the explosive charge nestling against its outer face. It was 0134 on Saturday 28 March 1942. They were four minutes late.

By far the unluckiest place for a German sailor to be that night was on the *Botilla Russ*, a *Sperrbrecher*, or guard ship. Anchored off the east jetty she was squarely in the middle of the fairway up which Chariot Force would drive and had already been hotly engaged by Able Seaman Savage on MGB 314 as they passed. The treatment was repeated as, one by one, each little ship in the flotilla sailed by. During the course of the night she would survive an attempt to torpedo her, record 123 hits and suffer two men killed and eight wounded, but come morning she was still afloat.

When all attempts to obscure their identity had expired and fire was opened on *Campbeltown*, the two columns of launches coming up astern began to take casualties. The launches' own complement of Oerlikons and Lewis guns was augmented by commandos on deck manning their Bren guns. Their targets included the searchlights whose glaring beams, shining horizontally across the water, were making navigation extremely difficult. Several of the launches would initially miss their landing points and have to make a second approach. They had encountered the same problem in their practice raid on Plymouth.

The overall plan had allowed for assault troops to be first ashore to silence the defences as the demolition troops needed to plant their charges without interruption. Leading the port column, therefore, to land assault troops at the Old Mole, was ML 447, commanded by Lieutenant Platt, RNR, who was carrying the parties of Captain Birney and Lieutenant Clibborn, charged with silencing the two guns, one on the landward end of the Old Mole and one a little inland of it, that commanded the whole stretch of water in which all the launches would have to manoeuvre. Platt made straight for the north side of the Old Mole but was hit during the approach and drifted round to the south side on fire. He had been unable to land any troops.

50. Light craft which may become damaged during the approach are to do their utmost to reach their landing positions even if this may be some time after the main assault. During this stage other craft will not stand by them and they must fend for themselves.

Operation Chariot – Combined Plan

With these two dangerous guns still in action the plan now began to unravel further due to an incident that had occurred some hours earlier. Shortly after 2000 hours the previous evening, after the force had formed up in battle order on passing Point E, Lieutenant Briault, RNVR, in ML 341 had reported engine trouble. Unable to keep up, her troops had been transferred to one of the spare launches, ML 446, commanded by Lieutenant Falconar, RNVR, and by the time this transfer had been completed it was well behind and would not regain its place in the battle order.

The launch had carried the assault troops of Captain Hodgson and Lieutenant Oughtred whose task was to silence the two guns on the east jetty of the southern entrance. Eventually reaching the Old Mole he overshot but turned in the estuary and approached again and was once more repelled. With several casualties, some severe, he withdrew and reached the pre-arranged rendezvous at sea. The following launches carrying the demolition troops now had to run the gauntlet of the four deadly guns lining the shoreline of the approach.

In the absence of Briault's ML the next in the line, ML 457, commanded by Lieutenant Collier, RNVR, had closed the gap and sailed straight in to the Old Mole. He carried the demolition party of Lieutenant Walton for Bridge D and the lock gate in the Southern Entrance and their attendant protection party under Second Lieutenant Watson. Also on this ML were Captain Pritchard and his party of four corporals who would control all the demolitions in this area. Leaving them to their tasks and promising faithfully to return for them later, Collier pulled out into the river to wait but on returning to keep that promise he was hit and drifted down river on fire.

Following Collier was Lieutenant Wallis, RANVR, carrying in ML 307 the demolition party of Captain Bradley whose protection party under Lieutenant Houghton was, for some unaccountable reason, on ML 443. He set course for the Old Mole but was driven off. Pulling out into the relative safety of midstream he crossed to the east bank and contented himself with engaging the guns there. He then withdrew and eventually reached Falmouth.

Lieutenant Joe Houghton, of the Queen's Own Cameron Highlanders and 2 Commando would not survive the war, falling victim to Hitler's infamous Commando Order. In September 1942 he took part in the daring Operation Musketoon, the raid on the electricity generating station at Glomfjord in Norway, where he was one of seven commandos to be captured. They were ordered to be shot under the terms of the order and travelled via Colditz Castle, where they were held from 7 to 13 October, thence to Berlin and finally, on the 22nd, to Sachsenhausen Concentration Camp where they were shot just before dawn on the following morning. The bodies were cremated.

Another survivor of the raid on St Nazaire, Lance Corporal Richard O'Brien, also took part in Musketoon. He had travelled to St Nazaire on ML 447 as a member of Birney's party. He was fortunate enough to avoid capture at Glomfjord and return home.

On the east bank of the Loire, not more than two sea miles across the estuary from the Normandie Dock, is a promontory which was home to elements of Mecke's Marine-Flak-Abteilung 809 (MFA.809) and Dieckmann's Marine-Artillerie-Abteilung 280 (MAA.280). There were three batteries commanding the neck of the Loire where it narrowed opposite the docks. At Saint-Brevin-les-Pins was 4./MFA809 while to the north of that was 6./MFA809 at Mindin. Both these installations deployed four dual-purpose light flak guns, but even more of a danger to the Chariot flotilla was 2./MAA280 at le Pointeau. This naval artillery battery fired 1,300 rounds on the night of the raid and caused enormous damage amongst the motor launches as they attempted to land their commandos. It was to silence this battery and to douse the 150-cm searchlight behind it that ML 307 set off to the east bank after being unable to land its troops at the Old Mole. Nowhere in the plan for Operation Chariot was there provision made to neutralise the threat from this area, all effort being confined to the dock area on the west bank.

Coming up astern of Wallis was Lieutenant Horlock, RNVR, in ML 443. He carried the three demolition parties of Lieutenant Wilson, Second Lieutenant Bassett-Wilson and Lieutenant Bonvin who were charged with destroying the strategically important boiler house, impounding station and hydraulic power station, all in the Southern Entrance. These buildings provided the power to drive all the machinery for the locks, pumps, bridges and winding gear in the dockyard. Horlock overshot the Old Mole, as would Falconar later, and after turning to approach a second time was once more driven off, withdrew and eventually reached Falmouth safely.

Nominally the last launch in the port column, but with Falconar still straining every sinew to catch up astern, Lieutenant Henderson in ML 306 sailed in to approach the Old Mole but was driven off. He had aboard the demolition group of Lieutenant Swayne and their protection party under Lieutenant Vanderwerve. Deciding to attempt a landing at the Old Entrance instead, he was again driven off and withdrew downstream to the rendezvous.

The landings at the Old Mole had, to say the least, been less than successful. Only Collier in ML 457 had been able to put his commandos ashore and none of them had achieved their targets. Walton, charged with blowing Bridge D, had been killed. Watson had been tied down in the dockyard. Of the commandos, Wheeler would walk across France and then travel through Spain to Gibraltar and home. Bradley and Searson would later escape from prisoner of war camp and reach Switzerland. Pritchard, to whom a vast debt was due for his work in planning the demolition programme for the raid, having visited the power station, ran round a corner onto a German bayonet and was killed. Those of the remainder who were still alive would spend the rest of the war as prisoners.

Of the launches, two were adrift in the estuary and on fire, two had withdrawn and would make Falmouth and two had set off for the rendezvous where they would come once more under the watchful eye of the RAF who would again patrol the Bay of Biscay to see them home.

The launches in the starboard column were to land their troops at the Old Entrance and it was not long before they began to take casualties. Leading the column was the senior ML commander, Lieutenant Commander Stephens, RNVR, in ML 192. Sailing a little astern of *Campbeltown* he fielded all the ordinance that was missing the destroyer and was soon hit in the steering and the engine room. Even before the first launch of the port column had made its attempt to gain the Old Mole, Stephens' ML, out of control, had veered across in front of it and bounced off the Old Mole on fire. The launch carried the assault party of Captain Burn, destined for Bridge M at the extreme north of the dockyard. Commandos and sailors alike abandoned ship. As we have seen, this launch was soon to be joined in this area by two others, also on fire.

The Germans would not detain Billie Stephens long. A constant desire to escape saw his first attempt take place at Rennes, where the survivors of the raid had initially been taken, his last from Colditz Castle. In between he had made bids for freedom from Marlag Nord and Stalag VIIIB at Lamsdorf. He made his home run from Colditz with Pat Reid, Hank Wardle and Ronnie Littledale after successfully breeching the walls of that formidable fortress and by October 1942 he was in Switzerland. Captain Michael Burn, who was in command of a protection party on Stephens' launch, also gravitated to Colditz where he saw out the war.[27]

Seeing Stephens come to grief, Lieutenant Burt, RNVR, in ML 262, hurried to close the gap. He was carrying a demolition group under Lieutenant Woodcock and a protection party under Lieutenant Morgan. Their target was Bridge G and the lock gate in the Old Entrance. Before it was blown, Bridge G had to be held until troops landed from *Campbeltown* to destroy installations in the northern part of the dockyard had passed through. Like two launches at the Old Mole, he overshot but turned and came in again, successfully landing his troops. Backing out he was hailed by Morgan from on shore who thought he had seen the withdrawal signal. Burt went back in and took them on board. Backing out a second time he was again hailed from the shore and went back in to pick up Lieutenant Smalley who had landed from *Campbeltown* and successfully destroyed the southern winding house. It was not to be third time lucky, for as he backed out yet again and manoeuvred in the Old Entrance he was twice hit and set off downstream. Stopping to help another launch, Burt's ML was hit three more times, catching fire and drifting into midstream. With fourteen or more dead they abandoned ship.

Lieutenant Beart, RNVR, in ML 267, bore a headquarters party under RSM Moss and successfully landed them in the Old Entrance but they were repulsed and re-embarked. Backing out, the ML was hit and drifted away on fire. Eight of the eleven commandos and eleven of the sixteen sailors on board were lost.

Next up came Lieutenant Tillie, RNVR, in ML 268, with the demolition party of Lieutenant Pennington, whose target was the swing bridge M. He had with him a protection party under Lieutenant Jenkins. Approaching the Old Entrance he was hit and blew up. Fifteen of the seventeen commandos and half of the crew were lost. The assault party for Bridge M had been carried in Stephens' ML 192 which had perished at the Old Mole but in a remarkable solo effort Captain Burn made his way through the occupied dockyard to his target and finding no-one there he had withdrawn to Newman's headquarters.

Carrying an assault party under Captain Hooper, whose task was to silence two guns on the shoreline between the Old Mole and the Old Entrance, next in came Lieutenant Fenton

---

[27] Of the other Charioteers, Corran Purdon and Dick Morgan would also end up in Colditz, as would Micky Wynn, who was later repatriated on medical grounds. Sergeant Steele, too, would spend a short while there having swapped places at Lamsdorf with an officer, Colditz bound, intent on escape.

in ML 156. Coming up river his steering had been put out of action and he had followed a haphazard course around the estuary while the hand steering gear was rigged. He eventually withdrew to the rendezvous.

ML 177, under the command of Sub-Lieutenant Rodier, RNVR, was carrying an assault party under TSM Haines to attack any ships in the dry dock and to act as headquarters reserve. His was another launch to overshoot but he turned in the river, came back in and landed his troops on the south side of the Old Entrance. He then crossed to the stern of *Campbeltown*, now well and truly embedded on the caisson, took off thirty surviving crew and withdrew downstream, but was shot up and sank with heavy loss of life.

The achievements at the Old Entrance mirrored those at the Old Mole. Only one ML had left troops ashore and that was an assault group without any demolition capability. It addition to Stephens' launch at the Old Mole three others were on fire and the whole scene was reminiscent of Dante's Inferno. Fire was to cause as much loss of life as enemy action for the sea itself was ablaze and no-one could survive in that, neither could they be rescued. It was now left to the troops on *Campbeltown* to bring a successful conclusion to the whole operation.

From the moment *Campbeltown* had rammed the caisson, the groups of commandos, in an orderly fashion, emerged from their positions on deck where, although provided with steel barriers behind which to shelter, they had taken casualties. Those who had travelled below deck also came forward in a pre-arranged order and all groups were seen off to their targets by Copland, standing as unconcerned on the fo'c'sle as a headmaster seeing his children off on a school outing.

As had happened at the Old Mole and the Old Entrance, it was the assault troops who were first to disembark. Over the starboard side went a party under Lieutenant Roderick detailed to silence the guns on the dockside and to attempt to fire the oil storage tanks. They were then to form a bridgehead at the caisson to prevent infiltration by German troops while the demolitionists were about their work.

First off on the port side was Captain Roy with a party to attack the guns on top of the pumping station. Finding these already silenced by fire from the river he destroyed the guns by charges wrapped around the barrels. He then proceeded to Bridge G which he was detailed to hold until all the commandos from *Campbeltown* had passed through having completed their demolitions.

Following the two assault teams was a protection party commanded by Lieutenant Dennison whose task was to secure the area at the north of the dry dock and provide an environment in which the demolition teams could lay their charges. This already small team had been weakened by men sustaining wounds during the run-in but they went willingly about their work.

Lieutenant Burtinshaw was next to land with a group to destroy the southern caisson, but with the success of *Campbeltown* this was not necessary and they were sent to assist with the destruction of the northern caisson. Burtinshaw would later be killed while engaging the guns on two tankers that were in the dry dock.

The other teams Dennison's troops were to support, those of Lieutenant Brett and Lieutenant Purdon, came next doubling up the side of the dry dock to their targets at the far end. Brett and his team were to destroy the northern caisson and were augmented by those from the southern end. The plan was to enter the caisson through the manholes in the road that ran across the top but the tarmac had sealed them and they could not be opened. The troops resorted to hanging charges from the rails and connecting them with a ring main. After this had been detonated water could be heard entering the caisson.

The target for Purdon and his four corporals was the northern winding house. Finding it locked they finally broke it open, entered the building and placed their charges. Having waited outside for the signal to pull their igniters they eventually had the satisfaction of watching the whole building rise a few feet into the air and collapse like a house of cards.

The last parties were led off *Campbeltown* by a protection party under the command of Lieutenant Hopwood, charged with securing the area at the southern end of the dry dock for the demolition parties of Lieutenant Smalley and Lieutenant Chant to operate without disturbance. Smalley and his four corporals made straight for the southern winding house and like Purdon, found the door locked and climbed in through a window, placed their charges and retired to pull their igniters. When nothing happened, against all the rules of demolition, they went straight back in, re-set the detonators and tried again, this time successfully. Seeing an ML close at hand they hailed it and clambered aboard but Smalley was almost immediately shot dead.

With *Campbeltown* so well and truly embedded on the southern caisson with her charge in place, perhaps the next most important target was that of Lieutenant Chant. With a demolition team of four sergeants he was to destroy the pump house which contained the four great pumps used to empty and fill the Normandie Dock. As with the two winding houses, the door was found to be locked, but it was blown open with a small charge and, leaving one to guard the door, Chant and the other three sergeants descended into the depths of the building, laid their charges and retired outside until a huge explosion announced that they had been successful. They then went back in to destroy the motors but the floor of the room had collapsed onto the pumps below and they contented themselves with smashing the electrical installations with sledgehammers.

There was one other group of commandos on *Campbeltown* and that was the headquarters party of Major Copland. Numbered among them was Captain Montgomery who, with Captain Pritchard, had been responsible for planning all of the demolitions for the raid and was now in charge of those taking place in this area of the dockyard. Indeed it was he who, wandering by at the critical moment, had provided the charge to blow open the door of the pump house. The succeeding series of explosions in the area of the Normandie Dock brought to a shattering conclusion the exploits of *Campbeltown's* commandos, sufficient to compensate for the gallant but unsuccessful efforts of their comrades who did not get ashore at the Old Mole or the Old Entrance. It now only remained for the charge in the bows of *Campbeltown*, in the fullness of time, to crown the operation with dazzling success.

Those men in the area of the dock who were still able now withdrew to Newman's headquarters close by Bridge G where, joined by the few who had landed from the MLs, they were sent on their way to the collection point close to the Old Mole to await the return of the launches to take them home. Now, for the first time, they saw the full outcome of the battle that had taken place in the river. The sea itself was on fire as petrol from the burning launches spread far and wide. It was impossible that anyone or anything could survive within that awful scene. For the commandos, now stranded ashore, there was no alternative but to organise themselves to break out into the town and thence into the country beyond. There, now, we shall leave them.

While the little commando-carrying ships had been striving to put their troops ashore and the men from *Campbeltown* had been about their destruction, there were five other craft whose exploits must now be recounted.

Leading the flotilla upriver had been MGB 314, commanded by Lieutenant Curtis, RNVR, and carrying the two force commanders and their headquarters. Having led *Campbeltown* to the caisson the gunboat veered away to starboard to clear the run for the destroyer on to her altar. Curtis circled and brought the gunboat into the Old Entrance where he tied up on the south side while Newman and his team leapt ashore and made for their chosen headquarters nearby. Crossing the Old Entrance to the north side Curtis again tied up and Ryder went ashore to check that *Campbeltown* was securely impaled on the caisson and that the scuttling charges had been fired. When he returned he found that Sub-Lieutenant Wynn, RNVR, in MTB 74 had arrived and tied up alongside.

The eccentric little craft commanded by Wynn had been specially adapted with the torpedo tubes mounted on the fo'c'sle to attack the *Scharnhorst* in Brest harbour but the 'Channel Dash' in February 1942, had made her redundant. Ryder, however, foresaw a role for her at St Nazaire for should the *Campbeltown* fail to reach her target (and there were moments on the Loire shoals when there was a real danger that she might not) MTB 74 could deploy her torpedoes against the Normandie Dock. Now satisfied that *Campbeltown* would carry out her destiny, Ryder ordered Wynn to fire his delayed-action torpedoes against the lock gates of the Old Entrance, take aboard survivors from *Campbeltown* and make best speed for Falmouth.

Best speed for MTB 74 was in excess of forty knots and fully laden with survivors and crew she set off down the estuary. Six miles out Wynn stopped, against orders, to collect two commandos from a Carley raft. He was immediately blown out of the water and of the thirty-six men who made it to a life raft, by morning only four were left.

Following Ryder on either hand upriver had been the MLs of Lieutenant Boyd, RNVR, in ML 160 and Lieutenant Irwin, RNR, in ML 270. Carrying no commandos but armed with torpedoes they had been given roaming commissions to draw fire and to attack any vessels giving trouble. Soon after *Campbeltown* had rammed the caisson Irwin was hit in the steering gear but, while stopped in a dangerous position off the oil storage tanks, managed to rig the hand steering and limp away to the rendezvous. Boyd set off upstream in search of two tankers reported to be there but they were, in fact, in the dry dock. Returning to the scene of the action he silenced a gun on shore, torpedoed a ship, possibly the *Sperrbrecher*, had his electrics severed but quickly repaired and gone to the aid of Platt, picking up men from the launch and from the water. Hit several times and with enough excitement for one day he left the river and made for the open sea.

51. During the withdrawal every effort must be made to get damaged boats out to sea, assisting each other as necessary.
Operation Chariot – Combined Plan

The last launch in the flotilla was the sole surviving 'spare' as Falconar in the other had taken on Briault's troops at sea. This was the ML 298 of Sub-Lieutenant Nock, the youngest of the launch commanders. He sailed around the estuary engaging targets on shore before going into the Old Entrance seeking survivors, but he was driven out and caught fire when burning petrol on the surface of the water washed over the transom, becoming yet another addition to the inferno.

The toll is now complete. It only remained for Ryder to leave the relative shelter of the Old Entrance, which he did at about 0230. Coming out into the open river he now saw for the first time the carnage that had been inflicted on the force of little ships. Under fire that was hotly returned by AB Savage, who we have already seen shooting up the *Botilla Russ*, on the forward pom-pom, Ryder had no alternative but to withdraw downstream, a passage during which Savage again excelled himself, but sadly, at the cost of his life. For his exploits that night and in recognition of the bravery of all the men of Coastal Forces, he was awarded the Victoria Cross.

RETIRING COURSE

43. All craft on retiring will proceed at maximum speed until clear of shore batteries. They will then pass through position 'Y' (47° 01' N, 2° 43' W) thence on course 248° at their best speed with due regard to fuel consumption.

44. The escorting destroyers will pass through position 'Y' at 0600 on course 248° spread 5 miles apart in order to pick up craft which may be in difficulties, take onboard personnel from M.L.s and generally rally the forces.

Operation Chariot – Combined Plan

The remnants of Chariot Force that limped out of the Loire numbered eight launches. Boyd (160), Wallis (307) and Horlock (443) would make it all the way to Falmouth while Curtis (MGB 314), Fenton (156), Irwin (270) and Falconar (446) would arrive at the rendezvous at Point Y where we shall later find them under the protection of the RAF. Henderson's ML 306 would be captured in a stirring little action with one of the German torpedo boats that had left St Nazaire as a result of the delayed sighting report of U-593 the previous evening. That, however, is another story, one in which Sergeant Tom Durrant would win the only VC ever awarded to a soldier in a naval engagement.

CHAPTER 9

ENTER THE LUFTWAFFE

In August 1939, with Europe on the brink of war and German forces poised to invade and overrun Poland, Reichsmarschall Hermann Goering sent a message to his airmen. Goering may well have been a braggart, never shy of trumpeting his own achievements, but few at that time would argue with his claim that "I have done my best, in the past few years, to make our Luftwaffe the largest and most powerful in the world". He went on to say, "The creation of the Greater German Reich has been made possible by the strength and constant readiness of the air force".

The truth of his assertion became self-evident as the Blitzkrieg swept across Europe, consuming nation after nation as it went until, with the BEF withdrawn through Dunkirk and many other French ports, including St Nazaire itself, the summer of 1940 saw the Luftwaffe at the zenith of its power. The conquest of Britain was to be a formality. However, what Goering did not then know was that the Battle of Britain would remain its zenith as defeat in the skies over England would herald the start of a steady decline until, in 1944, the Luftwaffe was conspicuous by its near absence from the skies over Normandy.

Having been forced, with the invasion of Russia, to fight on three fronts and weighed down by the responsibilities heaped on it by the egotistical aspirations of its commander, it was finally reduced to what was virtually a home-based force whose sole task was the defence of the Fatherland. The inability of the Luftwaffe to match the growing strength of the Allied air forces, boosted by the entry of the Americans into the war, meant that the mighty war machine, about which Goering had boasted in 1939, had been the precursor of both the rise and the fall of Hitler's Germany, and was admitted as such by Field Marshal von Rundstedt when he declared that the swing in the balance of air power was "the first decisive factor in Germany's defeat".

The Treaty of Versailles, signed in 1919, had been designed to eliminate the possibility of such a global Armageddon as the Great War being inflicted again on mankind, but there were many who held that it did, in fact, sow the seeds of the Second World War, making further conflict virtually inevitable with the ignominy of defeat and the malign oppression of its provisions burning like a slow fuse within the hearts of the German people. The treaty had allowed for a small German military force, to total no more than 100,000 men split between a standing army (Reichsheer) and a small defensive navy (Kriegsmarine) with no provision at all for an air force. In practice, however, the Luftwaffe existed in all but name virtually as soon as the ink was dry.

Into the permitted manpower level was embedded a covert number, approaching 200, of former Great War pilots who would form and develop the nucleus of a new air force. Under the guise of recreational flying numerous glider clubs sprang up which would soon boast a total of some 50,000 trained pilots. In addition, civil aviation developed to such a degree that it was soon carrying more passengers than the British, French and Italian airlines combined and over much greater distances. The airline's flying school became a prolific source of trained pilots. Further, in complete defiance of the terms of the treaty, three secret air bases had been set up in Russia which was, at that time, in a treaty of alliance with Germany.

When the National Socialist Party came to power in 1933 the charade did not last long and two years later the Treaty of Versailles was renounced and the existence of the Luftwaffe officially announced. Then fell into Goering's lap the outbreak of the Spanish Civil War. What better way to train pilots? With the formation of the Condor Legion the Luftwaffe gained a priceless opportunity for the development of battle and fighter tactics. Many pilots who later became 'aces' in the air war against Britain honed their skills in Spain and thus, blooded and battle-hardened, did the Luftwaffe enter World War Two.

Following the successful expulsion of the BEF from France the Germans swept ever westward to occupy the whole of northern and western France. With the Channel and Biscay ports now available Hitler could move his U-boat operation to more advantageous locations and the Atlantic Wall gained bases at Lorient, Brest, St Nazaire, La Rochelle and Bordeaux. Whilst this removed the long and dangerous route around Scotland for U-boats to gain the Atlantic and thus facilitated Germany's stranglehold on the convoy routes essential to Britain's survival, it also placed an added burden on the Luftwaffe to defend them, a responsibility that was stretched even further by the presence of the great capital ships *Scharnhorst*, *Gneisenau* and *Prinz Eugen* at Brest, a presence that acted as a magnet for the attention of the RAF.

The organisation of the Luftwaffe varied in one significant respect from that of the Royal Air Force. Whereas the RAF formed commands based on the type of aircraft and their role – Fighter Command, Bomber Command, Coastal Command, etc. – the Luftwaffe formed air fleets (Luftflotten) on a geographical basis and each had, therefore, in its establishment fighters, bombers, reconnaissance and rescue units all under one command.

There were six Luftflotten in existence in March 1942, and of these it was Luftflotte 3 that would be tasked with providing the response to the raid on St Nazaire. Formed in February 1939, in Munich, following the fall of France it had been given responsibility for the area of north-west France bounded by the Seine and the sea. Here, from airfields at Brest, Lannion, Rennes, St Malo, Dinan, Cherbourg and others it had shared the Luftwaffe effort to subdue the RAF in 1940 with Luftflotten 2 and 5, the former taking the lion's share in north-east France and the Low Countries and the latter operating from Norway. However, with the Battle of Britain lost and Luftflotte 2 by now in the Mediterranean theatre, flying in North Africa, Italy and Greece, 1942 saw Luftflotte 3 covering the whole of northern Europe from Brittany to Holland. We will see that even those as far from St Nazaire as Amsterdam would be mobilised to seek and destroy the remnants of Operation Chariot as they withdrew, even though they did not make it to the scene of the action.

With headquarters in the Palais de Luxembourg in Paris, Luftflotte 3 was commanded by Generalfeldmarschall Hugo Sperrle, an officer of much experience for he was foremost among those who had benefitted from action in the Spanish Civil War where he had commanded the Condor Legion. Being also a veteran of the First World War he was arguably more experienced than his chief and had not only the prescience to realise the futility of Goering's decision to switch the focus of his attack on Britain from airfields to towns, but he also had the courage to openly argue against it, recognising that the will of the British people would not be broken by indiscriminate bombing and that, given the respite the change in tactics would bring, the RAF would recover and rebuild. Goering was adamant and ignored him.

Sperrle shared the Palais de Luxembourg with his chief and like him was given a sumptuous apartment where he enjoyed the good life in the luxurious surroundings. It did not escape the attention of Albert Speer, the armaments minister, during a visit, that "the Feldmarschall's craving for luxury and public display ran a close second to that of his superior, Goering; he was also his match in corpulence".

In August 1944, following defeat in Normandy, Sperrle was relieved of his command and in 1945, captured by the Allies, was tried for war crimes and imprisoned. The Palais de Luxembourg was, from 29 July to 15 October 1946, to play host to the Paris Peace Conference.

Luftflotte 3, over which Sperrle held sway, comprised two separate formations, widely dispersed geographically, but each of which would be mobilised to seek out and destroy the survivors of Operation Chariot.

Based in Holland, IX Fliegerkorps, a formation equivalent to an air corps, flew from airfields at Schipol, Soesterberg, Gilze Rijn and Leeuwarden and comprised Kampfgeschwader 2 (KG2), and a flight each of Kampfgeschwader 40 (II/KG40) and Kampfgruppe 506 (KGr 506), all except the latter equipped with Dornier 217E aircraft. It also had a test detachment (Erpr.Kdo 100) flying the Heinkel 111H, based at Chartres. Of these units only two flights of KG 2 would be mobilised but in the event would not see action.

The Dornier 217E had originally been designed as dual-purpose, able to be deployed in a level or dive-bombing role. However, an intractable problem with the dive brakes resulted in that aspect of its capability being abandoned. It somewhat resembled a dragonfly, its slim fuselage headed by a bulbous nose which housed the four-man crew. This arrangement made for a close-knit team but left them all vulnerable to a single strike by a fighter. With a bomb load approaching 9,000 lbs it would pose a significant threat to those few small craft that had escaped destruction in the Loire.

The other arm of Luftflotte 3, Fliegerführer Atlantik, the equivalent of an RAF wing, covered a large area which included that already noted as stretching westwards from the Seine to the sea and operated from the Brest peninsula from airfields at Lannion, Dinard and Brest, the latter, in March 1942, also playing host to a detachment of floatplanes from Cherbourg. Commanded by General Ulrich Kessler, who had held the position for less than two months, Fliegerführer Atlantik had its headquarters in a chalet at Brandérion, some 14 kilometres east of Lorient.

Unlike IX Fliegerkorps, which was a bomber formation, Fliegerführer Atlantik was a mixed establishment in common with normal Luftwaffe practice of geographical formations. In addition to bombers its units included maritime reconnaissance and search and rescue planes, flying from both land and sea. There were three reconnaissance and bombing units, Küstenfliegergruppen (KüFlGr), 106 at Dinard and 406 and 906 at Brest, one reconnaissance unit, Aufklärungsgruppe 3.(F)/123, and a flight of Kampfgeschwader 40 (9./KGr 40) at Lannion. The detachment from Cherbourg, attached to KüFlGr 406 at Brest, was 5./ Bordfliegergruppe 196.

Of these disparate units, two were equipped with variations of the Junkers 88 (Ju 88), KüFlGr 106 flying the Ju 88A and Aufklärungsgruppe 3.(F)/123 the Ju 88D-1. However, whilst the former played a large part in the ensuing action the latter took no part at all.

The twin-engine Ju 88 was a most successful machine, made so by its extreme versatility, being able to assume the roles of light or medium bomber, deliver conventional bombs or torpedoes and act as a night fighter, reconnaissance or transport aircraft. Its crew of four – pilot, bombardier, wireless operator and machine-gunner – found the flight compartment too small and far from comfortable. Able to carry 6,600 lbs bomb load, it had a range of 1,250 miles and a maximum speed of 280 mph and had played a large part in the Battle of Britain.

The Heinkel 111 (He 111), flown by 9./KGr 40, was a child of the deception practised by Germany to circumvent the prohibitions of the Treaty of Versailles, for it was developed as a high-speed airliner but was capable of rapid conversion to a warplane. A twin-engine medium bomber, like the Ju 88 it, too, was a versatile machine, able to attack ships with torpedoes or to carry personnel or cargo and had played a significant part in the Battle of Britain. It had practised and proved its skills operating in the Spanish Civil War. With a crew of four or five it could carry a 7,275 lbs bomb load, had a range of 1,200 miles and a maximum speed of 270 mph.

The remaining units at Sperrle's disposal were all equipped with float planes at Brest-Sud, so-called to distinguish it from the conventional field to the north-east of the town. KüFlGr. 406 flew Dornier 18s and 26s together with Blohm and Voss 138s but none of them would be deployed against the Chariot survivors. However, two of the planes attached to KüFlGr. 406 from Cherbourg, Arado 196s, did take off and we will later encounter one of them circling the British boats out at sea. The final unit involved was KüFlGr. 906 and flew the Heinkel 115 (He 115).

The Arado 196 was one of the most successful float planes of the war and, like other planes mentioned above, was extremely versatile, able to insert agents off enemy coasts as well as affect rescues at sea and carry out coastal patrols. It was best known, however, as a scout plane, launched by catapult from the great German capital ships. In a nice twist to our story, an Arado 196 had been deployed on the *Bismarck*, the sinking of which had appeared early in the planning for the raid on St Nazaire and now one was seeking the raiders who had just gallantly destroyed the very dock to which the *Bismarck* had been heading. The Arado 196 had a range of 665 miles, a ceiling of 23,000 feet and a maximum speed of 193 mph. It carried no bombs but was heavily armed with two 0.79 in cannons forward firing from the wings and one or two 0.31 in guns mounted in the rear cockpit.

As successful as was the Arado 196, even more successful was the Heinkel 115. A slim-bodied, twin-engine plane with a crew of three – pilot, observer and wireless operator/air gunner – it could be employed in a torpedo-bomber, minelaying or reconnaissance role and could carry three 550-lb bombs or one 1,760-lb torpedo. The A-1 variant was capable of loading two more 550-lb bombs under the wings. It had a range of 1,300 miles and a maximum speed of 200 mph.

These albeit brief details of the formations and machines available to the Germans to pursue the destruction of the remnants of Operation Chariot show that, without doubt, they possessed the wherewithal to do so. We shall shortly discover the reasons why they didn't, but first let us follow the sequence in which their intervention developed.

Like an ill-mannered guest the Luftwaffe arrived late for the party. Having put in no appearance at all during the night while the diversionary air raid pursued its tortured course, the Luftwaffe was no doubt grounded by the 10/10ths cloud that blanketed St Nazaire, in this respect coming to the relief of the British bombers whose efforts it was frustrating. It is a fine point whether or not the RAF would have preferred a clear sky from which to see the target and bomb successfully, running the gauntlet of any patrolling night fighters, rather than the climatic conditions which kept the Luftwaffe on the ground.

It was not until 0355 hrs on the morning of 28 March, more than an hour after Ryder had left the scene of the raid in MGB 314, the last to set course down the river to the open sea, when a telephone call from Seekommandant Loire, the senior officer of the Kriegsmarine in the west, was received in the sybaritic headquarters of Luftflotte 3 in faraway Paris alerting it to the attack on St Nazaire. Luftflotte 3 lost little time in sending an order to the headquarters of Fliegerführer Atlantik in the chateau at Brandérion requiring them to get planes airborne in order to establish the position of the retiring raiders.

It was not until 0420 that a reply was sent to the effect that a plane would be despatched but that it would take a further hour before it could take off and would do so at 0520. By this time Ryder would have been nearly three hours out of St Nazaire. Quite what the delay was is not known but suggests that no plane was kept on instant standby and was further testimony to the surprise with which the raid had been carried out. Whatever the reason, in the scramble to get the plane in the air a grievous omission was made and it departed without the flares essential for a sea search at night. It was not surprising, therefore, that the Ju 88, thought to belong to KüFlGr. 106 and piloted by Major Friedrich Harlinghausen, failed to establish the whereabouts of the retiring launches.

Meanwhile, over in Paris, Luftflotte 3, seeking to increase its firepower against the British boats, had sent an order to mobilise elements of KG 2 from their base in distant Holland. Consequently the commander of IX Fliegerkorps, General Joachim Coeler, ordered two flights to leave immediately for France to bomb up for an attack on the launches. These flights were II/KG 2 under Hauptmann Walter Bredel, which flew from Soesterberg to Rennes and III/KG 2 under Oberstleutnant Hans von Koppelow, which flew from Schipol to Nantes. Oberstleutnant Georg Pasewaldt, commanding KG 2, could have every confidence that his powerful Do217Es would hunt down and destroy the enemy.

Although Schipol Airport is now a huge international airport and a hub for flights all over the world, its origins were as a military airfield in 1916, but with Holland declaring itself neutral in WWI it did not see a shot fired in anger. Again declaring neutrality at the start of WWII, a declaration not recognised by Germany, Holland was overrun in five days and Schipol became a main airfield for the Germans. It was bombed several times by the Allies but was eventually destroyed by the Germans themselves when, on 17 September 1944, the day following the Allied airborne assault on Arnhem, they blew it up and left it unusable.

Soesterberg, like Schipol, had its origins in WWI when its activities were confined to pilot training using aircraft that had been confiscated after landing on Dutch soil in breach of its neutrality. Also, again like Schipol, in September 1944 Soesterberg was deemed by the Germans to be more or less useless and they abandoned it, but this time the damage had been caused by the heavy and relentless bombing throughout the war by the Allies.

Meanwhile, out at sea, news of the Dorniers bombing up at Rennes would reach Ryder and become a factor in his decision to transfer the surviving personnel to the escorting destroyers, scuttle the launches and make all speed for England. Ryder had other cause to make this decision for the little boats carried men who were grievously wounded and without the care that could be provided by their home bases many would not survive. Had he known he need not, however, have worried about the bombers at Rennes and Nantes for they had arrived there far too late in the day to have any chance of launching a strike against his little flotilla. The following day they returned to their bases in Holland.

With the dawn came increased confidence that it was only a matter of time before the British ships would be found as the Germans launched a series of reconnaissance flights. First in the air, soon after 0800 hours, was a He 115 of 2 KüFlGr. 906 from Brest-Sud. Successfully locating the flotilla the He 115, finding itself the sole German presence, contented itself with circling at a safe distance. In preparation for the raid the motor launches had replaced their normal armament with 20mm Oerlikons to upgrade their anti-aircraft capability in realisation that their greatest threat would come from the air and now the arrangement bore fruit as the He 115, not daring to run the gauntlet of the combined firepower of the destroyers and launches contented itself with bombing and sinking Fenton's ML 156 which had already been abandoned, although gunfire from HMS *Atherstone* had failed to sink it. It no doubt made a good tale for the brave Luftwaffe pilot to recount to his colleagues in the mess that evening.

At 0913 the Luftwaffe increased its efforts by launching an attack by ten Ju 88s of 1/KüFlGr. 106 from Dinard shortly followed by three He 111s of 9./KG40 from Lannion. Lastly, two Arado 196s of 5./Bordfliegergruppe 196 took off from Brest-Sud and we shall later see one of these little planes circling HMS *Brocklesby* out of range of the destroyer's guns.

This, then, was the sum total of the sorties mounted by the Luftwaffe to seek out and destroy those few gallant little ships that had escaped from the burning hell of St Nazaire and, although the story of their effort is not yet complete, it must be recorded here that it was a complete failure. Having arrived late on the scene due to their lack of readiness, their reluctance to face the combined firepower of the little ships and their escorting destroyers and, on the arrival of aircraft from Coastal Command, whose intervention we will now witness, lacking a defensive capability for air-to-air combat, they were unable to stop the British force continuing on their way. This, together with their absence from the skies during the diversionary raid, meant that the Luftwaffe had played no effective part against Operation Chariot.

CHAPTER 10

FROM DAWN TO DUSK

```
To 236 Squadron - Operation 'Chariot'
Two aircraft to be immediately available. Remainder at
one hour's
notice from one hour before dawn 27/3/42 until dusk 27/3/42.
T.O.O 1000.
```

HQ 19 Group – order PL/G1/26/3

The airfield at Predannack, which would share with its Cornish neighbour at St Eval the responsibility for launching all the sorties to protect and escort home the remnants of Chariot Force, is situated on the southernmost tip of the Lizard Peninsula, close to Mullion. The south-west of England had found itself dragged into the Luftwaffe firing line by the fall of France in 1940 which rendered it liable to attacks and a rash of airfields were constructed to counter the threat. RAF Predannack opened in May 1941, as a satellite for RAF Portreath and welcomed as its first squadron the Hurricanes of 247 Squadron, one of which we have seen overflying the Chariot flotilla as it set out on its momentous enterprise on 26 March.

The airfield was subjected to regular Luftwaffe attention, the first occasion being in October 1941 when a returning Beaufighter was followed home by a German fighter. Gradually, however, defence gave way to attack and the station grew larger, housing as many as 3,400 personnel by 1944, partly as a result of the lengthening of the runways in 1943 which allowed the operation of larger aircraft. Accommodation on the airfield was limited and the personnel were widely spread amongst the community with the officers housed in two large hotels, the Mullion Cove and the Polruan.

After the war Predannack was used by Barnes Wallis to test his revolutionary swing-wing planes which, with their swept-back wings, top-mounted engine and launch ramps were somewhat reminiscent of Hitler's flying bombs.

When 236 Squadron was ordered to Predannack on 26 March 1942, it was going home for it had been formed at Mullion in August 1918. By May 1919, it had been disbanded having spent its war flying anti-submarine patrols off south-west England. When reformed in October 1939 it was as part of Fighter Command, but by February 1940 it had transferred to Coastal Command and found itself stationed at North Coates. After another short spell with Fighter Command, from April to July, it re-joined Coastal Command and assumed fighter and reconnaissance duties, flying from Carew Cheriton in South Wales and St Eval.

In January 1942, the squadron received orders to go non-operational as the crews were being posted immediately to the Middle East. However, of the nineteen Beaufighters held by the squadron, eight were to form a 'cadre unit' for 12 Operational Training Unit at Catfoss. On 14 February they were advised of the posting to them of fourteen crews from that unit, to be based at Wattisham. Local flying, air tests and army cooperation exercises formed the flying programme until on 15 March, the squadron became operational again. Then on 24 March came the order for eight aircraft to proceed to Predannack immediately to stand by for orders to play their part in Operation Chariot.

```
MOST SECRET          MESSAGE            1804A/19th March   IN
From C-in-C Plymouth                         Date    19.3.42
                                             Recd.  2203

        NAVAL CYPHER 'D' BY T/F. RECIRCULATION
```

```
Addressed Admiralty Repeated CCO
583.
        Request a squadron of Beaufighters may be placed under
Orders of AOC 19 Group for CHARIOT.

                            1804A/19
```

The move was not all together a smooth one. Four aircraft, led by Squadron Leader Wood, took off at 1500 that afternoon, but one, captained by Pilot Officer Schaefer, swung to starboard and crashed on take-off, the pilot and navigator, Sergeant Lawton, receiving cuts and suffering from shock and the aircraft eventually burning itself out. Sergeant Avern and his navigator Sergeant Crossan, set off at 1730, but the weather conditions at Predannack precluded a landing and he returned to Wattisham. The following day, the 25th, Wing Commander Glover and Squadron Leader Pike flew to Predannack, landing at Roborough en route, and Sergeant Smith made the flight direct. There was no flying on the 26th but finally, on 27 March, Sergeant Avern caught up with his colleagues and the seven surviving aircraft of the eight detailed were finally in position, awaiting their call to action.

The proposal to build the Beaufighter came from the Bristol Aeroplane Company itself. With the development of the Westland Whirlwind stalled, BAC felt that by using parts already available from the current development of the Beaufort a fighter version could quickly be produced and a fighter born out of a Beaufort became a Beaufighter. It outlasted its parent and served in nearly every theatre of World War II. An order was placed in February 1939, based on Air Ministry Specification F.11/37. The use of Beaufort components to speed development was somewhat set back by the need to redesign the fuselage, but even so, the prototype flew on 17 July 1939, two weeks after an order had been placed for 300 to be produced.

The Beaufighter was equipped with Bristol Hercules engines, the Taurus of the Beaufort not being powerful enough. This led to the engine nacelles protruding forward to the detriment of the centre of gravity and so the cockpit was moved back, giving the aircraft its iconic snub-nosed appearance. The armament was four 20-mm Hispano Mark III cannons firing forward from mountings in the lower fuselage. These had the disadvantage of having to be re-loaded by hand by the observer which could be most inconvenient when in the midst of an action. They were later replaced by six 0.303-inch Brownings in the wings. With a maximum speed of 335 mph and a ceiling of 16,800 feet it was slower and heavier than the conventional fighter but was a godsend for the RAF as the planned Westland Whirlwind never reached production. The first Beaufighter entered trials at Tangmere on 12 September

1940 and three weeks later the first operational machines were delivered. In 1941 a Mark 1C (the 'C' denoting Coastal Command) was developed as a long-range, heavy fighter.

Although now on station at Predannack on 27 March as ordered, the seven of those eight Beaufighters of 236 Squadron that had successfully arrived there from Wattisham were not immediately required as the Chariot flotilla was still at sea on its approach to St Nazaire. It would not be until the following day that the first aircraft would take off at dawn to start the searches and patrols to protect and shepherd home the survivors of the raid.

We last saw the remnants of Chariot Force, numbering but seven MLs and MGB 314, in varying states of distress, leaving the burning, fiery furnace that was now the water off the dockyard area of St Nazaire and making best speed for Point Y and the comforting presence of the Hunt Class destroyers HMS *Atherstone* and HMS *Tynedale*. They would also soon come under the protective umbrella of the squadrons of Coastal Command that had been ordered by HQ Plymouth to cover the withdrawal.

The plan for the withdrawal had been for surviving launches to make best speed for a rendezvous at Point Y (47° 01'N, 02° 43'W), a mere twenty miles from St Nazaire and from there along a course of 248° to Point T, seventy miles further on. *Atherstone* and *Tynedale*, following an overnight patrol crossing this course at right angles, would make for Point Y at 0530 and then also sail the same course of 248° to sweep up any withdrawing launches. Any launches not caught up by this sweep should continue on this course until reaching 7°W when they should turn north and make their own way to Falmouth.

First to leave the estuary was ML 306, commanded by Lieutenant Henderson, RNVR, and carrying the disgruntled commandos who formed the demolition and protection squads of Lieutenants Swayne and Vanderwerve, not at all happy at having failed to get ashore. Being far too early at Point Y, Henderson set off for Point T but had the misfortune to stumble across the five German torpedo boats that had sailed out of St Nazaire as a result of the belated sighting report from U-593 the previous evening. All slipped by except the third in line, Kapitänleutnant Paul in *Jaguar*, and a sharp battle ensued that was heard from their various positions in the bay by U-593, *Atherstone*, *Tynedale* and the other four German torpedo boats. Whilst having little chance and enormously outgunned, the ML put up a gallant fight in which it caused significant damage to *Jaguar*, but finally, with many dead and wounded, it was compelled to capitulate. It was a fight in which Sergeant Tom Durrant, RE and 1 Commando, won his Victoria Cross.

The last to leave the estuary had been Ryder in Curtis' MGB 314. Pulling out from the shelter of the Old Entrance he saw for the first time the devastation in the river and, unable to regain the Old Entrance, reluctantly set off downstream. Forty-five minutes out he almost ran into a German patrol boat and in the fierce action that followed Able Seaman William Savage, who had manned his gun with great gallantry throughout the raid, was killed. He was awarded a posthumous Victoria Cross and, in circumstances we shall soon see, was taken back to England and buried in the cemetery at Falmouth. Shortly after, the gunboat passed Lieutenant Fenton, RNVR, in ML 156 and signalled to him to follow.

The ML of Leslie Fenton, himself badly wounded, had been for some time in a perilous situation with the engines stopped and the steering out of action, but, working in appalling conditions, the crew had rigged the hand steering and an engine had been restarted, enabling withdrawal. At 0315 they met up with ML 446, commanded by Lieutenant Falconar, RNVR, carrying the commandos that had, on the outward journey, been transferred at sea. Thus arriving late at the dockyard he had been unable to land his troops and had withdrawn.

Lieutenant Irwin, RNR, in ML 270, had sustained damage off the oil storage tanks in St Nazaire and, with his steering gear disabled, had led a charmed life during which he had sailed aimlessly around the estuary while the hand steering gear was rigged. When this had been done he was able to creep past the defences and out to sea. An hour and a half later he met with MGB 314 and the two proceeded together. At 0430 they passed through Point Y.

Ten minutes earlier *Atherstone* and *Tynedale* had completed the last leg of their overnight patrol and set course for Point Y where they were to rendezvous with retiring launches. However, the plan for Operation Chariot had provided for launches to leave St Nazaire at 0330, after the commandos had been ashore for two hours to carry out their tasks. In the event Ryder had been the last to leave, almost an hour earlier than this, and consequently the two destroyers found no-one at Point Y. Whilst sailing there, however, they had passed two MLs, thought to be ML 156 and ML 446, and later passed two more, almost certainly MGB 314 and ML 270, who had sailed through Point Y at 0430. No matter. Their orders were to sweep up surviving launches on the way back, which eventually they did.

An hour after leaving Point Y along a course of 248° *Tynedale* sighted four of the German torpedo boats, the fifth having detached to follow up its sighting of ML 306. A short, inconclusive action followed which ended when *Tynedale* made smoke and returned to its primary task of finding the MLs. First light had been at 0548 and as the visibility improved MGB 314 and ML 270 sighted ML 156 and ML 446 and they joined forces. Shortly after, *Atherstone* and *Tynedale* were also sighted and by 0720 the four launches and two destroyers were all together.

The condition of ML 156 was not conducive to a safe journey home and after all personnel had been transferred to *Atherstone* the launch was scuttled but showed a marked reluctance to sink, while the destroyers and three remaining launches set off together. It was not long before German aircraft appeared and a Heinkel 115 bomber attacked and sank the abandoned launch.

```
To : S.O. 10th A/S Striking Force
     TYNEDALE
       (R) Admiralty 687
           C.C.O.
From : C-in-C Plymouth

1. Beaufighters will escort you from 0630 28th Blenheims
standing by.
2. CLEVELAND and BROCKLESBY will be available to reinforce
you p.m. 28th
= 1422A/27.
```

At 0830 HMS *Cleveland* and HMS *Brocklesby*, sent from Plymouth to give added support to the retiring launches, arrived and by 0900 the force was fully formed up. Thus it proceeded for the next five hours, its speed the while held back by the parlous state of the little ships whose captains were naturally determined to return home with their craft. At 1350, therefore, Commander Sayer in *Cleveland*, senior to Ryder and thus now the senior naval officer, gave orders to evacuate the launches. They were carrying men whose wounds, if not properly and promptly treated, would result in unnecessary loss of life. Without the launches to hold them back the destroyers could increase speed and make a dash for Plymouth where facilities were available to save these precious lives. Once all were embarked, including the body of Able Seaman Bill Savage, MGB 314 and the two MLs were set alight by gunfire and left to drift, while the destroyers made all speed for home. It was a wise decision, for it was now that news reached Ryder that Luftwaffe planes were bombing up in Rennes for an attack, but in the event it never materialised.

During the morning of 28 March the convoy of four destroyers and three launches had been constantly under surveillance by enemy aircraft. The weather was overcast with a slight mist and HMS *Brocklesby* recorded being aware of shadowers through her RDF equipment even though they were in cloud and there were constant warnings up to ten miles. However, there were always at least three of these aircraft in sight and they included Ju 88s, Heinkel 115s and Arado 95s. The little convoy was then making 14 knots on a course of 265°.

Every now and then a shadower would venture too close and at 0940 *Brocklesby* engaged a Ju 88 which had dropped a 250-lb delayed-action bomb from 500 feet which had landed astern of *Atherstone*. As the Ju 88 passed across the stern of *Brocklesby* at 2,000 feet it was engaged by X turret in director control and was shot down, a success witnessed by the crew of the destroyer and those of the launches. Then at 1006 another Ju 88 ventured to attack and two 100-lb delayed-action bombs, dropped from 500 feet, landed harmlessly in the sea on the port side of HMS *Cleveland*. Engaged when at 500 feet on the starboard quarter the Ju 88 was seen to be damaged by a 4" shell bursting under its nose and tracer pads from the pom-pom were seen to deflect off the fuselage. The aircraft was last seen flying erratically and was losing height rapidly when it disappeared into the mist.

The gunnery teams of HMS *Brocklesby* had fired 210 rounds from its 4 x 4" Mark XVI and 300 from its 2-pounder pom-pom, but the smaller calibre Oerlikons and Lewises had not been in action. The gun teams were in good form, for eight days earlier they had shot down a Dornier 215 and a Ju 88 whilst escorting a convoy off Trevose Head and a number of decorations were awarded for these two actions. The first lieutenant, Lieutenant A.J.M. Miller, RNVR, received an immediate DSC, while Able Seamen A.T. Blake (director layer) and W. Henderson (director trainer) received immediate DSMs. There were five immediate Mentions in Despatches including one for the commanding officer, Lieutenant M.N. Tufnell, DSC RN.

During the course of their participation in Chariot the four Hunt Class destroyers would see four aircraft – two Beaufighters and two Hudsons – giving cover and support. Another Hudson would later make contact with *Atherstone* and *Tynedale* as they sped for Plymouth with their rescued sailors and commandos. These aircraft were part of the comprehensive cover put out by Coastal Command as we shall now discover.

```
To 236 Squadron Predannack
Commence Operation Chariot on 28/3 as instructed. First
sortie to be in position 0630/28. Sorties to be arranged
by O/C 236 Squadron. General instructions including orders
for communications have been issued personally to O/C 236
Squadron. T.O.O.1155.
```

HQ 19 Group – order PL/G2/27/3

Under instructions to have two aircraft available from one hour before dawn on 27 March the crews of the Beaufighters of 236 Squadron had stood by until, at 1155, the order came from Headquarters 19 Group that their part in Operation Chariot would commence the following day when the first aircraft should be in position at 0630. Given the responsibility to arrange the sorties for his squadron Wing Commander Glover had sent off first the crews of Squadron Leader Wood and Sergeant McNichol in aircraft ND-Z and Pilot Officer Rankin and Sergeant Pickering in ND-K.

Setting off for the search area they flew over Ushant and reaching 48°N turned southeast towards the expected position of the surviving launches. When due west of Belle-Île K sighted a motor vessel and shortly after four destroyers which it presumed to be British and of the Hunt Class. However, K having given the recognition signal, both visually and by flares, the destroyers opened fire and the aircraft, which had been suffering engine trouble throughout the trip, was forced to take evasive action and was unable to identify them. It is tempting to assume they were the four German ships of the 5th Torpedo Destroyer Flotilla making their way post-haste to St Nazaire, the fifth having detached to fight its sharp engagement with ML 306, but at that time, having just withdrawn from their brief action with HMS *Atherstone* and HMS *Tynedale* half an hour earlier, they were far away.

When K had turned east towards Belle-Île aircraft Z had flown on towards the search area where K, having extracted itself from the encounter with the enemy destroyers and flown on to Belle-Île before turning south, formated with it and together they searched for Chariot without success. K eventually lost Z in cloud and with the engine still being troublesome, at 0957, requested a QDM[28] and set off for home. This was the crew's first operational sortie.

Aircraft Z had also set course for home and, at 0930, while flying at sea level off Ushant, it was attacked down sun by a single-engine enemy aircraft firing cannon and tracer, but without scoring any hits. The ground defences at Ushant also opened up with light anti-aircraft fire, also without success. Both Beaufighters landed safely at Predannack at 1025 neither having seen any sign of survivors from Chariot.

Lifting off from Predannack at 0730 the next aircraft to be despatched was ND-Y piloted by Sergeant Taylor with Sergeant Parfitt as his observer. Making straight for the expected position of the retiring launches they were almost immediately lucky and around 0900 appeared above the little group, now numbering four destroyers, MGB 314 and two MLs. Patrolling in a square pattern above them, at about 0945 they attacked a Ju 88 which arrived and was threatening the ships below. Sergeant Taylor engaged the enemy so closely that when the Ju 88 exploded in mid-air the Beaufighter was unable to avoid the debris and was itself seriously damaged, both planes crashing into the sea.

This distressing incident was witnessed by many of the men on the ships who sent up a big cheer when the enemy aircraft was seen to be hit but this was quickly followed by a stunned silence when the Beaufighter itself plunged into the waves. Ryder was to comment on "our great admiration" and "the hawk-like ferocity and determination of the pilot in our defence". HMS *Tynedale* detached herself to search, but without success, for any survivors. Thus perished in glory Sergeant Archie William Taylor, RAAF, and Sergeant Hilary Rolfe Parfitt, RAFVR. They, like others of the squadron, were on their first operational sortie. Also were lost Oberleutnant Raymund Sheelke and his unnamed crew in Ju 88-A, Werk #8514

---

[28] QDM = Request magnetic heading to steer towards destination (in this instance, base) assuming no wind.

'M2+MK' of 2/Kü.Fl.Gr-106. They were posted as 'Missing in Action in the Bay of Biscay 28 March 1942, cause unknown'.

With fair hair, blue eyes, standing 5'8½" and weighing 138 lbs and listing games played as cricket, rowing, tennis, football, athletics, golf and swimming, it could reasonably be assumed that Archie William Taylor was a typical all-Australian boy. He had, however, been born in Wolverhampton, Staffordshire, on 20 September, 1913 the second child and only son of Charles and Nellie Selina Taylor and golden boy to his sister Hilda Annie (9 years older). In May 1924, they had sailed from Tilbury Docks, London, in the SS *Demosthenes* for the six-month voyage by way of Cape Town to Brisbane, where they arrived on 2 November.

The family settled in Rockhampton, Queensland, and Archie went to Allenstown State School, followed by Rockhampton Boys Grammar School where, in the junior public examinations he was successful in five subjects, four of them with first class passes, but failed in four others. Leaving school in February 1930, he took a job as an insurance representative, which provided the opportunity for travel through provincial towns along the north Queensland coast.

Archie was a spirited lad and on occasion would find himself in court, on both sides of the law, over the next eight years. The first, in December 1931, was described as a "most unusual case" when he and another lad were charged with "having ridden their bicycles across an intersection at a rate faster than four miles an hour". The actual speed was estimated to be between twelve and fifteen miles per hour and their case was not helped by the fact that each had a girl on their crossbar.

On 12 December 1938 Archie had married Phyllis Margaret Brown, an eighteen-year-old whose occupation was described as 'domestic', at the district registry office in Cairns. They did not have the best of starts to their married life for on Boxing Day Archie was hospitalised after a road accident while riding his motorcycle. He had a broken ankle and lost part of a toe. In August 1939 he successfully claimed damages from the car driver involved.

The following month, with the outbreak of war and the Mother Country in peril in Europe, Archie felt the desire to rally to the cause and in February 1940, he applied for air crew training. He was by then living in Sydney and working for Qantas Empire Airways at Rose Bay. He had learned to fly with Kingsford Smith Air Services, going solo after 16½ hours and clocking up 27 hours subsequently. In the event, he was not enlisted until 19 August when he was sent as an AC2 to 2 Initial Training School at RAAF Bradfield Park which had been formed as part of the Empire Air Training Scheme. Here he learned the basics of military life and was taught subjects such as mathematics (one of those in which he had failed at school), navigation and aerodynamics. Leaving Bradfield Park as an LAC, he sailed out of Sydney for Canada to undertake pilot training on 19 Course at 4 Service Flying Training School at Saskatoon, also part of the Empire Air Training Scheme. Here, no doubt, his previous flying experience would have stood him in good stead and in May 1941, he left Canada as a qualified pilot arriving back in the UK the following month. Posted in September to 12 Course at 2 (Coastal) Operational Training Unit at Catfoss, four miles west of Hornsea in Yorkshire, he joined 236 Squadron at Wattisham on 21 February 1942, and was part of the detachment of eight Beaufighters sent to Predannack on 24 March, four days before he was destined to lose his life over the Bay of Biscay.

With no known grave Archie William Taylor is commemorated on the Runnymede Memorial. He left not only his widow, Phyllis, but also a little daughter called Jill who had been born in 1939. His sister, Hilda, mourned his loss for the rest of her 84 years.

For a man whose surname derived from the French word for 'perfect' (*parfait*) Hilary Rolfe Parfitt Senior had a skeleton of some magnitude in his cupboard. His saving grace was that he had married an angel. A marine engineer who had served in the Royal Navy in the First World War he had married the former Rachael Elena Richards, always known as Lena, the daughter of a farmer in Ystrad Mynach. It was more than he deserved, for her caring and forgiving nature was to rescue him from the follies of his own infidelity. Lena had borne him two sons before he upped and left her and travelled with her sister to Australia. There the couple had two daughters together but the relationship did not last and she left him and the two young girls, and he returned with them to England where he placed them in the care of Dr. Barnardo's.

Hearing of the girls' plight Lena visited them and finding one in such poor health that she would likely not survive and being unwilling to take one without the other she took them both home and brought them up as her own. A reconciliation with her erring husband having been effected, Lena later gave birth, on 28 November 1915, to a son, Hilary Rolfe Parfitt Junior.

As the youngest in the family he grew up close to his mother and they were devoted to each other. Perhaps inherited from his farming forebears, young Hilary developed a great love of animals and kept many pets. Once, having arranged to visit his Welsh grandparents on their farm, together with two friends, and bedding having been borrowed and extra food laid in, he arrived alone, but carrying a basket. His two 'friends' were his tortoises, Sid and George.

On 20 May 1940, with the BEF about to be ejected from France at Dunkirk and this country seemingly destined to stand alone against Germany, young Hilary volunteered for service, joining the RAFVR at 2 Recruiting Centre and being posted as an AC2 to the 1 Initial Training Wing the following month. In November he moved on to specialist training at 10 (Signals) Recruiting Centre, which was housed in an annexe of the Imperial Hotel in Blackpool, and then in January 1941, to 2 Signals School. His qualification achieved, he was next sent to 51 Group Pool whilst awaiting a posting to a squadron, 51 Group being part of the fourth of the RAF's commands, Training Command.

It was three months before Hilary was posted and it was to 143 Squadron he was sent and which was reforming at Aldergrove, County Antrim, after having been disbanded in 1919. Within three weeks, however, he was on the move again, this time to join 12 Course at 2 (Coastal) Operational Training Unit at Catfoss where he met up with Archie Taylor who was to be his pilot and where, apart from a short spell in Rauceby Hospital, he would stay until they were both posted to 236 Squadron at Wattisham in February 1942. A month later they would go on detachment to Predannack from where they would fly their fateful sortie.

With no known grave, Hilary is commemorated on the Runnymede Memorial. His devoted mother was mercifully spared his loss, having died in late 1941. He left a young widow for he had married Aileen Margaret Mackenzie at St Andrew's Church, Ilford, on 23 March 1940, where he was living and working as an accountant. There were no children. Aileen later remarried and died in 2009.

Meanwhile, back at Predannack, two more aircraft had taken off to continue the search for Chariot survivors. Pilot Officer Smith and Sergeant Treadwell in ND-M were airborne at

0843 and reaching 48°N set off south-east to fly a figure of eight pattern which covered the area already searched by K and Z as well as a similarly sized area to the west, but without sighting Chariot. Having spent a fruitless two hours, at 1203 they set course for home, landing safely at 1420.

Next to fly, Beaufighter ND-O took off at 0958 and set course to play its part in the ongoing search. Like M before it, aircraft O, with a crew of Sergeant Avern and Sergeant Crossan, flew a comprehensive figure of eight during which it sighted an He 111 which immediately lost itself in cloud and with visibility rapidly decreasing O made course for base, landing at 1336. The crews of O and M were also flying their first operational sortie.

The squadron commander himself, Wing Commander Glover, was next to take up the search flying in aircraft ND-J with Sergeant Fern as his observer, getting airborne at 1056, half an hour after the first two aircraft had returned. Reaching the designated area they, too, were unsuccessful in their quest but sighted a He 115 flying at sea level and gave chase but the enemy aircraft was lost when it climbed into cloud. It seemed that the Luftwaffe were loath to come to battle.

So far, with the notable and distressing exception of Sergeants Taylor and Parfitt, there had been no sighting of the survivors at all, due not only to the low cloud but also to the fact that the withdrawing launches were on a course to the south of that which had been intended. The search to date had been too far north and too far east but now we shall see success achieved by the next three aircraft, two of which were from 233 Squadron.

The last Beaufighter of 236 Squadron to take off was aircraft ND-G piloted by Squadron Leader Pike, a vastly more experienced pilot than the young, fresh crews who had carried out the search to date. His observer was Sergeant Kent and their sortie was to be the most successful and action-packed flown by the squadron. Taking off at the same time as Wing Commander Glover, a little over an hour later contact was lost with him in poor visibility and then, at 1249, Pike sighted the four destroyers and four motor launches of Chariot Force and at 1314 noted two Hudsons circling. However, it had to break off escort duty to attack an He 115 which ventured to put in an appearance. Pike fired a short burst at a range of 200 yards and the Heinkel responded with a two-star recognition signal but it was the wrong colour for the time of day. Emulating its compatriots it entered cloud and was lost and Squadron Leader Pike returned to escort duty at 1357. He now saw three motor launches on fire and of the fourth there was no sign. During the time he had been engaging the He 115 Fenton's ML 156 had been abandoned and later sunk by the Heinkel, possibly one of those he had himself encountered, and the crews of MGB 314 and MLs 270 and 446 had been taken on board the escorting destroyers and the launches set ablaze by gunfire.

Once again, however, an He 115 appeared and was attacked from 200 yards, an attack which was seen to damage the enemy, but this time there was heavy and accurate return fire. Aircraft G was hit in the nose and the port side of the cockpit. An oil leak was started which caught fire but went out after burning for five minutes.

We have noted earlier that a disadvantage of the Beaufighter was the need for the observer to re-load the cannons by hand, an operation that took him away from the cockpit, and it was while Sergeant Kent was engaged in this task that this second action against an enemy aircraft was taking place. With petrol now short it was necessary to make tracks for home and finding himself unable to lower the undercarriage Squadron Leader Pike made for St Eval where there was sufficient grass to afford him the opportunity to make a successful crash-landing which he accomplished at 1630 without injury to either himself or Sergeant Kent.

```
One Hudson to take off forthwith and proceed to 46 32N 04
16W thence on track 062 degrees T for 60 miles and return
to base as soon as recce completed. Aircraft to locate
and report all surface vessels on return to base. Second
Hudson to take off forthwith - same procedure as above
on completion of recce to reinforce our own fighter effort
to PLE.
T.O.O. 1035.
```

HQ 19 Group - order PL/G2/28/3

233 Squadron was formed late in World War I, on 31 August 1918 and flew various anti-submarine patrols and sorties against enemy fighters before being disbanded six months after the end of the war. It was reformed in 1937 as a Coastal Command squadron flying Avro Ansons until in August that year it moved to Scotland and converted to Lockheed Hudsons, last flying the Anson on 10 October when a flight of Bristol Blenheims were added to the strength.

Operating out of RAF Leuchars in 1940, the squadron flew sorties over the Norwegian and Danish coasts until those countries were overrun, when they switched their attention to land targets such as airfields and to shipping. During this time a detachment also operated out of Aldergrove in Northern Ireland. In August 1941 the squadron was posted to St Eval from where it flew shipping patrols over the Bay of Biscay. Now, in March 1942, we shall see two of their number, flying the Hudson V, come to the support of the withdrawal from the raid on St Nazaire.

The Hudson was built for the RAF shortly before the outbreak of war by the American Lockheed Aircraft Corporation. With commendable timing and no doubt with an eye on the brewing conflict "in a far off land", in 1937 the Corporation had published plans for a civilian aircraft that could be converted to a light bomber. It was not surprising that it caught the eye of those in England who were viewing with some alarm developments in Germany and who were already engaged in a rapid expansion of airfields. As a light bomber and reconnaissance aircraft it was ideally suited to use by Coastal Command with whom it flew for the duration of the war.

The initial RAF order for 200 machines was not only a great boost to its own capability but also a contract with considerable significance for Lockheed who had never produced aircraft on this scale before. A somewhat portly fuselage betrayed an aircraft which, although lacking in the performance needed for combat, was smooth handling and popular with its crews. The Hudson Mark V was powered by two Pratt and Whitney Twin Wasp engines giving it a range of 1,955 miles, a maximum speed of 245 mph and a ceiling of 25,000 feet. It was armed with seven 0.303 machine guns – two in a dorsal turret, one in a ventral position, two in beam positions and two firing forward. A total of 1,400 lbs of bombs or depth charges could be carried in an internal bomb bay. It was crewed by a pilot, navigator and two wireless operators/air gunners.

At 1125 on the 28th two Hudson Vs of 233 Squadron left the tarmac at St Eval and made a course for the search area in the Bay of Biscay. Hudson ZS-G was piloted by Flight Sergeant Johnstone, with his all-sergeant crew of Hunt, Daniel and Poole, and Hudson ZS-N by Flight Sergeant Barling with a crew of Pilot Officer Thompson and Sergeants Forbes and

Gasteen. They were to successfully arrive above the little flotilla of survivors where they found Squadron Leader Pike giving fighter protection. Chariot Force was in the process of transferring the crews of the little ships when at 1306 Barling, in N, recorded four British destroyers with three motor launches, one of which was alongside a destroyer. At 1310 Johnstone, in G, also recorded the four destroyers with all three motor launches circling.

With the motor launch crews safely aboard the destroyers, Johnstone set off for St Eval, where he landed at 1600, while Barling, in accordance with orders, remained in the area to reinforce the fighter protection. At 1355 he recorded one motor launch on fire and sinking and, half a mile south, two more motor launches, also on fire and sinking. The escort force of the four Hunts could now make best speed for Plymouth.

```
To Carew Cheriton - Operation "Chariot".
Six Blenheims to proceed to St Eval AM/27/3.Instructions
for operations will be issued later
T.O.O. 1005.
```
H.Q. 19 Group - order PL/G2/26/3

254 Squadron had enjoyed but a short life in World War I, having been formed in May 1918 and disbanded in February 1919. It was reformed on 30 October 1940 as a shipping protection squadron in response to the heavy losses off the east coast early in the war, when twenty-one ships had been sunk in a period of fourteen days. Together with squadrons 235, 236 and 248 it was designated as a 'trade protection' squadron, taking over, in January 1940, convoy escort duties from the single-engine, short-range fighters that were not suited to the task. Initially placed in Fighter Command it was transferred to Coastal Command in February 1940. The squadron was deployed at various bases around the British Isles until February 1942 when it found itself at Carew Cheriton.

Carew Cheriton is a village tucked away in the far south-west corner of Wales in what was in 1942 known as Pembrokeshire. The town of Pembroke is three miles to the west and Tenby five to the east. During World War I the rural peace was disturbed by the development of an airship station, RNAS Pembroke, and named Milton Air Station after a nearby village. In the 1930s the airfield was further developed to accommodate fixed-wing aircraft which would operate in conjunction with the flying boats from Pembroke Dock. A decoy site was added close by.

With another world war looming, Carew Cheriton was recommissioned in 1938 as a grass field and in August 1939 the Avro Ansons of 217 Squadron made it their base from which they patrolled the coast protecting convoys. Upgraded to a Class A airfield in 1940 by the laying of three concrete runways, flying activities were also stepped up by the arrival of Beaufighters and Blenheims of 236 Squadron which would mount combat patrols over the Irish Sea and box in the huge German battle-cruisers holed up in Brest. Escorts were also provided for the BOAC Lisbon-Chivenor service and the Fishguard-Rosslare Irish Mail boats. The Beaufighters and Blenheims of 236 Squadron left on 9 February 1942 to be replaced two days later by the Blenheim IVFs of 254 Squadron who arrived from Dyce, whither they would return on 1 June 1942. Operational flying from Carew Cheriton would cease later that year.

The Bristol Blenheim, like the Short Sunderland we met in Chapter 5, was unusual for a war plane in that it grew out of a design for a civilian aircraft, in this case a small one that

THE BOMBERS OF THE DIVERSIONARY RAID

Above: Armstrong Whitworth Whitley, flown by 51, 58 and 77 Squadrons. (Ed Coates Collection)
Below: Vickers Wellington 1C, flown by 103 and 150 Squadrons and 304 and 305 Polish Squadrons. (IWM HU 104762)

SQUADRON PERSONNEL

Above left: Wing Commander D.C.T. Bennett, CO of 58 Squadron, who later formed Pathfinder Force. (IWM CH 13645)
Above right: Wing Commander P.C. Pickard, CO of 51 Squadron, later lost on the Amiens prison raid in February 1944. (IWM HU 98865)

Above left: Flight Lieutenant 'Bill' Sise, who led the Blenheims of 254 Squadron in the search for survivors of Operation Chariot on 28 March 1942.
Above right: Squadron Leader David Holford, DFC, who flew with 103 Squadron on the diversionary bombing raid.

Above left: Sergeant A.T. Price of 254 Squadron, captured when his aircraft force-landed near Brest. He spent the rest of the war as a POW. (Alex Price)

Above right: Sergeant P.P. 'Johnny' Pohe of 51 Squadron, New Zealand's first Maori pilot, shot by the Gestapo following the 'Great Escape' from Stalag Luft III.

Above left: Sergeant Brian Nation, rear gunner with 51 Squadron in MH-A which carried Group Captain Willetts on the raid. (Sue Pendry)

Above right: Rear gun turret of a Whitley bomber, 'a grandstand view of the action'. (IWM C 924)

Above: A Lysander of 277 Squadron which operated in the east of the English Channel whilst 276, which rescued the crew of MH-S, operated in the west. (IWM CH 7571)
Below: A Spitfire of B Flight 1 PRU which operated from RAF St Eval and brought back valuable reconnaissance photographs of St Nazaire. (IWM HU 86528)
Bottom: Danesfield House, near Marlow, which became RAF Medmenham, home of the Photographic Interpretation Unit, later renamed the Central Interpretation Unit. (Crown Copyright – courtesy of the Medmenham Collection)

THE LOSS OF BEAUFIGHTER ND-Y

Above left: The pilot, Sergeant Archie William Taylor, RAAF. (Michael Dunbavan)
Above right: The observer, Sergeant Hilary Rolfe Parfitt, RAFVR. (Ann Inglis)
Below: A Beaufighter Mark 1C of 236 Squadron. Based at RAF Wattisham, a detachment was flown to RAF Predannack to take part in the search for survivors. (IWM C 2733)

TO THE FALLEN

Above left: The grave of Sergeant Douglas Murton Colledge RAFVR at the Church of St John the Baptist, Leeming. (Author)

Above right: The Commonwealth War Graves plot at the church. (Author)

Bottom: The panels commemorating Sergeants Hilary Rolfe Parfitt and Archie William Taylor at the Air Forces Memorial, Runnymede. (The War Graves Photographic Project)

THE FORCE-LANDING OF BLENHEIM Z6103

Above: The aircraft on the Plage de l'Aber, on the Crozon peninsula, being guarded by a German soldier from the nearby base.

Below: The aircraft after being painted in German livery and markings before being flown to Germany.

THE ANTI-AIRCRAFT DEFENCES
OF ST NAZAIRE

Above: A 60-cm searchlight. Each battalion had a total of fifteen 60 cm and 150 cm which were widely dispersed to follow aircraft across the whole area. (Collection Luc Braeuer)
Left from top to bottom: A 12.8-cm Flak 40 of Dragon battery (5/MFA 703) at Marsac (Collection Alfred Hörnchen/Luc Braeuer); The quadruple 20-cm Flak gun on the roof of the Frigo building next to the U-boat pens. This was ineffective against bombers flying at high altitude. (Collection Luc Braeuer)
Below: The dual-purpose 20-mm Flak position on the seaward end of the west jetty. (Collection Luc Braeuer)

would carry six passengers and a crew of two. Ordered by Lord Rothermere, owner of the *Daily Mail* and who had at one time been Secretary of State for Air, it was motivated by a desire to see a British plane that was the fastest civilian plane in Europe and could also be used to carry his reporters to the scene of breaking news stories before his competitors. When the plane first flew at Filton on 12 April 1935 it proved to be even faster than any RAF fighter and thus quickly attracted the attention of the Air Ministry who promptly issued a specification for a bomber version. The eventual outcome was the Bristol Blenheim Mark I. A Mark IF fighter version would follow.

In due course an improved version, the Mark IV, appeared in which several shortcomings of the original had been addressed. The short nose, which had proved cramped and uncomfortable for the navigator/bomb aimer, had been extended and the Perspex canopy stepped back to give the pilot good all-round vision. The range, too short for the long patrols over water which the plane was destined to carry out, had been increased by placing a ninety-four gallon fuel tank in the outer wing. This, however, brought its own problems, as it made the plane too heavy to land when fully loaded and a system with which to jettison fuel had to be added. Further, experience in combat showed up a need to increase the armament.

The basic specification, therefore, was of a three-seat light bomber – pilot, navigator/bomb aimer, wireless operator/air gunner – with a maximum range of 1,460 miles, a ceiling of 27,250 feet and a maximum speed of 265 mph. It was powered by two Bristol Mercury XV radial piston engines, armed with five .303 machine guns and could carry a bomb load of 1,250 lbs. Like the Mark I a Mark IVF fighter version, was built and this was the aircraft being flown by 254 Squadron in March 1942.

Arthur Price was born in 1919 at Peterhead, in the far north of Scotland, a son of the Manse. He had joined the RAF in 1939 and was posted as a wireless operator/air gunner to 235 Squadron on the east coast where early sorties had included shooting up barges massed in ports along the Dutch coast and scouring the Norwegian fjords for the German pocket battleships that lurked there, and on one occasion finding the *Deutschland*. During this time Arthur was shot down and spent three days in a dinghy before being rescued, but he had no fear of the sea for as a lad he had earned pocket money sailing with the herring skippers out of Peterhead. Now with 254 Squadron at Carew Cheriton, Arthur would later remember:

> "One night we were awakened and told to take off for Falmouth[29], where we would receive our briefing. Well, landing in Falmouth we went to the operations room and we were told where we were going. We were going to St Nazaire. Now, unknown to us, the night before the naval people, commandos and marines, went into St Nazaire with an old destroyer called the *Campbeltown*, which was filled with explosives....
>
> "It was blown up so that it became useless to the Germans and then they had to make their way out in small MTBs and our job was to pick them up in the estuary of the river and escort them out to naval vessels which were lying a bit out to sea."

The Blenheims having been flown to Predannack and the crews briefed, the aircraft of

---

[29] This was, in fact, RAF Predannack, about 14 miles south-west of Falmouth.

Flight Lieutenant Illingworth piloting QY-H and Pilot Officer Lown in QY-D got airborne at 1140 to begin the search for Chariot survivors. Arriving at the rendezvous at 1322 and having seen only three fishing vessels and a trawler, all stationary, and no sight of withdrawing forces from St Nazaire, they commenced a square search around the rendezvous. Arriving at the south-east corner of the search area at 1420 they saw, almost immediately, a Focke-Wulf Kurier about 400 yards ahead. Flying at 200 feet at 130 knots the enemy aircraft was on a course of 150°, the Blenheim on 308°, almost a reciprocal. However, when the Blenheims banked to attack, the Focke-Wulf climbed into cloud and though followed was not seen again. Their search for Chariot having proved fruitless, at 1445 Illingworth and Lown set course for base.

Leading the second wave an hour later Flight Lieutenant G. D. 'Bill' Sise took off in QY-P with Pilot Officer Wright in QY-C and Sgt Parnell in QY-K. Bill was a New Zealander, born in Dunedin in 1917, and had joined the RNZAF in 1939, a few weeks after the war had started. Posted to fly the Blenheim IVF with 254 Squadron he very nearly blew his chances of a career as a pilot. Sent up to familiarise himself with both aircraft and locality he came in a little short and left his undercarriage decorating the stone wall that bordered the airfield. To compound the felony his passenger, there to check him out, was none other than his flight commander, Flight Lieutenant Bain, and the resulting inevitable 'wheels-up' landing inflicted injuries to that part of Bain's anatomy that required him to spend his recovery time in a face down position. It being a familiarisation flight it was no more than justice done when the cause of the mishap was put down to 'pilot unfamiliarity' and Sise remained with 254.

From then until 1942 Sise took part in many raids, varied in both type and danger, one of which being, of course, this search for survivors from St Nazaire which would have ranked as one of the least arduous and most frustrating of his war. During his time with 254 he was to rise to squadron leader and in November 1942, after the squadron had converted to Beaufighter VICs, he survived an attack by three FW190s during a sortie against a convoy off the Hook of Holland. Having with great difficulty shaken them off he limped back to England and made a successful crash-landing near Frinton-on-Sea. He was awarded a DFC shortly after and in April the following year, as just reward for two years continuous operations with 254, a DSO.

Before the war was out he would attain the rank of wing commander and add bars to both his DSO and DFC. The citation for his second DSO could well stand as the summation of his wartime service:

> "This officer has displayed great gallantry in operations against the enemy. He
> is a brilliant leader whose personal example and untiring efforts have done
> much towards raising his squadron to the highest standard of efficiency."

Sise set a course for the start point of their patrol at 48°N 06°W which they reached at 1342. For the next hour they flew a course of 128° and found themselves near the mid-point of the eastern boundary of the square search flown earlier by H and D and, like them, had not seen any Chariot survivors. Turning to starboard they now flew a creeping line[30] ahead along a mean course of 288°. At 1530 they turned about and started a back search ten miles either side of the track but when halfway down the line and still having drawn a

---

[30] A creeping line ahead follows a track like the crenellations of a castle.

blank they turned to port and set course for their starting point at 48°N 06°W.

Fifty minutes later they sighted an aircraft which they decided was a Beaufighter and so took no action. It was flying at 300 feet on a course of 40° and, unless their aircraft recognition skills were wanting, it was not part of the search for Chariot forces for at this time, the last Beaufighter of 236 Squadron to return, Squadron Leader Pike in ND-G, was within ten minutes of crash-landing at St Eval.

Seven minutes later, however, another aircraft sighting saw them turning to starboard to intercept. Pilot Officer Wright, in QY-C had spotted a Heinkel 111 at 200 feet flying due east, but it had no stomach for a fight with three Blenheims and dived to sea level. It was last seen banking seaward into haze, having fired a four-star green recognition signal. The rear gunner fired fifty rounds without effect and although a search was made no further contact ensued. Arthur Price remembered the incident which was soon to have serious consequences:

"On the way back we got tied up with a Heinkel 111. Actually there were three planes in the formation and all pilots, against the regulations we had been given, decided to have a go at this first. Since we had the faster plane we started a scrap with this Heinkel."

The action having lost them their bearings they turned north to make a landfall and fix their position. They crossed the coast at Audienne and continued across the Baie de Douarnenez. Pilot Officer Wright was experiencing engine trouble and turned for home and after being fired on in the vicinity of Cap de la Chèvre flew on over Ushant and landed safely at base at 1920. Aircraft P and K continued north, gathering useful intelligence as they went. Five miles east of Crozon they saw a dummy airfield with up to twenty-five dummy Heinkels up on props. They also saw, when crossing the Crozon peninsula, an airfield with camouflaged buildings and four runways but, ironically, no aeroplanes. Nearing Brest they encountered heavy anti-aircraft fire and Flight Lieutenant Sise took evasive action by heading out to sea, noting as he did six large barges anchored in the Goulet de Brest. At about 1700 Sergeant Parnell, in QY-K, broke away and was last seen heading south. Arthur Price again:

".... We were so far off course that instead of going on up to Falmouth we hit the French coast at Brest. Once we sailed in there the fortifications that they had were very heavy because it was only a few weeks before this that the *Scharnhorst* and *Gneisenau*, which were the big German battleships [sic], had left, with the result that we were pretty well knocked about and eventually crash-landed on the beach. Now as soon as we hit the beach there was quite a crowd of German soldiers came running over the sand hills firing at us so, drop everything and stick our hands up as high as we could, and wait for them."

For Sergeants Parnell, Mullineaux and Price the war was over, but we shall meet them again later. For Blenheim Z6103 the war would continue, for the Germans salvaged it and it was flown to Germany by a crew from Wettererkungdungstaffel 2 (Wekusta 2), a German weather reconnaissance squadron based at Brest Lanveoc. It later reappeared in German livery. The letter K was not to be a lucky one for the Blenheims of 254 Squadron for three weeks later Z6102, which had now adopted it, ran out of runway when landing at Carew Cheriton and even raising the under-carriage to bring it to a halt failed to avoid it being written off.

As the crew of Parnell's QY-K were being taken into captivity Sise flew on, over Pointe Saint-Mathieu, where he suffered more flak, towards Ushant and safety. He had received hits in the starboard wing, rudder and port elevator, the latter causing some loss of fore and aft control. Nevertheless he landed safely back at Predannack at 1905, a quarter of an hour before Pilot Officer Wright who had successfully nursed his sick aeroplane home.

```
To St Eval.
On Hudson aircraft becoming available A/A escort to be
maintained continuously on convoy Chariot. Sorties to
consist of three Hudsons last sortie to leave Chariot at
last light. Latest intelligence re position and composition
of convoy will be passed by phone.
Aircraft are not to carry bombs or DCs.
T.O.O. 1350.
```

HQ 19 Group - order PL/G5/28/3

The airfield at RAF Thorney Island was situated halfway between Portsmouth and Southampton, an ideal location for a Coastal Command base covering as it did those two important centres of naval activity. However, it had been built in 1938 as a fighter airfield and had seen action during the Battle of Britain. It would also have an important role to play in the D-Day landings in 1944 and the subsequent progress across France and during that time would be used by numerous squadrons, some of which stayed only a few weeks.

407 (RCAF) Squadron had been formed at Thorney Island on 8 May 1941 and was one of the eight Article XV[31] RCAF units to serve with Coastal Command. The squadron trained on Blenheim IVs but soon converted to the Hudson and operated initially in a strike role, earning itself the nickname of the 'Demon Squadron'. In January 1943, it became a general reconnaissance squadron involved in protecting shipping from U-boat attacks. It was disbanded at Chivenor in June 1945.

Part of 16 Group, which was at that time commanded by Air Commodore L.T. Lloyd, CBE, 407 Squadron had spent the morning of 28 March 1942 on formation and normal flying training and the squadron had been deemed ready for operations. All available aircraft had been ordered to St Eval to stand by for orders and by noon seven of the squadron's Hudson Vs, led by their OC, Wing Commander A.C. Brown, DFC, had taken off, bound for the airfield on the north coast of Cornwall where they joined a growing number of aircraft from other squadrons similarly deployed. However, only six were to arrive in a serviceable condition, the OC having tangled with the cable of a barrage balloon at Falmouth during the flight. The dent in his aircraft was of a nature that had, in the past, been sufficient to cause a total loss but the aircraft landed safely, although it was unable to take any part in the operation.

In accordance with the orders received from HQ 19 Group at Plymouth, three aircraft lifted off that afternoon at 1445 to search for the survivors of Operation Chariot and to act as their anti-aircraft escort. Not to miss out on a sortie and possible action, Wing Commander Brown, having damaged Hudson E, took over F with three of his own crew and Pilot Officer Armstrong and with Squadron Leader Douglas in B and Pilot Officer Ross in D set course for the search area.

---

[31] Article XV Squadrons – Australian, Canadian and New Zealand Air Force squadrons formed from graduates of the British Commonwealth Air Training Agreement (1939).

Starting their patrol due west of Ushant at 48°45'N, 06°17'W they flew in company along a course of 185° for a little over 100 miles before turning east on to a course of 100° to a point 120 miles south-west of St Nazaire. Then, doubling back on themselves, they flew an almost reciprocal course until shortly before 47°N, 06°W from where they returned to base.

At regular intervals throughout the patrol fishing boats and, at 1825, a motor vessel of about 900 tons, were sighted. The motor vessel was a three-island type with the funnel amidships, well loaded and proceeding at a speed of between eight and ten knots on a course of 100 degrees T, but as orders had precluded the carrying of bombs or depth charges it was left to pursue its journey. They also sighted a Dornier 217, again taking no action, but of Chariot Force there was no sign and the Hudsons returned to St Eval, landing at 2032.

Taking off an hour and two hours respectively after 407 Squadron were Hudson Vs drawn from 53 and 59 Squadrons, also of 16 Group, based at North Coates. These two squadrons led a somewhat parallel existence for much of the war. Both had been formed in World War I and flew as army cooperation squadrons in France. Both had been disbanded in 1919, 53 in October and 59 in August.

Reformed at Farnborough in June 1937, 53 Squadron, flying Hawker Hectors, was once again engaged on army cooperation and in January 1939, converted to the Blenheim and later that year moved to France. 59 Squadron, too, had been reformed in 1939, also with the Hawker Hector, before converting to Blenheims and deploying to France in October of that year. Both squadrons, like all those of the RAF in advanced bases in France, were forced out in May 1940 in the face of the German onslaught but continued to attack targets in France from bases in England. Having been transferred from Fighter Command to Coastal Command they now flew from their respective bases – 53 at Detling in Kent and 59 at Thorney Island in Hampshire – the lions' share of raids on the invasion ports, although they were also engaged on anti-shipping strikes.

On 17 September 1940 both squadrons, this time flying together on the same mission, acted as a diversion for Beauforts on a bombing raid against Cherbourg, the Blenheims successfully causing confusion with the dropping of bombs, flares and incendiaries while the Beauforts caused significant damage to the docks and the shipping within them.

In July 1941 the squadrons converted to the Hudson, 53 to the Mark V and 59 to the Mark III, but in September it followed 53 when it, too, converted to the Mark V. Early 1942 would find them based at North Coates from where, on 28 March 1942, 59 would fly four Hudsons to St Eval to provide anti-aircraft cover to the retiring Chariot forces while 53 would fly four machines to St Eval from Thorney Island where they were on detachment.

RAF North Coates, in common with so many other airfields, was named after a nearby village and was situated in Lincolnshire about four miles from the coast. It, like so many others, had a short life during World War I having been opened in mid-1918 and closed in June 1919. However, it was not part of the rash of airfield building of the late 1930s in anticipation of the war, having been re-opened in 1927 and until February 1940 it was occupied in armament practice and training. During this time it was known as North Coates Fitties and hosted Fleet Air Arm as well as RAF units, an arrangement that continued after it had become North Coates and its role become maritime. Torpedo bombers arrived in the shape of Blenheims and they and Marylands carried out strategic reconnaissance while the Fleet Air Arm flew their Fairey Swordfishes on minelaying and bombing operations.

At the outbreak of war its geographical position had led to invasion worries and North Coates had been evacuated but it now became, for the same geographical reason, a very busy airfield indeed. Not only did many Coastal Command squadrons form, pass through or send detachments there, but it also became a forward landing ground for fighters based at Digby and also maintained a detachment from 278 Air-Sea Rescue Squadron flying the Lysander.

Taking off for their sortie an hour behind the Hudsons of 407 RCAF Squadron, PZ-Y and PZ-Q of 53 Squadron lifted off from St Eval at 1553 in the afternoon of 28 March and set course for the start point of their patrol about an hour away due west of Ushant. Flying south along a course of 170° to 46°53'N, 05°W they swung on to 110° and, three hours into their flight, they encountered an enemy aircraft in the shape of a Heinkel 111 at position 46°38'N, 04°40'W. The aircraft were separated by a distance of only 400 yards with the Heinkel at about 300 feet on the same course of 170°. Its pilot, however, had no stomach for a fight for on sighting the Hudsons it increased speed and quickly departed the scene.

Maintaining their course for a short while longer they then turned about and flew an exact reciprocal of their outward flight until, virtually at the same point as they had earlier started their patrol they at last sighted part of Chariot Force in the shape of two Hunt class destroyers. It was 1937 hours and the destroyers *Atherstone* and *Tynedale* were making twenty-five knots along a course of 350° that would take them safely round the Brest peninsula before turning north-east for Plymouth with the survivors of the four little ships they had taken aboard earlier. Half an hour previously *Cleveland* and *Brocklesby* had been despatched to search for the three MLs that had earlier set their own course for Falmouth and from whom a signal had recently been received.

Following this sighting PZ-Y and PZ-Q parted company and set course for their base at St Eval. PZ-Y, fifteen minutes from touchdown had reported seeing a light on the water which was identified as the masthead light of a stationary trawler, fishing off the north Cornish coast. More bizarre, however, was a sighting in the same position of an orange glow at 1,800 feet which passed from starboard to port about a quarter of a mile ahead. PZ-Y landed safely on the tarmac at St Eval at 2159, to be followed twenty minutes later by PZ-Q.

A further hour behind the Hudsons of 53 Squadron, PJ-D and PJ-F of 59 Squadron lifted off to take over the search for Chariot Force. Commencing their patrol at 1753 from the same start point west of Ushant they flew the same course, a little east of south, until at 1840, at 46°35'N, 05°34'W, they sighted two Hudsons on a course of 330°. This could not have been the aircraft of 53 Squadron for at that precise moment they were encountering their Heinkel 111 over fifty miles away. It is just possible that they were two of the three Hudsons of 407 RCAF Squadron who were in that area a little earlier, but no identification was made and it is most probable that they were totally unconnected with the Chariot search. Following this encounter PJ-D and PJ-F commenced a square search but found no trace of Chariot and an hour later they parted company, D setting course for base where they landed at 2222. After parting, F flew a short leg to the south-west before returning to St Eval at 2159.

The sortie flown by 59 Squadron was to have consisted of three aircraft but PJ-E, taking off shortly after the others, found his wireless to be unserviceable and eight minutes later he was back on the tarmac at St Eval.

It was well after 2200 on 28 March that the last plane returned to base, bringing to an end the first day's search for Chariot survivors. It had been a comprehensive effort to find, protect and escort the force and it had covered a large area of the Bay of Biscay. The RAF had flown from dawn to dusk and beyond and twenty-two aircraft, with seventy aircrew, had flown over 100 hours during the day's sorties in the course of which a Dornier 217, a Heinkel 111 and two Heinkel 115s had been encountered, one of the latter having been engaged in inconclusive combat. A Ju 88 had been attacked and destroyed but sadly at the cost of the crew of Y/236 who shot it down. Another aircraft, K/254, was forced down and its three-man crew condemned to a life as prisoners for the remainder of the war. A total of five aircraft had made contact with Chariot Force, but most importantly, no harm had come to the force from the air. The search, however, was not over and the next day further efforts would have to be made to locate the three MLs that were still unaccounted for.

HMS *Atherstone* and HMS *Tynedale* arrived in Plymouth at 0145 on the morning of Palm Sunday, 29 March. Thus returned to England some of the men who had sailed out of St Nazaire following the raid – the crew and commandos of MGB 314 and the MLs 156, 270 and 446. We must now return to the three MLs – 160, 307 and 443 – who had passed through Point Y at 0415 the previous morning and, being too early for the rendezvous with the Hunts, had set out in accordance with the instructions for making their own way home.

Lieutenant Boyd, RNVR, in ML 160, had limped out of St Nazaire on fire and with only one engine, the other being temporarily disabled and on the way down the estuary he had linked up with ML 443, commanded by Lieutenant Horlock, RNVR. Together they had proceeded to Point Y where they met up with ML 307, the command of Lieutenant Wallis RANVR.

Following the withdrawal route of 248° to Point T, seventy miles west of Y, at 0830 they had observed, with some trepidation, the approach of two warships. Hastily destroying their charts and confidential papers in a move they were soon to regret, they awaited the inevitable. The warships, however, through an exchange of signals with ML 443, revealed their identities as HMS *Cleveland* and HMS *Brocklesby* who had been despatched from Plymouth to support the withdrawal and were hastening to the rendezvous at Y. After enquiring the whereabouts of the rest of the launches they dashed away leaving the three MLs chartless in the middle of the Bay of Biscay.

The launches were carrying several wounded men but also a doctor, Captain Paton, RAMC, and at midday they came together so that he could visit and tend to the wounded on the other two MLs. One man in particular, Motor Mechanic T.G. Parker, who had been plucked from Lieutenant Platt's doomed ML 447 by Boyd's crew in the maelstrom of the dockyard, was grievously wounded, but was maintaining a fierce determination to see England once more. Sailing on again and hampered by their lack of charts they had to estimate the point at which they would turn north and this they did at 1700. The instructions had been to turn at 7°W but Ryder, in his book *The Attack on Saint Nazaire*, records them not turning until 8°W, thus extending the journey home by many miles and putting them in a position not anticipated by the aircraft that would search for them.

Maintaining this course for 100 miles, during which they were attacked by a Heinkel 111 which they shot down and a Blohm and Voss seaplane which was frightened into departing the scene by the combined weight of fire from the MLs, they eventually turned north-east for the long run to Falmouth. At 1850 signals from the launches were picked up by the Hunts as they sailed for England and at 1904 Commander Sayer detached *Cleveland* and *Brocklesby* to search for them. They would fail to find them, no doubt because they were sailing further west than was expected and probably with more distance between them and home than was anticipated and *Cleveland* returned to Falmouth, arriving in the afternoon of 29 March. However, the hunt for the missing MLs had not been abandoned.

```
To St Eval.
Three Hudsons to carry out parallel track search. From
50.30N. 06.20W   50.30N 06.40W. 50.30N 06.00W. Thence on
tracks 180 °T to 49.20N - 270 °T for 7 miles - 360 °T to
datum line. If no surface craft sighted re-commence patrol
20 miles further west. Aircraft to take off forthwith.
T.O.O. 0945.
```
HQ 19 Group – order PL/G3/29/3

```
Reference PL/G3/29/3 amend datum to read 50.45N. 06.20W.
50.45N. 06.40W. 50.45N. 07.00W.
T.O.O. 0955
```
HQ 19 Group – order PL/G4/29/3

Of the seven serviceable aircraft of 407 RCAF Squadron that had flown from Thorney Island to St Eval to take part in the cover for Operation Chariot, four had flown on 28 March. Now, the following day, it was the turn of the other three to play their part. Pilot Officer Mullen in N, Flying Officer Race in S and Flight Sergeant O'Connell in O took off a few minutes apart, the first at 1020, and set off for their respective start points. Pilot Officer Mullen started at the co-ordinates of the original message, but the others used the correct positions and all flew the parallel track search as ordered.

With the three MLs now seriously overdue came the realisation that the planned route north along 7°N, if pursued for too long, would result in them missing Cornwall altogether and not reaching land until the Irish coast at Waterford. By flying the search ordered these three Hudsons of RCAF would cover the vast majority of the area bounded by 48°N, 06°W, 50°N and 08°W, a huge area of sea due west of Land's End in which they would be sure to find them should they have overshot Cornwall. Of the MLs, however, there was no sign although N did sight an ML off the Isles of Scilly and exchanged recognition signals.

ML 341, commanded by Lieutenant Douglas Briault, RNVR, was second in the port column and carrying Captain E.S. 'Bertie' Hodgson, of the Bedfordshire and Hertfordshire Regiment and 2 Commando, and his important assault party, important because its task was to silence two guns on the east jetty. These two guns were the first that would be encountered by the flotilla as they neared their target. At 2000 on 27 March, the force had adopted its assault formation and sailed towards Point Z where the submarine *Sturgeon*, acting as a navigation beacon, awaited them.

During the course of this stretch of their journey Briault, in ML 341, reported that he could not keep up as his port engine was unserviceable and in need of repair. Ordered to transfer his commandos to the spare launch ML 446, commanded by Lieutenant H.G.R. Falconar, RNVR, Briault continued gamely on until realisation dawned that he could not make it to St Nazaire and he was left to pursue a lonely and disconsolate course for home. At a speed of six or seven knots he would not make England until much the same time as those MLs which, withdrawing from the estuary after the action, would themselves reach Falmouth.

```
To St Eval.
One Hudson to locate M/L on bearing 146 °T from Lands End
Radio to maximum depth 60 (R) 60 miles. If located the
position of M/L to be passed to M/L by visual signal and
reported by W/T. Hudson to supply escort to PLE. Aircraft
to take off forthwith.
T.O.O. 1045.
```

HQ 19 Group – order PL/G5/29/3

There is some confusion regarding the sighted ML and the search ordered to be carried out by Hudson ZS-G. This aircraft had been flown in the original search for Chariot the previous day by Flight Sergeant Barling. Now piloted by Pilot Officer Broadhurst, it took off to investigate and set a south-westerly course which took it parallel to the north Cornish coast and heading directly for the reported position of the ML, but this was on a bearing of 246° from Land's End Radio rather than the 146° along which Broadhurst had been instructed to search.

Ten miles off Land's End, Broadhurst sighted two destroyers which he identified as of the Javelin Class. After exchanging identities he turned 90° to port on to a south-east course that would take him to the position defined in his orders. At 1222, however, when due south of the Lizard, he was recalled to base where he landed at 1308 without having sighted an ML. By 1445 the three Hudsons, O, N and S of 407 RCAF Squadron, which had carried out parallel track searches to the west of Land's End, were also safely back on the tarmac at St Eval.

Many questions arise from this episode. Why did Broadhurst set a course to a point 246° from Land's End when his orders gave a bearing of 146°? Was this an error, realised when he turned 90° to port after his encounter with the destroyers? Was there a second ML or was 146° given in error and should have been 246°? Was his early recall to base a result of the realisation that an error had been made or had news of the arrival of Boyd, Wallis and Horlock become known?

The likelihood is that the ML sighted by N/407 was ML 341. It was most unusual for an ML to be out on its own, being a craft that normally operated in groups. It was in a position and at a time quite consistent with the circumstances of the sad return from the brink of glory at St Nazaire.

```
To St Eval.
Three Whitleys to carry out search for M/L's from positions
50.00N. 04.30W. 50.00N. 05.25W. 50.00N. 06.20W. Thence
210 °T to latitude 48° - 270 °T for 18 miles - 030 °T to
datum line thence to base. M/L's or similar craft to be
escorted and reported by W/T. Aircraft to pass position
of any M/L located to M/L by visual signal. Aircraft to
take off forthwith
T.O.O. 1300.
```

HQ 19 Group – order PL/G6/29/3

Within twenty minutes of this order being issued aircraft WL-L of 612 Squadron lifted off from St Eval for a final sweep of the Western Approaches to locate the missing MLs of Boyd, Wallis and Horlock. Closely followed by Sergeant Hill in YG-H and, a quarter of an hour later, by Sergeant Coates in YG-J, both of 502 Squadron, the three crews made for their starting points, spread out along 50°N at 04°30'W, 05°25'W and 06°20'W respectively.

WL-L followed the ordered course of 210°T from his datum point until having crossed 5°W when for some unexplained reason he turned on to 245°T for about forty-five miles before setting a new course for the designated point on 48°N where he was to turn due west. Eighteen miles later he turned on to 30°T to fly a parallel return course to 50°N and thence to base. Although numerous S/E contacts were investigated nothing was seen and of the MLs there was no trace.

Sergeant Hill, in YG-H sighted three destroyers early into his sortie but they remained unidentified, as did the trawler also sighted close by. Hill flew his ordered course to 48°N and returned on a parallel track with an eighteen-mile separation during which he, too, made no sightings of the MLs.

Sergeant Coates, in YG-J flew his ordered course but on reaching 48°N continued for some time until at 47°25'N he turned due west as per his orders and after eighteen miles turned on to 30°T to fly his parallel track back to his datum line and from there to St Eval.

These three aircraft had covered in comprehensive fashion the area between 06°W and 08°W which should have found the motor launches had they been following the planned withdrawal route north along 07°W. However, unknown to them and also, presumably, to the RAF authorities, Boyd, Wallis and Horlock were unloading their wounded in Falmouth even as the order to search for them was issued at 1300. The ML skippers had sighted the Lizard at 1000 that morning and around midday had entered Falmouth harbour.

The obsession with security that had driven Ryder to issue orders that no soldier was to be seen on the decks of HMS *Campbeltown* or any of the launches, still prevailed and this may well have accounted for the absence of advice to the RAF of their safe return. A signal was received requiring the commandos to remain below deck and out of sight while the RAF, providing further service to the operation, transferred the casualties to the RAF ambulances in which they were taken to hospital for the urgent treatment that many of them required.

When YG-J landed at St Eval at 1850 hours on 29 March the sorties flown by the Royal Air Force in support of Operation Chariot came to an end. In addition to the bombing raid a constant presence in the air had been maintained for all the hours of daylight since 1940 hours on 26th – less than one hour short of three full days. Nine aircrew had been lost and three were to languish in POW camps until the final victory more than three years later. It is to these three men that we shall now turn our attention.

CHAPTER 11

GUESTS OF THE THIRD REICH

Morgat is a small town on the south coast of the French department of Finistère which occupies the western tip of the Brittany peninsula. Two kilometres south of Crozon, the largest town, Morgat was originally a fishing village, but in the 1930s it was discovered by the brothers Peugeot, of motor car fame, who developed it into a holiday resort where the family still maintain a villa. Whilst Crozon has little to recommend it, Morgat is one of the prettiest resorts in Brittany and retains the atmosphere of the period in which it was developed.

The beaches of the area face south and the sunny aspect attracts visitors to swim, sail, sunbathe and explore the many caves that line the coast. To the east of the main beach of the town is La Plage de l'Aber, a straight, flat length of golden sand popular with tourists wishing to disport themselves. However, on the evening of 28 March 1942, it welcomed three visitors, uninvited and much against their will, when Blenheim QY-K of 254 Squadron RAF force-landed upon it. It was a feat of some magnitude by the pilot to land a damaged aircraft in such a place and without injury to himself or his crew. The soldiers who quickly overwhelmed them were, no doubt, the men who manned the casemates and blockhouses which were dotted along La Plage de l'Aber and the other beaches on this part of the Atlantic Wall.

Anthony George Parnell, known to all as Tony, the pilot of QY-K, was born in September 1921 and was still four months short of his nineteenth birthday when he enlisted in the RAF in May 1940. He described himself as a clerk and was living in Wallington, Surrey. Whilst a prisoner in Lamsdorf he preserved his sanity and filled the long hours by helping the camp dentist. This was to mark his future career for on his return to England he enrolled at the Royal College of Dentistry in London. In the mid-1960s he emigrated to Canada where he became chief of the dental department at the local hospital and professor of Dentistry at the University of West Ontario. Tony died at London, Ontario, in July 2013, aged ninety-one.

Herbert Joseph Mullineaux, the wireless operator/observer, was the 'father' of the crew, having been born in October 1913. He lived in Blackburn and had enlisted in 1939. In civilian life he was a member of the Chartered Institute of Secretaries. Although originally sent to Lamsdorf with his fellow crew, in July 1943 he was moved to Stalag Luft III at Sagan. Herbert spent his time as a prisoner studying for the final exams of the CIS and was awaiting the results when he was repatriated.

Arthur Thomas Price, the wireless operator/air gunner we met earlier, filled his time in Lamsdorf by volunteering to work in the post office, of which more later. After his return to England, in 1947 he moved to Prestatyn where he worked firstly in a hardware business and then in a café/supermarket, while being active in local politics. Arthur died in 2006.

It had still been light when Tony Parnell had force-landed his aircraft on the beach at Morgat and no sooner had he brought it to a halt than the crew were overwhelmed by soldiers from a nearby base. Not even having enough time to set fire to the aircraft they were made prisoners of war. Three days later they arrived at Dulag Luft (Durchgangslager der Luftwaffe – air force transit camp) which was the main collection and interrogation centre for all aircrew, where at least Sergeants Parnell and Mullineaux were prepared for what was to come. Parnell had been lectured in how to behave in the event of capture while at 2 (Coastal) Operational Training Unit at RAF Catfoss, while Mullineaux had received similar instruction at RAF Squires Gate, now Blackpool International Airport. Price had received no such preparation at all.

At Dulag Luft captives were stripped and their clothes searched on arrival, allocated to a cell and interviewed by an interrogating officer. A form was presented for completion which contained far more questions than a POW was required to answer under the Geneva Convention and the interrogator would endeavour to get the form fully completed. The prisoner's willingness or otherwise to complete this form was used to judge whether he could be made to talk or not. Psychologists were involved and the techniques were very sophisticated including trading food, clothes and cigarettes for information and sometimes releasing a prisoner to his permanent camp after only a few days 'to encourage the others'.

The first few days were spent in his cell and during this time the rations were minimal and he was subjected to extremes of heat and cold. Many POWs were often taken by surprise by the information the Germans held about them, including knowledge of the airfield from which they had flown, gathered from sources such as captured papers. In the case of the crew of Blenheim QY-K their aircraft had been captured intact and would have yielded up much useful intelligence.

After two weeks interrogation they were taken to Stalag VIII-B at Lamsdorf, also known as Stalag 344. Here would also be imprisoned many of the commandos from St Nazaire, of whom Dick Bradley, Alf Searson and Jimmy Brown would make a successful home run from a working party.

Dulag Luft was relieved by the American 7th Armored Division at the end of March 1945. Many of the permanent staff, who were themselves POWs, had been there since 1940.

Arriving at Lamsdorf the Blenheim crew joined the third generation of prisoners of war to be held there. The camp had been built in 1862 in a huge area of forest cleared for use as an artillery range, but in 1870 it was put to use as a camp for prisoners from the Franco-Prussian War. Used again for that purpose in World War I it welcomed its first prisoner of the second, a solitary Polish officer, as early as 3 September 1939.

One of the features of Stalag 344, Lamsdorf, was the number of working parties – some sources suggest in excess of 250 – that were organised by the Germans to factories and other locations in the vicinity. It was quickly recognised that joining one of these parties offered better opportunities for escape than staying in the camp and many volunteered for them with this express purpose in mind.

There was much for the prisoners to do. They had within their number men versed in a variety of skills and the Stalag school offered tuition in a hundred different subjects. There was a theatre and the opportunity to make music. All types of sport were catered for and there were churches of several denominations. In October 1943 great excitement pervaded the camp when a guard was persuaded to bring in a radio, having been advised it was bread for the prisoner he was escorting. Accurate news could now be gathered and disseminated and the morale boost of the sound of Big Ben was substantial.

Another way to fill the long hours was to take a job in the camp. As we have seen earlier, Tony Parnell spent his time helping the camp dentist. Arthur Price had taken Latin, French and German at school and was sufficiently fluent in the latter to get a job in the camp post office where he was quickly promoted to chief sorter and responsible for ensuring that, not only did the mail get to people in the camp, but also that it was correctly redirected to those who were out on working parties:

> "Well, of course, anyone who wanted to escape, their only way was to change places with a soldier who was going out to the working parties and if he did this he used to come to me to tell me all the arrangements so I could sort the mail out and see that it got to the right people. Also I felt that I had to be in a sort of Robin Hood way that any parcels that came in for people that had escaped, then these parcels mysteriously disappeared and in the camp I distributed them to the people who were in want, because I had a list – 'next time we got a good pair of socks I've got nothing left in mine', or 'my jersey is in holes, etc, etc.' So I worked my way through the list with any parcels that came in."

On 20 July 1943 Herbert Mullineaux was taken from Lamsdorf and the following day arrived at Stalag Luft III at Sagan. The camp at Sagan had not opened until 21 March 1942, only a week before the St Nazaire raid, with the arrival of about 100 officers from Stalag Luft I at Barth. The Germans thought that the sandy soil would make tunnelling impossible and to ensure that this was so, microphones were buried to detect any effort the prisoners might make to prove them wrong. However from here two of the most celebrated escapes of the war – the Wooden Horse Escape and the Great Escape – would take place.

In April and May 1942, the population of the camp was increased by the transfer of RAF prisoners from camps all over Germany. In April a new centre compound had been added to the original east compound and others followed – the north in March 1943, the south in September 1943 and the west in July 1944. As the Russian armies advanced on Germany from the east and plans were put in hand to evacuate the prisoners to the west, Stalag Luft III, together with Belaria, held 12,000 Allied prisoners of war.

At around 2000 on Saturday 27 January 1945, with the Russians a mere 60 miles away, the word went around Stalag Luft III to prepare to leave immediately. There had been some discussion at Führer Headquarters about trucking the POWs out but Hitler would have none of it. There was no transport for his own troops. The prisoners would have to walk to the railhead at Spremberg from where they would be taken to various camps by train.

There was a scramble among the men to gather their belongings and to put together makeshift sledges on which to transport them. A schedule of departures and destinations had been drawn up which allowed for 2,000 RAF personnel from Belaria and 1,000 from the east compound to go to Stalag IIIA at Luckenwalde, forty miles south-west of Berlin. Among their number was Herbert Mullineaux.

At 0300 the following morning a roll call was held in the compound in deep snow but it was not until after 7 am that the column moved out. As they left, each man was handed a Red Cross parcel. That day they marched 18 km to a village where they stayed the night before parading ready to move on again at 0900. However, they did not move all day and at 1500 a roll call was held and they settled down to stay another night.

The next day, Tuesday 30 January, they moved off at 0700, stopping for ten minutes every hour and for half an hour for lunch. At 1330, after covering 17 km they arrived at Sichdichfür where they were billeted in a school and a church. The following day it was cold and snowing as they set off at 0615, all the while encountering both refugees and, occasionally, German troops on their way to the front. At 1800 they arrived at Bad Muskau where they would stay for two nights. The weather now turned warmer and the snow was turning to slush.

On Friday 2 February they were on the road again and marched the 21 km to Steindur. It was now raining and they spent the night at a farm. Setting off the following morning they joined up with the group from Belaria to march the last leg to Spremberg where they were given soup at a Luftwaffe barracks. The marching was now nearly over for after another 3 km to the station they were put on a train. With the men packed fifty to a freight car the train pulled out at 1900.

It was 1730 the next day before they arrived at Luckenwalde, the journey having been prolonged by Allied air raids. After alighting, a march of 4 km took them to the camp to join the 16,000 prisoners already there. Conditions at the camp were bad. Seriously overcrowded, all the beds were taken and hundreds of men were sleeping on the floor. Rations and Red Cross parcels were in short supply and medicines were totally inadequate as were the washing and toilet facilities. Here the men would stay until liberated by the Russians on 22 April. The previous day the commandant had handed over control to the senior Allied officer, the Norwegian General Ruger, and the guards had marched out of the camp. However, it would be some time before repatriation as the men became pawns in Stalin's power game.

At 1823 hours on 25 March 1942 a Wellington II of 12 Squadron took off from RAF Binbrook as part of a twenty-seven-aircraft night-bombing raid on St Nazaire. Captained by Sergeant Einar Ernest Due, RAAF, and with Sergeant Robert Eric Greenhall, RAAF, as second pilot the other members of the crew were Pilot Officer Timbury Alan Mayo, RAAF, navigator, Flight Sergeant Gordon John Sheahan, RAFVR, wireless operator, Sergeant John Henry Ives, RAFVR, wireless operator/air gunner and Sergeant Alister McGregor Currie, RAAF, air gunner in the rear turret. This aircraft was the only one of the bombing force to fail to return to base.

Having circled over the target for thirty-five minutes they bombed from 16,000 feet but after the bomb doors had been closed a strong smell of burning was evident throughout the aircraft and it appeared a flare had hung up on the bomb rack. Certainly no flak had been near to them. The fire quickly caught hold and the captain gave the immediate order to abandon the aircraft. The intercom then failed and the aircraft went out of control and into a steep dive. Tim Mayo was the first to bale out, at about 15,000 feet and soon after the aircraft must have blown up for he never saw it again. He had, in fact, been fastening his parachute when he was pushed out of the aircraft by the wireless operator. Landing in the sea he managed to swim ashore.

Mac Currie was turning his turret to see what the trouble was when the hydraulics went. With the turret not turned far enough to jettison the doors and no time available for manual operation he managed to force one of the doors and was able to squeeze out. The aircraft was now at 12,000 feet. Currie was drifting down and resigning himself to landing in the sea when a change in the wind took him over the coast and he made a heavy landing, injuring his ankle. Within ten minutes he had been captured.

Pilot Officer Mayo and Sergeant Currie were the only two survivors. The other members of the crew were later washed ashore and they now lie buried in the Commonwealth War Graves Cemetery at Escoublac-la-Baule, where also lie many of the fallen Charioteers. Parts of the aircraft were picked up in the estuary the following day. Reunited in the afternoon of the 27th the two prisoners were taken to Nantes and then on through Paris to Dulag Luft at Frankfurt-am-Main where they were interrogated. Tim Mayo was then sent to Stalag Luft III where he arrived on 10 April and Mac Currie to Stalag 344 at Lamsdorf, arriving on the 15th.

Alister McGregor Currie was born on 19 March 1908, at Claremont, Western Australia. He enlisted in the RAAF at Adelaide on 6 January 1941. At that time he was living in Toorak, Melbourne, married to Isabel and working as a sheep station manager.

Mac Currie would become the 'man of confidence' at Lamsdorf and as such he would lead the men on the so-called 'Death March' from there to Stalag IXA at Ziegenhain during the months of January, February and March 1945. His award of an MBE, gazetted on 28 December 1945, would record that he "worked tirelessly to mitigate the hardships of those under his charge". Two of those under his charge would be Tony Parnell and Arthur Price.

As at Sagan, so it was also at Lamsdorf. The prisoners were given scant notice of imminent evacuation. On 22 January 1945, they were told to prepare to leave and later that day, in groups of about a 1,000, they marched out. Red Cross parcels and German rations had been issued to each man before leaving. The weather was fine and frosty and the hard ground made for difficult marching with many painful falls.

It soon became apparent that the large amount of belongings the men were carrying could not be sustained and much of it was soon discarded. The first day's march covered twenty-six kilometres and it was 0300 before all had arrived at the barns in which they spent the night. Many were sick and thirty-five were left behind the following morning. By the time they reached Stalag VIII-A at Görlitz on 3 February, 377 had dropped out and only 600 of the original column were still marching.

By Wednesday 31 January the weather was turning warmer and a thaw set in. This brought its own problems for they were now marching on hard roads instead of soft snow. The snow melted fast and on 3 February, with the weather now quite mild, they finally reached Görlitz. Here they would rest while each day saw the arrival of some of those who had dropped out earlier through sickness and who now re-joined the group. On 10 February they all marched out again on the next stage of their odyssey. They had already covered 280 km from Lamsdorf and another 520 km stood between them and their final destination.

The party reach Meiningen on 1 March and the next day was separated into three groups. One, numbering about 1,340 men, mostly sick and wounded, was bound for Stalag IXC at Bad Sulza, another, of 1,000 men , for Bad Orb. The third group, led by Mac Currie and including Tony Parnell and Arthur Price, set off for Stalag IXA at Ziegenhain.

Night stops were again in barns or, on some occasions, in military barracks but in all cases the accommodation was overcrowded and the food diminishing, sometimes not arriving at all. Disease claimed four lives on this section of the march, due entirely to the conditions in which the men were living. The main cause of illness among the marchers was dysentery and this was to cause the death of many of them. It rendered its victims unrecognisable. Tony Parnell was one of those to succumb and he endured its privations for three weeks without access to adequate medical attention. The medical officer had advised the men, when they got their bread ration, to burn it to charcoal before eating it and this undoubtedly brought relief to those who followed his advice. Also at this time another danger was that the Germans were getting short-tempered and were not averse to using their rifle butts and bayonets with which to encourage the marchers.

The ever resourceful prisoners let no opportunity slip to augment their meagre rations. Put into a barn one night for shelter, Arthur Price noticed a lady carrying two steaming buckets across the farmyard. Arranging for the guard to be engaged in conversation, Price waited for the lady to return to the house before slipping out unobserved. Opening the door to the building the lady had visited he found it to be a pig sty. Pushing the pigs out of the way he scooped up a hatful of the steaming mixture, filled his pockets as well and returned to the barn to share with his pals a marvellous feed —"warm, a little bit gritty, but it was food".

At some stage on this march Arthur Price got involved in a daring night sortie by a group of Australians aiming to improve their diet. He had palled up with a commando, Corporal Beattie, and a paratrooper, Sergeant Peek. Arthur later recorded:

> "Another night one of the chaps I met along with, there were three of us, actually, who went along together, this particular chap, Bob Beattie his name was, he was from my home town up in Peterhead and he was a butcher. Well, there were some Australians in this march and they had spotted one or two sheep up in the hills behind the barn we were in this particular night so they asked Bob if he would come with them and cut up the sheep for them. They could catch it and kill it but they wanted someone who knew about butchery to cut it up, which he did, and when Bob got back to us late that night he showed us what his share of the sheep was and it was the sheep's head. So we sat and scraped all the brains out of the sheep's head and ate them like that, raw, that night. Well, it was food!"

The remnants of the group – 700 had been left behind in reviers and lazarets – arrived at Ziegenhain on 12 March. Here they would stay until they were liberated on Good Friday, 30 March 1945, by General Patton's tanks. Parnell and Price had been captives for three years and two days and although now free they would have to endure another two weeks before being flown home. Arthur Price, however, was to take a different route.

Shortly before reaching Ziegenhain gunfire had been heard and thinking themselves now to be close to the front, Price, Beattie and Peek decided to leave the march and make their own way to freedom, as did many other marchers. Slipping out of the back of the barn in which they were quartered for that night they crossed the small river running alongside it and walked until daybreak. Hiding up in a field they soon saw proof of their proximity to the action when a group of German tanks sped along the road, closely followed by their American counterparts.

Making their way into a village they found themselves well treated by the inhabitants who were clearly exhausted by the war and very much aware that it was about to come to an end, resulting in their occupation. A little ingratiation, therefore, would not go amiss. The three men were able to collect milk and eggs daily and when a farmer killed a pig they were given a generous joint. On baking day, a communal exercise in the village, they were given first choice of the bread and cakes produced. On another occasion they were invited to dinner by a family whose son was a prisoner of war in England, providing, perhaps, an explanation of the way they had themselves been received.

Two miles down the road at another village they found an abandoned car, but it had only three wheels,

> ".... but enquiring around, the villagers told us the fourth wheel was at the bottom of the village pond. So we had to go in there and eventually we managed to get it out and got the fourth wheel back on the car. Now, we had noticed that all the American tanks that had gone through had a big star on the side, so we thought, 'well, it looks as if this is the sign now of the Allied army' so we painted big white stars on the top of the car and the sides of the car and eventually got it going. There was no ignition key in it – we had to pull the wires out and tie two together to start it up, but that was it and off we went to the Channel, as we thought."

Two days later, finding themselves in a camp for displaced persons, Arthur sought out the officer in charge and explained their situation. The officer wrote them a pass 'to all American troops' which proved to be "the most valuable piece of paper .... we could do anything in the American army". They stopped tanks to obtain petrol and on arrival at an American camp their 'passport' would obtain for them food and cigarettes. Arriving at a bridge about to be blown, the military traffic was halted for them while they drove across, and in this swashbuckling fashion they finally arrived in Brussels, where prisoners of war were being collected for their flights home.

Now that the various groups of prisoners had been liberated from the Germans it was time to put in train the arrangements to get them home, although it would take a little while longer before those at Luckenwalde could be prised free from the grip of their Russian liberators. Plans for repatriation had been discussed as early as the middle of 1944. Two priorities dominated the plans – that there should be a minimum of delay in getting the men home and that there should be adequate provision for their welfare. Having been long away from home and loved ones and in poor physical condition, the latter priority would best be served by the former. These plans now all came together in Operation Exodus.

Repatriation flights began in late April 1945 and continued throughout May. The men were first flown to transit centres in Belgium and France, most notably to Brussels and Reims, by Transport Command Dakotas returning from forward areas where they had delivered supplies. From these holding centres they were then flown to England in Lancaster bombers and other aircraft, now relieved of the task of bombing Germany.

The authorities were overwhelmed by the sheer number of men to be repatriated and an unseen factor in the organisation was the large number of men who, like Arthur Price and his two colleagues, had been unwilling to kick their heels in the liberated camps and set off for home on their own. However, by the end of Operation Exodus, over 350,000 men had been repatriated.

It is entirely appropriate that the final episode in this story should concern the man who had been part of it from the beginning, Group Captain A.H. Willetts. He had been appointed to COHQ on 5 November 1941 and had cut a lone RAF figure at all the meetings at which Operation Chariot had been planned. In the absence of an official appointee in the role he had been, de facto, the RAF force commander. It was an invidious position, combining as it did responsibility without power. That such an office had not been filled was one of the lessons of the operation.

Earlier we have seen the group captain disappearing "like a rat out of a trap" from a stricken Lancaster of 7 Squadron on which he had gone along for the ride on a Pathfinder mission over Berlin. Condemned to spend the rest of the war as a prisoner Willetts was sent to Stalag Luft III at Sagan where he was the senior British officer at the time of the famous Wooden Horse escape when three officers made a successful home run. He relinquished that position when a more senior officer, Group Captain 'Wings' Day, arrived. During his time at Stalag Luft III he was also housed at Belaria, an overflow compound to the north-east of Sagan, the main camp being to the south. Belaria was opened on 10 January 1944, when about 500 Royal Air Force prisoners of war were transferred there from the main camp.

As the squeeze on Germany from east and west gathered momentum and following the forced marches of prisoners of war away from the advancing Russians, Willetts found himself in Stalag VII-A at Moosburg. Here he was once more the senior British officer and, indeed, the senior Allied officer, for he was senior to the American Colonel Paul 'Pop' Goode who led the large contingent of US prisoners.

On Saturday 28 April 1945, 14th Armored Division crossed the Danube at Inglostadt and were hot on the heels of the German troops who were withdrawing towards Moosburg where two important bridges crossed the river Isar, one there and one at Landshut. By 2300 the Americans were only four miles from the camp. That night the German commandant sent for Willetts and suggested they go and meet the Americans, but none were found and they agreed to set off again at 0230 the following morning. Throughout the night the prisoners heard continuous gunfire and woke in the morning to find USAAF planes flying overhead.

In the early hours of the following morning, 29 April, a car under the protection of a white flag approached a road block at Mauren, eight miles north-west of the camp. The occupants were a representative of the Red Cross, a major in the SS, Group Captain Willetts and Colonel Goode, and they asked to speak with a senior officer. They carried a proposal, written in English, from the area commander. After a brief discussion with an American lieutenant colonel, at 0600 they were taken to see General Karlstad, commanding officer of Combat Command A of 14th Armored Division. The American servicemen noticed that Colonel Goode was somewhat dishevelled with ill-fitting and ill-matched uniform with a single badge of rank pinned to the collar. Group Captain Willetts, however, was seen to be well attired in a uniform of excellent condition and even carrying a swagger stick.

Willetts and Goode were not party to the discussions regarding the German proposal, which was turned down out of hand, and they returned to the camp, followed down the road by 14th Armored Division who immediately resumed their progress towards the town of Moosburg which fell after a short engagement. Taking a captured German captain as his guide, General Karlstad led a small convoy to the camp. The prison guards were paraded and disarmed and the general accepted the unconditional surrender of the commandant, Colonel Otto Burger. The first prisoners to greet their liberator were Group Captain Willetts and Colonel Goode. It would be several days before repatriation would begin and during that time the two senior officers took control of the camp.

With the return to England of Group Captain Willetts and the repatriation of the crew of Blenheim QY-K the story of the Royal Air Force and their participation in the raid on St Nazaire is complete. In due course the reports would be written and the post-mortems held. In the case of the naval and military forces, much of this would have to await the return from captivity of the 200 men who had languished for three years as prisoners of war. As for the RAF the recriminations would start almost immediately, as we shall now discover.

CHAPTER 12

REPORTS AND RECRIMINATIONS

When the time came to write reports, on 28 March, with aircraft of 19 Group still searching for survivors, C-in-C Bomber Command, Sir Arthur Harris was first in the field. Sending his preliminary report to the chief of the air staff, Sir Charles Portal, Harris recounted the planning process from 16 March as a precursor to outlining the confusion that had arisen in the issuing of the executive order to Bomber Command that Chariot was proceeding, and when. The burden of his complaint was that no direct order had been received by Bomber Command.

There was no doubt at COHQ that supreme force commanders were inclined to overlook the need to keep air force commanders fully informed and here again was demonstrated the weakness of the Chariot structure created by the non-appointment of an RAF force commander. Even so, when C-in-C Plymouth issued the executive orders for the operation, Willetts, whose brief was to liaise with Bomber Command, did not receive a copy. When he did see one it was in the routine circulation of papers within combined operations. Until now, Willetts had dutifully kept Bomber Command fully informed but responsibility for the prosecution of the raid had now passed from Combined Operations to Admiral Forbes, C-in-C Plymouth, as supreme force commander. The executive orders "Prepare Chariot" and "Carry out Chariot" were not copied by the Admiralty to Bomber Command.

A further complication arose with the use of Commander Ryder's cover name for the Chariot Flotilla. Obsessed with security he had called it the '10th Anti-Submarine Striking Force'. When the signal advising that the force would sail in the afternoon of 26 March was originated it was addressed to CCO, assistant chief of the naval staff and 'Air Striking Force 10'. The signal bore no priority marking and with an unrecognised address was delayed in the Admiralty teleprinter room.

It was Willetts who rescued the situation. On discovering the message in the file at Combined Operations HQ on the evening of the 26th he had immediately phoned Bomber Command to ask whether they had received a signal regarding the sailing of Chariot Force. Advised by Group Captain Barnett that they had not, Willetts immediately contacted C-in-C Plymouth who copied the original order to Bomber Command. First issued at 1804 on 25 March it was finally received at Bomber Command at 0159 on 27th, an unacceptable delay about which Bomber Command had every reason to be aggrieved.

The message having arrived in the early hours of the 27th, Bomber Command telephoned Willetts at 0915 that morning seeking confirmation that the force had indeed sailed. Such confirmation being given, the signal was finally sent to the headquarters of 1 and 4 Groups at 1440 by the director of operations at Bomber Command, Wing Commander Elworthy. It was short notice – the first bombers were to take off soon after 1930 that evening.

No praise can be too high for Group Captain Willetts. His sharp and immediate assessment of the import of finding the copy of the order to "execute Chariot", an order to which he, of all people, should have been privy in his capacity as air liaison officer, circulating in the files at Combined Operations HQ, saved the day. It is not too fanciful to wonder if, without his prompt action, the diversionary bombing raid would, quite literally, have got off the ground.

After outlining how the initiating of the bombing raid had unfolded, Harris turned his ire to another bone of contention. "No attempt appears to have been made to utilise Bomber Command's meteorological operation in ordering this operation." The weather conditions over St Nazaire were the critical factor in the difficulties encountered by the bomber force in carrying out their highly restrictive orders. It should be remembered, however, that the weather conditions were different things to different people. It kept the Luftwaffe on the ground and assisted the stealthy approach of the Chariot flotilla.

Others were to enter the debate on the meteorological situation. Invited by the chief of the air staff to comment on Harris' preliminary report, Mountbatten drew attention to the difficulties of getting a long-range forecast for operations of this nature. Conceding that closer cooperation between all naval and RAF commands was required, he reported that such arrangements had been made for any future combined operation. Mountbatten further pointed out that although the Bomber Command forecast was extremely unfavourable on the morning of the 27th when Willetts and Hughes-Hallett briefed the pilots of 51 Squadron, they were told that conditions over the target would be good.[32]

The imponderable weather had led to the drawing up of a contingency plan regarding the bombing raid in the event of conditions at the bases in England grounding any or all of the squadrons. The 1 Group Wellingtons had been ordered to fly to forward bases from where they would mount their attack and should 4 Group aircraft be unable to fly the Wellingtons would attack the three phases of targets in the ratio 5:10:10. Should 1 Group be grounded the 4 Group squadrons would attack in the ratio 5:15:15. Should none of the bomber force take off the force commander at sea would be signalled at 1800 on the 27th and he had been given full discretion to decide between continuance or cancellation of the operation. In the event all the aircraft took off – the meteorological problem was not in England but over St Nazaire.

Willetts' admirable report, referred to above, also contained details of the briefing of the pilots of 51 Squadron, which show up further shortcomings in the planning which are illuminating in the context of the problems encountered by all the pilots over the target. Most surprising is the revelation that "insufficient information of the operation as a whole was available to the squadron for them to fully appreciate the nature of the operation". All that was thought possible in the circumstances was for Willetts and Hughes-Hallett to fully explain the operation to the crews and to recommend that strict adherence to the instruction to drop single bombs was less important that dropping all their bombs, but this was at only one of the three 4 Group squadrons sending planes on the raid. Was this a lack of acknowledgement that the RAF was a full partner in this enterprise or another manifestation of the problems caused by the lack of an RAF force commander? Whether more discretion granted to all the pilots in phases two and three would have enabled more

---

[32] Willetts' report, drawn up to brief Mountbatten for his reply to the chief of the air staff, is a succinct and comprehensive recital of the position regarding both the untidy issue of the operation order and the prevailing weather and is reproduced in full in Appendix 4.

to bomb can only be a matter of conjecture.

Replying to the chief of the air staff on 3 April, Mountbatten reported that he had sent his deputy CCO, Air Vice-Marshal J.M. Robb, to Bomber Command to talk the matter over with Harris. The issue of non-appointment of an RAF force commander, he wrote, had been dealt with at the chief of Staff's meeting of 30 March – one such appointment would be made for all future raids of this nature. In agreeing with this proposal, Sir Charles Portal said that Air Officer Commanding-in-Chief (Harris) would have been ready to appoint a force commander for this operation. The stable door was now shut – the horses had long since departed.

It was not only at Bomber Command that difficulties were experienced. A report on conditions at Predannack, from where, with St Eval, all the Coastal Command sorties had been flown, was sent to Ops 1 at 19 Group by Flight Lieutenant Dolman from the operations room at Carew Cheriton, the home base of the Blenheims of 254 Squadron. He was clearly not impressed. Whilst admitting that personnel at Predannack had given every possible assistance, being a fighter station there were certain matters in respect of which none was available.

In another indication of the lack of information afforded the RAF, it was found that, with the tied lines to group always busy, the use of the code word 'Chariot' did not attract priority. With the traffic office two miles from the temporary operations room, the need to dictate messages over the telephone led to delay and inconvenience.

Dolman found that Predannack was a widely dispersed station and the provision of only one transport caused further delays. The officers' mess was five miles away and the sick bay in the village of Mullion.[33] Dolman also found that the station met office closed at 0800 and that the operations room was understaffed. Were these deficiencies further examples of the lack of any meaningful briefing of the RAF on the nature and importance of Operation Chariot?

The report of Admiral Forbes, C-in-C Plymouth, as supreme force commander, dated 13 April 1942, would later, with amendments, be published as a despatch in the *London Gazette* of 30 September 1947. It was his paragraph headed 'Surprise' that would become the subject of dispute with the Air Ministry:

"Surprise in the final approach was .... due to the methods employed by Commander Ryder to deceive the enemy."

There is no doubt that the methods Ryder employed – the flying of a German Ensign on *Campbeltown* and the responses by the MGB to German signals from the shore using code books captured at Vaagso – were effective in delaying hostile action but by then surprise had been lost and these ploys were to delay recognition, not to conceal presence. Admiral Forbes continued:

"That surprise was not complete was principally due to the bombing policy adopted. The weather, always a doubtful factor, prevented accurate location of targets by bomber aircraft, who consequently did not drop their bombs,

---

[33] The doctor's house at Mullion, used by the airfield as its sick bay, would later become the home of Sam Beattie, VC, captain of HMS *Campbeltown*, in his retirement.

but their presence overhead was sufficient to ensure that every AA gun in the neighbourhood was manned and ready to open fire at any moment. As these guns were in no way worried by falling bombs they were able to concentrate their fire on the MLs when the alarm was given. The noises of the ML's engines, which on a still night are clearly audible three miles away, were an additional handicap."

We have to fast-forward to November 1946, when the report was being prepared as a despatch, to find a more accurate narrative regarding the bombing raid and the achievement of surprise. Sent a copy and invited to comment, the director of staff duties at the Air Ministry rightly bristled at the import of such a statement. He noted that:

"One of the ideas behind the use of bombers was that their engines would drown the noise of the MLs' engines, and this appears to have been largely accomplished, since a very high degree of surprise was achieved."

The Air Ministry also pointed out that, whereas the Forbes Report criticises the "bombing policy adopted" it was now proposed to omit from the original text an admission by Forbes that "I ordered the bombing". The Air Ministry thus proposed that the paragraph should read:

"That surprise was not complete was principally due to the noise of the MLs' engines (which, on a still night, are clearly audible three miles away) and the inability of our bomber aircraft to locate their targets in the difficult weather conditions. Though the bombers (for whose services I had asked) fulfilled a useful purpose by helping to drown with their engines the noise of the MLs' approach, their presence overhead ensured that every AA gun in the neighbourhood was manned and ready to open fire at any moment. Whilst air activity covered the approach of the seaborne forces, it thus meant that these guns, unimpeded by falling bombs, were able to concentrate their fire on the MLs once the alarm was given."

This suggested version was an accurate description of the facts and, after submission to and approval by Admiral Forbes, was adopted verbatim.

Enclosed with Forbes' report were the remarks by Ryder, the naval force commander. In paragraph 1, on which Forbes chose not to comment, Ryder wrote:

"The bombing plan was not sound. With large numbers of aircraft overhead every single gun, large and small, was already manned and was able to depress in a matter of seconds onto the craft coming up river."

This assumes a fact not in evidence – that the unusual nature of the bombing raid pointed eyes to the sea. The commander of the German flak defences in St Nazaire, Kapitän-sur-Zee Karl-Conrad Mecke, suspicious of the actions of the aircraft, issued an injunction to "beware landings". This injunction has too often been taken to refer to landings from the sea. Not so. The German report on the raid admitted that "the enemy did succeed in approaching unperceived to within four miles of his objective, and surprising us". In making this concession they had, in addition to the poor visibility, considered the following:

1. It had already been reported at 0100 by the Naval Flak Regiment that the behaviour of the enemy aircraft suggested the possibility of parachute landings[34]. In spite of this warning of unusual tactics by the enemy the possibility of a landing from the sea was hardly taken into account. At that time we were not predisposed to believe in the possibility of a surprise attack – such as that of Zeebrugge in 1918 – on strongly fortified points.

2. Although the enemy's powerful air bombardment was not maintained, yet from 0300 onwards he did succeed, by sporadic attacks, in distracting attention from the seaward sector, and also in covering the sound of his ships' engines by the propeller noise of low flying aircraft.

This is the first time we have heard from the defenders and it is surely they, rather than the attackers, who are best placed to admit to surprise or not.

On his return from captivity, Lieutenant Commander Beattie reported on a conversation he had with a German NCO toward the end of 1943, who stated that "had it not been for the air raid warning no gun crews would have been closed up". The attack by sea, so far as he knew, was entirely unexpected. Here is perpetuated the myth that, had there been no air raid, the guns would not have been manned. It is impossible to believe that, without the distraction of the air raid, the attackers in the river would not have been discovered earlier. We have seen ample evidence that eyes were 'in the sky' and that the ships' engine noise had been drowned by that of the aircraft, circumstances which would not have prevailed without the air raid.

The report of Lieutenant Colonel Newman, the military force commander, necessarily had to wait until his return from a prisoner of war camp in 1945. Writing three years after the event, time and captivity appear to have dulled the memory. "When we landed, however, the air raid seemed to cease," he wrote, adding that the poor visibility over the target "made decision necessary at the RAF Command – should they continue with the raid during the action on land, poor visibility making their bomb aiming very inaccurate together with the added danger of hitting us or the naval vessels – or should they call off the raid as soon as we were due to land. It would appear that the latter was the decision."

The operation order (CHAR ONE) had clearly set out the phases of the bombing raid and at 0120, ten minutes before the commandos were due to land, it would be switched away from the dockyard to the shipyards at the northern end of the Penhoët Basin. Set alongside Ryder's remark that "the bombing plan was not sound" it is arguable whether either of the force commanders fully understood the RAF plan for the diversionary raid and yet they had been party to the whole planning process.

At COHQ, the NACO and AACO set out their 'Lessons Learned' report. Not unnaturally,

---

[34] The commandos had been issued with rubber-soled boots to deaden their footfall and this reinforced the belief that they came from the sky rather than the river. Several commandos, when captured, were asked if they were paratroopers.

only one paragraph of the naval assistant's list related to the bombing raid and he got that spectacularly wrong.

> "1. A mistake occurred in the carrying out of the bombing plan. The mistake arose because crews of aircraft had not been properly briefed. The plan was for bombs to be dropped whatever the weather, so as to provide the necessary diversion. Actually very few bombs were dropped, owing to inaccurate briefing. The crews followed the precept that over French territory bombs were not to be dropped if the target was obscured. Therefore guns were fully manned and no bombing diversion took place. The guns were therefore able to engage the craft in the river."

The instructions for the crews were set out quite categorically in Bomber Command Operation Order 141. Aircraft were to attack at heights best calculated to achieve accuracy under the prevailing weather conditions but should not come below 6,000 feet, and in order to increase the effect of the attack all aircraft were to drop their bombs singly on separate bombing runs. The precept not to bomb French territory was written in stone by Cabinet edict. The problem with the bombing was that the crews had been accurately briefed and, in spite of Willetts' attempt to relax the restrictions when briefing 51 Squadron, the crews *had* bombed in accordance with their briefing.

It was unsurprising that Willetts could not agree. In his view, a diversionary raid such as that at St Nazaire should not be undertaken if it could not be delivered with certainty and the ability to damage the enemy defences. (The question of damage to the defences had never been raised in connection with St Nazaire, merely that of distraction.) If such were not possible it would be better to bomb after the enemy had become aware of the assault. As at the briefing he had given to 51 Squadron, he further felt that more latitude should be given to pilots to bomb on estimated positions. He supported the granting of full discretion for force commanders to proceed or to cancel the operation, as it had been for Chariot, if the air diversion was not possible through adverse weather conditions. Finally he stressed the importance of coordination of the meteorological services between air force groups and commands and the naval meteorological service.

Winston Churchill had the first word on St Nazaire back in January 1942, when he had pointed the spotlight at the Normandie Dock and had stressed the strategic importance of the *Tirpitz* and the utmost necessity of keeping it out of the Atlantic. Now we will grant him the last word. Having dictated the conditions on which targets in France could be attacked and completely forbidding bombing that would put at risk the lives of French civilians, he bore much responsibility for the difficulties encountered by the Royal Air Force at St Nazaire.

After Charles Newman had returned in 1945 from captivity and had been awarded a richly deserved Victoria Cross, he was invited by Churchill to dine at Chartwell. Dinner over, Churchill beckoned to Newman to follow him outside. There, in the rose garden, Churchill apologised. "I'm sorry about St Nazaire, and leaving you with no air support. Six months later I would not have bothered."[35]

---

[35] Quoted in *St Nazaire Commando*, by Stuart Chant-Sempill.

EPILOGUE

The raid on St Nazaire had been a true combined operation and the Royal Air Force had been involved throughout. The raid was a resounding success and the naval and commando forces were rightly feted and decorated, winning five Victoria Crosses and eighty other decorations. For the RAF, however, there was little other than opprobrium and a legacy of perceived failure that persists to this day. Although not the only phase in the RAF contribution, it was the diversionary raid that attracted the controversy and gave voice to the critics.

At this point in the war the concept of combined operations was a new one and some in the individual services did not take to it kindly. They lost their independence of action when planning had to accommodate the requirements of the other services involved, and, more often than not, of political considerations too. This was particularly true of bombing operations over France which housed a civilian population who, although occupied, were still allies on whom we depended for assistance in the fight and who had to be kept on board politically.

Such a situation required constraints on the bombing of targets in France and on 31 May 1940, a directive on policy was published in which it was declared that, in enemy-occupied territory, targets must be clearly identifiable and care should be taken to avoid civilian casualties. Thus the pilots in the diversionary raid were instructed that they should drop their bombs singly on separate runs and only when the target was visible. On no account were they to bomb the town.

This policy was reinforced in 1941 following raids on Brest and Lille. The Vichy government maintained an ambivalent attitude towards RAF bombing of targets in occupied France but following these particular raids they made a formal complaint and Churchill felt the need to address the issue. At a meeting of the War Cabinet on 25 August 1941 it was agreed that pilots attacking occupied territory should be instructed not to bomb if accuracy was in doubt.

Notwithstanding this instruction, civilian casualties were still occasioned. On the night of 15/16 February 1942 the town centre of St Nazaire had been attacked for the first time and between then and the end of April eighty St Nazairiens would lose their lives in air raids. Finding 10/10ths cloud covering the town on 27th/28th and in ignorance of the commando activities below, it appears that the pilots in the diversionary raid were more scrupulous in the observance of their briefing.

Regardless of the restrictive nature of the bombing policy the biggest barrier to success of the diversionary raid had been erected early in the planning process when it was announced at a meeting at COHQ on 3 March that no RAF force commander would be appointed. This had proved to be a big mistake and the failure to appoint would be one of the lessons of Operation Chariot. The current practice to do so could well be said to date from this operation. With the authority that this appointment would have given him, Group Captain Willetts could have exercised his responsibility to greater effect and would have been given operational control of the RAF units involved once the size of the force had been agreed. Such was the haggling between Bomber Command and Combined Operations for a realistic effort, however, that it was not until 25 March, a mere twenty-four hours before Chariot Force set sail from Falmouth, that the final complement of aircraft was agreed.

Where Willetts would have most welcomed the power appointment as force commander would have brought him was in the authority to brief the crews fully, not only in their part of the operation but in the wider implications of the action taking place in the docks below. Willetts flew with 51 Squadron in the raid and was present at its briefing. His admirable report[36] reveals his realisation that "insufficient information of the operation as a whole was available to the squadron for them fully to appreciate the nature of the operation". The naval assistant, Captain Hughes-Hallett, RN, acquainted the crews with the full details and recommended that, in spite of instructions received to the contrary, it was more important that they dropped *all* their bombs, but the crews could not have been expected to disobey their orders.

The lack of such overall knowledge, coupled with the restrictions on bombing, led to several incidences of aircraft, unable to comply with them, failing to remain over the target for the duration of their phase. There is no evidence among the Whitley squadrons of such a failure – phase one required time over the target of one hour and phase two only fifty minutes. The records of the Wellington squadrons of phase three, however, betray a willingness to abort the mission once it had been realised that prevailing conditions made adherence to the bombing parameters impossible. This betrayed their complete ignorance of the purpose of their mission. Phase three was the longest of the whole diversionary raid, planned to last for two hours and forty minutes, and had particular importance in that the commandos were now ashore and diversion was sorely needed. Some pilots turned for home after as little as twenty minutes over the target and at least four others did not complete an hour and only one of the twenty-five aircraft managed to drop bombs. A comprehensive briefing on the whole operation would have avoided this.

The failure was not made easier to bear with the admission by Willetts that the target area was clearly disclosed to the pilots "by the flash of flak through the clouds". He was further discomforted by a squadron leader who said to him the following day, "If only you had told us what it was all in aid of, we would have come down to nought feet and given them everything we had".[37] This was an admirable sentiment which had echoes of Newman's unsuccessful request on 3 March for a low-level attack as the commandos went in, but such an attack by Whitleys or Wellingtons would have been unrealistic.

There can certainly be no sanction on Bomber Command for the number of aircraft deployed on the diversionary raid. At a time when they were woefully short of machines and had priorities elsewhere they were continually pressed by the Chariot planners to increase the number to take part in the raid. Late in the day they agreed to provide thirty-five Whitleys, half of the total number of this aircraft in the RAF at that time, to which they added twenty-five Wellingtons. Four of the Whitleys did not make it back to base, losses which the RAF could ill afford. Happily, however, this was with the loss of only one life. This total of sixty-two aircraft compared most favourably with earlier raids on St Nazaire during March 1942, when seventeen attacked the town on 7/8 March and twenty-seven on 25/26 March.

Although the bombing raid was not the hoped for success, there were contingent effects which did, in some measure, assist the clandestine approach of the Chariot flotilla.

---

[36] See Appendix 4.
[37] Quoted in *The Greatest Raid of All* – C.E. Lucas Phillips.

The strange behaviour of the planes gave the impression to the German flak commander that a landing was imminent but his injunction to "beware landings" was in expectation of parachutists, not an amphibious assault as has been thought by some commentators. Indeed, such was the concentration on the bombers that a naval flak officer, reporting ships coming up river, was told to mind his own business and keep his eyes on the sky. The noise of the aircraft overhead had also greatly assisted in the surprise arrival of the flotilla by drowning the noise of the launches approaching up river. The Germans had admitted that the possibility of a landing from the sea was hardly taken into account.

In total, the contribution of the RAF to Operation Chariot was not inconsiderable either. Five hundred and forty-four aircrew had flown 108 sorties totalling 675 flying hours. They had maintained planes in the air for all the hours of daylight from 1940 hours on 26 March until 1850 hours on 29 March 1942 and had destroyed one enemy aircraft and found and chased off several more, losing nine men killed and three taken prisoner. At no time during the raid had damage been inflicted on the Chariot Force from either the air or the sea. Yet in spite of all this effort, the RAF has still found itself cast as the villain of the piece.

The role of the Royal Air Force in the raid on St Nazaire has to be taken as a whole and, while it had its deficiencies, without it the raid would not have been as successful as it was and a greater loss of life would have ensued. If it served no other purpose it laid down a bench mark for future combined operations which were, in March 1942, very much in their infancy. That is, perhaps, the true legacy of their involvement.

Sadly though, the enduring image of the RAF support for Chariot is one of failure. One lady, widowed at St Nazaire, had a stock riposte to any mention of the air side of the raid – "Bloody RAF!" – and yet her daughter traces such a reaction to having read C. E. Lucas Phillips' account in The Greatest Raid of All, published in 1958, fully sixteen years after the event.

David Paton, a commando captain and one of the two doctors in the Chariot flotilla, recorded in 1988[38], forty-six years removed from the action, that the medics manning a pair of RAF ambulances who met them on their arrival at Falmouth around midday on 29 March were booed by the survivors who harboured less than happy memories of the apparent absence of their bomber colleagues over St Nazaire. That such a feeling existed in men who had been in a desperate action and at sea in small craft for three days is understandable but they can have had scant knowledge of the circumstances impeding the pilots in the execution of their task. Nevertheless, it reflects little credit on the commandos as a welcome to RAF medical personnel, ignorant of the circumstances, whose sole purpose was to alleviate their suffering.

Even in 2015, now over seventy years after the operation, a serving RAF station commander, in response to a chance remark about the raid on St Nazaire, said quizzically, "We fouled up there, didn't we?" No, sir, you did not. It is important to understand the clear delineation between the planners and the aircrew who, at the risk of their lives, flew their missions, in this instance one in which they had insufficient knowledge of either its purpose or design.

Whence, then, cometh the myth? It is firmly rooted in the perceived and received opinions born of incomplete knowledge of the RAF endeavour for, until now, the full story has never been told. In this complete account of the role played by the Royal Air Force in Operation Chariot there can be found no basis for any suggestion that they carried out their duties other than to the utmost of their ability and in the best traditions of the service, given

---

[38] Quoted in Storming St Nazaire – James Dorrian (Leo Cooper, London, 1998).

the inclemency of the prevailing weather and the constraints imposed upon their actions. Judgement must be made only when considering that involvement as a whole. It is right that we now acknowledge the contribution of the RAF to the raid on St Nazaire and accord them their proper place in the annals of Operation Chariot.

**In particular we should honour the memory
of those who gave their lives.**

APPENDIX 1

SUMMARY OF SORTIES FLOWN

Sortie Type	Date	Squadron	Home Base	Flew from	Aircraft Type	Aircraft Number
A/S Sweep	26/03/1942	502	St Eval	St Eval	Whitley VII	3
		612	St Eval (detachment)	St Eval	Whitley VII	2
A/S Sweep	27/03/1942	10 (RAAF)	Mount Batten	Mount Batten	Sunderland III	4
		502	St Eval	St Eval	Whitley VII	3
		612	St Eval (detachment)	St Eval	Whitley VII	2
						Total: 14
Diversionary Air Raid	27/03/1942 28/03/1942	51	Dishforth	Dishforth	Whitley V	12
		58	Linton-on-Ouse	Linton-on-Ouse	Whitley V	11
		77	Leeming	Leeming	Whitley V	12
		103	Elsham Wolds	Pershore	Wellington 1C	11
		150	Snaith	Stanton Harcourt	Wellington 1C	13
		304	Lindholme	Stanton Harcourt	Wellington 1C	2
		305	Lindholme	Pershore	Wellington II	1
						Total: 62

Withdrawal Cover	28/03/1942	53	North Coates	St Eval	Hudson V	2
		59	North Coates	St Eval	Hudson V	3
		233	St Eval	St Eval	Hudson V	2
		236	Wattisham	Predannack	Beaufighter I	7
		254	Carew Cheriton	Predannack	Blenheim IVF	5
		407 (RCAF)	Thorney Island	St Eval	Hudson	3
					Total: 22	
M/L Search	29/03/1942	233	Thorney Island	St Eval	Hudson V	1
		407 (RCAF)	Thorney Island	St Eval	Hudson	3
		502	St Eval	St Eval	Whitley VII	2
		612	St Eval (detachment)	St Eval	Whitley VII	1
					Total: 7	
Other Activities		247 (dusk to dark)	Predannack	Predannack	Hurricane IIC	1
		276 (air-sea rescue)	Harrowbeer (with Spitfire escort)	Harrowbeer	Lysander	1
		276 (air-sea rescue)	Harrowbeer (with Spitfire escort)	Warmwell	Lysander	1
					Total: 3	
					Total number of aircraft: 108	

APPENDIX 2

OPERATION CHARIOT – COMBINED PLAN

(Short Title: CHAR ONE)

References:	Chart No. 1104	Bay of BISCAY
	No. 2646	FRANCE west coast
		BOURGNEUF to ILE DE GROIX
	No. 2989	Entrance to LOIRE
		River and approaches to ST
		NAZAIRE

Orders for the Passage (Short title: CHAR TWO)
Orders for the submarine (Short title: CHAR THREE)

Appendix -   A.   Times of High Water, etc.

ALL TIMES ARE BST.

OBJECT

The enemy is making great use of ST NAZAIRE as a base
for U-boats and light craft as well as a port of shipping.
The object of the raid in order of priority is to destroy:

(a) The lock gates and mechanism of the large dock.

(b) The smaller lock gates and their installation.

(c) Other key points, such as pumping machinery for the
     basin, etc.

(d) Any U-boats and shipping which may be accessible.

FORCES TAKING PART

2.   HMS CAMPBELTOWN

        M.T.B. 74

        M.G.B. 314

        12 M.L.s

        2 Hunt class destroyers.

OPERATION CHARIOT – COMBINED PLAN

Military Forces

    (16 officers and 68 Other Ranks: Demolition parties
    (from Special Service Brigade.
    (25 officers and 136 Other Ranks of No. 2
    Commando.

Air Forces

    Aircraft detailed by Bomber Command.

    P.R.U. aircraft after the operation - Admiralty
    to arrange.

INTELLIGENCE

3.   Intelligence will be issued separately.

OUTLINE PLAN

4.   It is intended that the force will proceed in
    company so as to approach ST NAZAIRE after
    dark on a moonlight night near high water. A
    submarine will act as a navigational beacon.

5.   The force will proceed up the estuary over
    the mud flats, CAMPBELTOWN being appreciably
    lightened to do this. The two Hunts will remain
    to seaward.

6.   The troops will be carried in the CAMPBELTOWN
    and the M.L.s. On arrival CAMPBELTOWN will
    ram the outer gate of the big lock and the
    troops on board will disembark over her bows,
    then proceeding to carry out their demolition
    tasks.
    The remainder of the force will disembark
    from their M.L.s at selected points in the
    dockyard area.

7.   After CAMPBELTOWN has come to rest, she will
    be scuttled and the large charge, which is
    stowed forward, will be fired with a delay
    action fuse.

8.   The whole force will withdraw in the M.L.s
    after a maximum period ashore of 2 hours or
    earlier if ordered.

AIR

9.   Bomber aircraft will carry out continuous
    attacks on ST NAZAIRE during the night of the
    operation with the object of:

    (a) Detracting attention from the main assault
    forces.

    (b) Disorganising local defences and lookout.

(c) Preventing any repairs being made to docks before the fall of the tide.

COMMAND

10. The operation as a whole will be under the supreme command of Commander-in-Chief, PLYMOUTH, under whose authority combined orders will be issued.

11. Naval and military forces will be under the joint command of two Force Commanders as follows:

Commander R.E.D. RYDER, Royal Navy, who will command naval forces taking part; referred to as the S.N.O.

Lieutenant-Colonel A.C. NEWMAN, No. 2 Commando, who will command the military units.

The Force Commanders will proceed in the CAMPBELTOWN during the passage and transfer to M.G.B. 314 at dusk on the evening of the operation.

12. Air forces taking part in the raid on ST NAZAIRE will operate under Commander-in-Chief, Bomber Command, in the normal manner. Group Captain A.H. WILLETTS, of Combined Operations Headquarters, will act as liaison officer between Commander-in-Chief, Bomber Command, Commander-in-Chief, PLYMOUTH and Air Ministry.

DATES

13. The operation can only take place between certain dates when the moon and tide are suitable. These are between the nights of 28th/29th March and 30th/31st March inclusive. This is a period of full moon. It is also essential to have calm weather for the passage.

ZERO TIME

14. Zero time will be 0130 B.S.T. and the landing will take place as near this time as possible. Zero time is the same for all nights on which the operation may be carried out.

PRELIMINARY MOVEMENTS

15. The orders for the assembly and training of the force will be issued separately.

OPERATION CHARIOT – COMBINED PLAN

OUTWARD PASSAGE

16.   Orders for sailing and outward passage will
      be issued separately.

SUBMARINE ACTING AS LIGHT BEACON

17.   The force will pass position "Z" (46° 48' N,
      02° 50' W) at 2230 approaching on approximate
      course 045°. STURGEON will be stationed in
      position "Z" and will act as a light beacon
      for navigational purposes.

18.   The light will be operated by STURGEON in
      accordance with paragraphs 7 to 9 of CHAR
      THREE.

19.   Both Hunt class destroyers will listen for
      STURGEON's signal as laid down in paragraph
      10 of CHAR THREE. Opportunity to practise
      inter-communication between destroyers and
      STURGEON will be made available prior to the
      operation.

RESTRICTIONS ON A/S OPERATIONS DURING APPROACH

20.   During the approach, submarines WILL NOT BE
      ATTACKED when within 20 miles of position "Z".

THE APPROACH

21.   After passing position "Z", the force will
      proceed on a course direct to the buoy in
      charted position 47° 7.6' N, 2° 20.2' W
      passing there at 0030, thence to a position
      2 cables to eastward of LES MOREES TOWER (47°
      15' N, 2° 13' W). The force will then proceed
      up GRANDE Road and then to its individual
      objectives.

22.   It is intended that the approach up the river
      from the buoy referred to in paragraph 21
      should be made at 10 knots; this reduction
      may be made without signal. Craft must be
      prepared for alterations of speed without
      signal particularly an increase when the force
      is fired on.

23.   After passing position "Z", the two escorting
      destroyers will part company and patrol about
      30 miles to seaward keeping clear of STURGEON
      as she proceeds to the southward. Further
      instructions for these destroyers are given
      in paragraph 44.

DISPERSAL OF NAVAL UNITS

24.   On arrival abreast the extremities of the
      southern breakwater of ST NAZAIRE the force

will disperse as follows:

(a) CAMPELTOWN proceeds towards the big lock gate.

(b) M.G.B. 314 hauls over to starboard towards PETITE Road.

(c) Group 1 of M.L.s proceeds alongside the north side of Old Mole.

(d) Group 2 of M.L.s proceeds alongside landing steps on both sides of Old Entrance.

(e) M.T.B. 74 takes up a position just south of the NAZAIRE shoal.

MOVEMENTS OF CAMPBELTOWN

25.   On passing the dispersal point, CAMPBELTOWN will steer to ram the centre of the big lock gate. She should pass about 100 yards off the end of the Old Mole increasing speed so as to strike the boom off the entrance of the lock at about 15 knots engaging dock defences with all available weapons. As the tide will be flooding it is probable that the stern of the ship will be carried upstream as the bow enters slack water just prior to hitting the net.

26.   After ramming the gate the ship is likely to slew across the entrance. It is most important, however, that she be kept against the gate after the first impact irrespective of her position in order to expedite the landing of the troops. This will be done by grapnels and warps and/or by working the engines.

27.   After the troops have disembarked, the Commanding Officer will arrange for the evacuation of the crew and having set off the delay action of the main charge, scuttle the ship. The delay action on the main charge will be two hours.

28.   The CAMPBELTOWN's crew will be taken off in M.L.s which will lie alongside the north side of the Old Entrance for this purpose.

M.G.B. 314

29.   M.G.B. 314 will land the Force Commanders at the Old Entrance after the troops have been landed and then act as required by the SNO.

OPERATION CHARIOT – COMBINED PLAN

GROUP 1 of M.L.s.

30. Group 1 consisting of 6 M.L.s will be in the
    port column. M.L.s will pass close to the
    end of the Old Mole engaging the shore defences
    and will round up sharply and go alongside
    the north side at the steps. After troops
    have landed, M.L.s will secure alongside bows
    outward under the orders of the piermaster.

GROUP 2 of M.L.s

31. Group 2, consisting of 6 M.L.s will be astern
    of CAMPBELTOWN during approach and will come
    up on her port quarter as she approaches the
    big lock. M.L.s will proceed alongside both
    sides of the Old Entrance using either the
    steps or ships alongside.

32. Three M.L.s will be detailed to remain
    alongside the north side of the Old Entrance
    to embark CAMPBELTOWN's crew and any casualties.
    When fully loaded these boats will proceed
    out of the LOIRE and in accordance with
    paragraph 43. If not fully loaded they will
    lie off within hailing distance of the Old
    Mole. The remaining M.L.s of this group will
    also lie off the Old Mole.

M.T.B. 74

33. M.T.B. 74 will be prepared to carry out any
    of the following roles if ordered by the SNO:

    (a) Should CAMPBELTOWN fail to reach the
    objective M.T.B. 74 will be prepared to
    proceed up to the boom and fire her
    "torpedoes" over it at the lock gate.

    (b) Proceed through the Old Entrance lock
    (East lock) passing under the footbridge
    if there is sufficient clearance and fire
    her "torpedoes" at U-boats in the pens.

    (c) Any other role such as attacking ships
    alongside. Etc.

OUTLINE MILITARY PLAN

34. The Military Force will be put ashore in three
    main groups as follows:

    Group 1: Consisting of 17 officers and 69 Other
    Ranks, will be carried in 6 M.L.s and will
    land at the Old Mole to execute tasks south
    of the Old Entrance (Exclusive).

    Group 2: Consisting of 11 officers and 76 O.R.s
    will be carried in 6 M.L.s and will land

within the Old Entrance to execute tasks in the sector north of the Old Entrance but exclusive of the dry dock.

Group 3: Consisting of 14 officers and 59 O.R.s will be carried in CAMPBELTOWN and will land at the south end of the dry dock to execute tasks in that sector.

35.   The Military Force will be divided into:

(a) Assault parties to deal with known defences and to seal the area within which demolitions are being carried out.

(b) Demolition parties each trained for a specific task.

(c) Protection parties accompanying demolition parties to ensure that the latter work undisturbed.

36.   It is of great importance that the area within which demolitions are taking place, is firmly held so as to prevent enemy troops from gaining an entry. All bridges, gates or other entrances over which access could be gained must therefore be held.

37.   It is equally important that the area should remain sealed during all but the final stages of withdrawal and re-embarkation. Only the most careful signal plan will ensure that this is successfully accomplished.

PRIORITY OF TASKS

38.   The order of priority of the tasks allotted to the Military Force is as follows:

(a) The lock gates and mechanism of the large dock.

(b) The smaller lock gates and their installation.

(c) Other key points such as pumping machinery for the basin, etc.

(d) Any U-boats and shipping which may be accessible.

DANGER AREA OF DEMOLITIONS

39.   ALL demolition charges, including those placed inside the destroyer, will be blown in accordance with a careful programme drawn up and agreed by the Naval and Military Force Commanders. This programme must cover not only the successful completion of the tasks but also the security

of naval and military personnel working within the area of those tasks.

PRECAUTIONS ON THE OUTWARD PASSAGE

40. In order to disguise the presence of the military personnel on board the destroyer and M.L.s, every precaution must be taken to ensure that at all times during the outward passage, NO military personnel are allowed on deck unless they are wearing duffle coats or naval oilskins.

TIMING OF THE WITHDRAWAL

41. (a) The Force will be withdrawn as soon as possible after the completion of its tasks.

(b) There is no necessity for the Force to effect its withdrawal as a whole. Individual boat loads may be sent away independently under Naval instructions as soon as their tasks have been completed. (See paragraph 42).

(c) The aim should be to have completed ALL tasks and re-embarkation by 0330 hours.

(d) It must accordingly be clearly understood that the completion of re-embarkation by 0330 hours is to take precedence over everything except the execution of any major demolition task which may be unfinished at that time.

WITHDRAWAL OF NAVAL UNITS

42. Except as described in paragraph 31 withdrawal will take place from the Old Mole. The outside M.L.s are to be loaded first and will be ordered to shove off as soon as 40 men have been embarked. M.L.s lying off will be called alongside by the piermaster.

As M.L.s shove off they will proceed independently to seaward and then in accordance with paragraph 43.

RETIRING COURSE

43. All craft on retiring will proceed at maximum speed until clear of shore batteries. They will then pass through position "Y" (47° 01′ N, 2° 43′ W) thence on course 248° at their best speed with due regard to fuel consumption.

44. The escorting destroyers will pass through position "Y" at 0600 on course 248° spread 5

miles apart in order to pick up craft which may be in difficulties, take onboard personnel from M.L.s and generally rally the force.

45. Return route for light craft and escorting destroyers is given in the passage orders.

OUTLINE AIR SUPPORT PLAN

46. (a) The critical time is from 0100 - 0300 hours, with the attack at its heaviest scale between 0100 and 0200 hours while the Force is approaching the objective and when troops are first ashore

  (b) From 2330 - 0045 hrs: Heavy bombs. M.P.I. on the Town.

  (c) From 0100 - 0300 hrs: Maximum number of sorties using light bombs and incendiaries. M.P.I. on the Town (and NOT the Docks area.)

  (d) From 0300 hrs for the remaining hours of darkness; small raids to prevent the sounding of the ALL CLEAR. MPI in dock area.

  (e) A P.R.U. to be flown at the latest moment prior to the operation in order to ascertain position of shipping in the harbour, etc. These photographs to be given to the Force Commanders before sailing.

CASUALTIES

47. Force Commanders will satisfy themselves that each Commanding Officer and Officer Commanding Units fully understands his own individual task. It must be clearly understood by them that they must proceed with their tasks with the utmost determination and speed irrespective of casualties to other craft or units. This particularly applies during the approach.

48. If heavy casualties occur during the approach which are liable to jeopardise the success of the original plan, the decision to send in CAMPBELTOWN alone must be considered, bearing in mind that if this only is done something will be achieved.

ACTION BY CAMPBELTOWN IF EITHER LOCK GATE IS OPEN

49.   (a)   If the outer lock gate is open the first task for CAMPBELTOWN is to disembark the troops as near the pre-arranged landing place as possible.

      (b)   If the outer lock gate is open and the inner one shut CAMPBELTOWN should carry out her role on the inner gate as originally planned for the outer one having previously complied with (a) above.

      (c)   If both gates are open, having complied with (a) above, it is at the discretion of the Commanding Officer whether he enters the basin and expends his ship on the most valuable target he can find or sinks his ship across the inner lock gate sill.

DAMAGED OR BROKEN DOWN CRAFT

50.   Light craft which may become damaged during the approach are to do their utmost to reach their landing positions even if this may be some time after the main assault. During this stage other craft will not stand by them and they must fend for themselves.

51.   During the withdrawal every effort must be made to get damaged boats out to sea, assisting each other as necessary.

ORDERS FOR THE CHARGE IN CAMPBELTOWN

52.   A charge of 24 depth charges is to be placed as far forward as can reasonably be expected to be undamaged by the impact. This charge is to be carefully secured so that it cannot break adrift and fitted with alternative firing methods. The delay action on firing the charge is to be 2 hours.

MEDICAL

53.   During the return journey accommodation for casualties will necessarily be extremely limited. It is therefore incumbent on the Force Commanders to make all possible arrangements for the comfort and well-being of wounded. To this end, the following steps must be provided for in the plan:

      (a)   Two M.O.s will be landed with the Force.

      (b)   Each sub-group will contain selected N.C.O.s or men who have been given training in advanced first aid. Each individual so trained will carry ashore a small medical haversack.

(c)   Special medical equipment will be issued
        to all officers. Special equipment will
        also be carried in each M.L.

(d)   Casualties will be transferred from
        M.L.s to larger ships as and when this
        becomes possible during the return
        journey. Advance arrangements must be
        made for their reception.

CANCELLATION OF THE OPERATION

54.   If during the outward passage, naval units
        become scattered by enemy action or stress
        of weather, and it is not possible to reform
        without delaying the operation, it is at the
        discretion of the Force Commander to cancel
        it. They must, however, inform C-in-C PLYMOUTH
        if they do so.

Appendix 11

CHARIOT

Commander-in-Chief's Office, Plymouth

25th March 1942.

MOST SECRET

Addendum No. 1.

Operation 'CHARIOT'

(Short title - CHAR TWO)

The effect which unfavourable weather conditions
in this country might have on the despatch of the
Bomber diversion has been discussed with the Air
Officer Commanding-in-Chief Bomber Command. The
A.O.C.-in-Chief Bomber Command has agreed to
arrange a 'Bad Weather' programme by which he will
have on the western aerodromes at least a part
of the bombing force. By doing this, he hoped that,
even should the main aerodromes be covered by fog,
some scale of air effort will still materialise.

2.   Should weather condition necessitate anything
        less than full bombing effort being delivered, the
        Force Commanders will be told that the 'Bad Weather'
        plan only will operate; or should circumstances
        arise in which no effort at all is available, that
        the force can expect no air assistance.

3.   A final decision to reduce or cancel the bombing effort will be made by 1800 hours on the day of the assault.

4.   On receipt of this information the Force Commanders must decide what their subsequent action should be, being guided by the following principles:

       (a)   If Force Commanders are reasonably certain that the force has not been sighted and therefore that surprise may be achieved, they should proceed with the operation, or as much of it as appears possible.

       (b)   If however, the force has been sighted and the Naval Commander feels in consequence, that surprise has been lost, then the operation should be abandoned.

If bad weather makes it impossible to carry out the operation on the dates planned, it may take place without "Campbeltown" and using coastal forces only with destroyer escort. In these circumstances the operation may be ordered to take place on one of the 3 further nights of 31st March–1st April to 2nd–3rd April inclusive. In this case "Sturgeon" will be informed accordingly.

———————————————

           (Sgd) C.M. FORBES
           ADMIRAL OF THE FLEET
       COMMANDER-CHIEF-PLYMOUTH

APPENDIX 3

BOMBER COMMAND OPERATION ORDER No.141

COPY NO:
DATE: 25th March, 1942.

INFORMATION

A night operation by naval and military forces has been planned and will shortly take place against a certain sea port in enemy occupied territory.

2.   It is essential to the plan that the enemy's attention should, so far as is possible, be diverted during the approach of the forces from the sea and during the operations on shore. This can best be achieved by bombing the seaport before the time of landing, thereby causing the population to take shelter and the defences to turn their attention upwards and by continuing the attack during the operations and for sometime after they are completed in order to keep as many people as possible still in shelters and to disorganise any efforts the enemy may make to minimise the damage.

INTENTION

3.   To bomb a certain seaport in order to cover the approach and subsequent operations of a combined naval and military force.

EXECUTION

Code Name

4.   This operation will be known by the code name CHARIOT.

BOMBER COMMAND OPERATION ORDER No.141

Date of Operation

5.   This operation will be carried out on the first suitable night between March 27/28th and March 30/31st 1942.

Bomber Forces Taking Part

6.   The following aircraft will take part in this operation:

      (i)   1 Group.   25 Wellingtons.

      (ii)   4 Group.   35 Whitleys
                           (numbers made up if necessary by Wellingtons).

Bases from which the Bomber Forces will operate

7.   In order to minimise the risk of the whole bomber force being unable to take part in the operation owing to weather conditions at home bases preventing aircraft from taking off, all aircraft of 1 Group will operate from advanced bases in South-West England, and all aircraft of 4 Group will operate from home bases. 1 Group are to make the necessary arrangements with the appropriate Commands and Groups in South-West England for accommodation and facilities. BOSCOMBE DOWN, EXETER, CHIVENOR and ST EVAL are the most suitable bases for this purpose.

Plan of Attack

8.   The bombing attack will be divided into three phases:

(i)   First Phase

      Target . . . . Target A
      Time over target 2330-0030
      Number of aircraft . . . 10 (4 Group)

(ii)   Second Phase

      Target . . . . Target A
      Time over target 0030-0120
      Number of aircraft . . . 25 (4 Group)

(iii)   Third Phase

        Target . . . . Target B
        Time over target 0120-0400
        Number of aircraft . . . 25 (1 Group)

Plan of Attack if 1 Group only are able to operate

9.   The plan of attack will be as detailed in paragraph
        8 above except that the numbers of aircraft in
        the first, second and third phases will be 5, 10
        and 10 aircraft respectively.

Plan of attack if 4 Group only are able to operate

10.   The plan of attack will be as detailed in paragraph
        8 above except that the numbers of aircraft in
        the first, second and third phases will be 5, 15
        and 15 respectively.

Targets

11.   All crews are to be most carefully briefed that
        they are to bomb no other target than that detailed.
        In particular the greatest care is to be exercised
        by those crews detailed to attack Target A not
        to bomb any ships outside the dock area, and by
        those detailed to attack Target B to confine their
        attacks absolutely to this more specific target.

Bomb Load

12.   All aircraft are to carry 500-lb GP bombs fused
        TD 0.025.

Height of Attack

13.   Aircraft are to attack from heights best calculated
        to achieve accuracy under the weather conditions
        prevailing at the time, but should not come below
        6,000 feet.

Flares

14.   No flares are to be used in any circumstances.

Method of Bombing

15.   In order to increase the effect of the attack
        all aircraft are to drop their bombs singly on
        separate bombing runs.

Secrecy

16.   It is essential that the utmost secrecy should
        be observed. Knowledge of the operation should
        be confined to as few persons as possible.

INTERCOMMUNICATION

17.   The signals procedure for the move of the 1 Group
        detachment to aerodromes in South-West England
        are to be in accordance with Bomber Command Signals
        Instruction No. 61, paragraphs 7 and 12.

18.   Normal Bomber Command Signals Organisation will
        be employed during the operation.

Executive

19.   The executive for this operation will be issued by
        this Headquarters by the signal EXECUTIVE CHARIOT
        followed by the date on which the operation is to
        take place and by definitions of Targets A and B.
        Approximately thirty-six hours notice will be given
        before the actual time of the operation.

20.   ACKNOWLEDGE BY TELEPRINTER.

                                (S. C. Elworthy, W/Cdr)

                                for Air Vice-Marshal,
                                Senior Air Staff Officer,
BC/S.26488/Ops.1(b).   BOMBER   COMMAND.

ISSUED BY D.R. AT 1900 hours

APPENDIX 4

REPORT BY GROUP CAPTAIN A.H. WILLETTS

Report by Group Captain A.H. Willetts, air assistant Combined Operations, to Vice-Admiral Mountbatten in response to a report on Operation Chariot sent by Air Marshal Arthur Harris to the chief of the air staff, Sir Charles Portal on 29 March.[39]

MOST SECRET

CCO

<u>Reference to C-in-C, Bomber Command's comments on Operation</u>
<u>"CHARIOT"</u>

1.   There is no doubt the "Supreme Force Commanders" are inclined to overlook the need for keeping cooperating Air Force Commanders fully informed of their plans. This was pointed out to Commander Luce early on in the CHARIOT arrangements. On the other hand, para.12 of the Combined Plan, states that AACO would act as liaison between C-in-C, Plymouth and AOC-in-C, Bomber Command, and C-in-C Plymouth may have assumed in consequence it would be sufficient to inform this Office. The point, however, is that the Combined Plan as issued by us was in a strict sense no more than a draft for C-in-C Plymouth's approval and only became executive on the issue of C-in-C Plymouth's orders. These were not sent to Bomber Command, nor was a copy seen by AACO.

2.   Bomber Command was kept fully informed, however, of the progress of planning and as the result of liaison by AACO produced their Operation Order on the 25th March. No comment was made on this by this Office since it fulfilled our requirements.

3.   The signal dated 25th March, referred to in para.3 of Air Marshal Harris's letter Ref.CAS, was first seen by AACO on the evening of 26th March, during it's normal circulation by CCO's Office. Since Bomber Command were not in the address Commander Luce was asked to confirm from C-in-C Plymouth that

---

[39] Transcribed from File AC71/9/1 by kind permission of the Trustees of the Royal Air Force Museum.

the information would be passed to Bomber Command. As a result of this intervention by AACO and after ascertaining from C-in-C Plymouth that Bomber Command had not in fact been informed, the signal was copied by teleprinter from Admiralty to Bomber Command that night. The delay, therefore, referred to in para.3 arose from the fact that the signal actually received by Bomber Command was, in fact, a copy of an earlier one and was not a direct signal's delay. The executive signals "Prepare Operation Chariot" and "Carry out Chariot" were not sent to Bomber Command, nor were they seen by AACO in the CCO's Office, but in order to make quite sure there would be no confusion through the absence of these signals, AACO informed SASO, Deputy SASO and Operations, Bomber Command of all progress as soon as information became available, i.e. on the evening of the 26th, as soon as news of the sailing of the Force was received in this Office, Group Captain Barnett, Bomber Command, was informed, as on the morning of the 27th this was confirmed to SASO.

4.   No advice concerning the cooperation of Bomber Command Meteorological Service was sought specifically to cover the night 27th/28th March since this matter had been discussed with AOC-in-C, and as set out in para.2, it appeared that any Bomber Command forecast could not be sufficiently reliable to either delay or cancel the sailing of the Force. When SASO pointed out the unfavourable forecast for the 27th, AACO consulted MA and NA, who concurred that the discretion allowed the Force Commander was sufficient for him to decide to continue or abandon the operation, and that beyond informing C-in-C Plymouth of Bomber Command's estimate of the weather, the actual decision to go on or not should be left to the Force Commander, without further recommendations being made. In arriving at this conclusion the Advisors were influenced by the instruction that in the event of no Air Support being likely a signal would be made at 1800 hours, to assist the Force Commander in deciding on his action.

5.   AACO and NACO were present at the briefing of 51 Squadron and were aware of the following limitations placed on the operations of the squadron:

   (a)   Pilots had to see and recognise their targets or bring back their bombs.

   (b)   The minimum height of attack was to be 4000 ft.

   (c)   Bombs were to be dropped singly, i.e. each aircraft was to make eight runs over the target.

      (d)   Insufficient information of the
Operation as a whole was available
to the Squadron for them fully
to appreciate the nature of the
Operation.

6.   AACO and NACO decided that all that was possible
in the circumstances was to:

      (a)   Explain the operation fully to
the crews. This was done by NACO.

      (b)   Recommend that strict adherence
to the instruction to drop single
bombs was less important than
dropping all bombs.

7.   No action was taken to reverse the instructions
concerning the need to see and recognise the target
or to reduce the minimum bombing height, for the
following reasons:

      (a)   The latest weather forecast made
at 1700 hours by Meteorological
Officer Driffield was that conditions
would be good over the target
area.

      (b)   It was not to be expected that
4 Group could or would reverse
the categorical instructions to
squadrons at that late hour,
when crews on many different
aerodromes were already briefed.

8.   The lessons that may be learned from this Operation
are:

      (a)   An RAF commander should be
appointed for all operations
and this officer must direct the
action of all aircraft taking
part.

      (b)   The briefing instructions to
Squadrons should be drawn up by
RAF Force Commander and agreed
by the Military and Naval
Commanders and RAF Operational
Commands.

      (c)   Supreme Force Commanders, when
appointed, must issue their
orders and executive signals
to RAF Operational Commands
in addition to RAF Force
Commander. This is particularly
necessary when the actual date

of the Operation is flexible
and aircraft are used for other
purposes while awaiting the
operation to be carried out.

31st March, 1942   AACO

BIBLIOGRAPHY

Acton, Viv & Derek Carter, *Cornish War and Peace*, Landfall Productions, 1995

Acton, Viv & Derek Carter, *Operation Cornwall 1940 – 1944*, Landfall Productions, 1994

Ashworth, Chris, *Action Stations 5, Military Airfields of the South-West*, Patrick Stephens Ltd, 1982

Ashworth, Chris, *RAF Coastal Command*, Patrick Stephens Ltd, 1992

Babington-Smith, Constance, *Evidence in Camera*, Chatto & Windus, 1957

Batteson, Ralph, *St Nazaire to Shepperton*, Highedge Historical Society, 1996

Berryman, Nick, *In the Nick of Time*, Woodfield Publishing, 2000

Bowyer, Chaz, *Beaufighter at War*, Ian Allan Ltd 1976

Bowyer, Chaz, *Coastal Command at War*, Ian Allan Ltd, 1979

Bowyer, Chaz, *Men of Coastal Command*, William Kimber & Co Ltd, 1985

Braeuer, Luc, *Fortresse Saint-Nazaire*, 2012

Braeuer, Luc & Bernard Petitjean, *Raid sur Saint-Nazaire*, 2012

Chant-Sempill, Stuart, *St Nazaire Commando*, John Murray Publishing Ltd, 1985

Conyers Nesbitt, Roy, *Eyes of the RAF*, Sutton Publishing Ltd, 1996

Cooke, Anthony, *Reflections of RAF Warmwell*, RAF Warmwell Preservation Group, 2000

Dorrian, James G., *Storming St Nazaire*, Leo Cooper, 1998

Downing, Taylor, *Spies in the Sky*, Little, Brown, 2011

Dunstan, Roy, *My Life with RAF St Eval*, Published privately, 1999

Falconer, Jonathan, *Bomber Command Handbook*, Sutton Publishing Ltd, 1998

Gammon, Victor F., *No Time for Fear*, Arms & Armour Press, 1996

Gammon, Victor F., *Not All Glory*, Arms & Armour Press, 1996

Halsall, Christine, *Women of Intelligence*, Spellmount – The History Press, 2012

Hastings, Max, *Bomber Command*, Michael Joseph Ltd, 1979

Hendrie, Andrew, *The Cinderella Service*, Pen & Sword Books Ltd, 2006

HMSO, *Coastal Command*, 1942

Hunter, Jim, *From Coastal Command to Captivity*, Pen & Sword Books Ltd, 2003

Lucas Phillps, C.E., *The Greatest Raid of All*, Wm Heinemann Ltd, 1958

Lyman, Robert, *Into the Jaws of Death*, Quercus Editions Ltd, 2013

McLelland, Tim, *Action Stations 6, Northern England and the Isle of Man*, Crécy Publishing Ltd, 2012

Millar, George, *The Bruneval Raid*, Doubleday & Company Inc, 1974

Otter, Patrick, *1 Group, Swift to Attack*, Pen & Sword Books Ltd, 2012

Pitchfork, Graham, *Shot Down and in the Drink*, The National Archives, 2005

Pomeroy, Colin, *Dorset: The Royal Air Force*, The Dovecote Press Ltd, 2011

Powys-Lybbe, Ursula, *The Eye of Intelligence*, William Kimber & Co Ltd, 1983

Purdon, Corran, *List the Bugle*, Greystone Books, 1993

Ryder, R.E.D., *The Attack on St Nazaire*, John Murray, 1947

Shepherd, Christopher, *German Aircraft of World War II*, Sidgwick & Jackson Ltd, 1975

Thomson, Adam, *Küstenflieger*, Fonthill Media, 2013

Ward, Chris, *4 Group Bomber Command*, Pen & Sword Books Ltd, 2012

Wetherspoon, N., A. Clark & M. Sheldon, *Aircraft Wrecks*, Pen & Sword
    Books Ltd, 2009
Younger, Calton, *No Flight from the Cage*, Frederick Muller Ltd, 1956

MEMOIRS

Mémoire et Savoir Nazairiens, Saint-Nazaire 28 Mars 1942. L'opération Chariot
    (Refonte Souvenances no1 et no2)

SOURCES

Note: This book contains public sector information licensed under the Open Government Licence v3.0

The National Archives, Kew, London

ADM 1/11888	Combined Operations – Operation Chariot
ADM 1/11970	Combined Operations – preparations for Operation Chariot
ADM 199/1199	Maps and Plans
AIR 2/4743	Air-Sea Rescue Search Reports
AIR 8/870	Chief of Air Staff Registered File – Operation Chariot
AIR 14/694	Bomber Command Register Files – Operation Chariot
AIR 15/611	Coastal Command Register Files – Operation Chariot
CAB 65/25/38	Cabinet Minutes
CAB 79/18	Cabinet Minutes Meetings 34-70
CAB 79/19	Cabinet Minutes Meetings 71-100
DEFE 2/125	Operation Chariot – Part 1
DEFE 2/126	Operation Chariot – Part 2
DEFE 2/127	Operation Chariot – Part 3
DEFE 2/128	Operation Chariot – Part 4
DEFE 2/129	Operation Chariot – Part 5
DEFE 2/130	Operation Chariot – Volume 1
DEFE 2/131	Operation Chariot – Volume 2
DEFE 2/132	Operation Chariot – Volume 3
MFQ 1/302	Maps and Diagrams
MFQ 1/304	Maps and Diagrams
MFQ 1/306	Maps and Diagrams
WO 208/3264	MI9 – Operations St Nazaire
WO 344/228	Prisoner of War Interrogation Questionnaires
WO 344/244	Prisoner of War Interrogation Questionnaires
WO 344/259	Prisoner of War Interrogation Questionnaires

Squadron Operation Record Books

AIR 27/656	77 Squadron
AIR 27/1010	150 Squadron
AIR 27/1431	233 Squadron
AIR 27/1447	236 Squadron
AIR 27/1488	247 Squadron
AIR 27/151	10 Squadron RAAF
AIR 27/152	10 Squadron RAAF

AIR 27/1515	254 Squadron
AIR 27/1597	276 Squadron
AIR 27/1668	304 Squadron
AIR 27/1672	305 Squadron
AIR 27/1793	407 Squadron RCAF
AIR 27/1959	502 Squadron
AIR 27/2114	612 Squadron
AIR 27/492	51 Squadron
AIR 27/500	51 Squadron
AIR 27/505	53 Squadron
AIR 27/544	58 Squadron
AIR 27/555	59 Squadron
AIR 27/814	103 Squadron

Station Operation Record Books

AIR 28/255	RAF Elsham Wolds
AIR 28/256	RAF Elsham Wolds
AIR 28/341	RAF Harrowbeer
AIR 28/450	RAF Leeming
AIR 28/455	RAF Leeming
AIR 28/456	RAF Leeming
AIR 28/478	RAF Lindholme
AIR 28/482	RAF Linton-on-Ouse
AIR 28/651	RAF Predannack
AIR 28/717	RAF Snaith
AIR 28/729	RAF St Eval
AIR 28/738	RAF St Eval
AIR 28/749	RAF St Eval
AIR 28/888	RAF Warmwell
AIR 29/415	Photographic Reconnaissance Unit

RAF Museum, Hendon

AC/71/9/1	Personal File – ACM Sir James Milne Robb

The London Gazette

Issue no 36089, 9 July 1943, Second Supplement (13 July 1943)
Issue no 38086, 30 September 1947, Supplement (2 October 1947)

INDEX

10th Anti-Submarine Striking Force, 65, 148

Advanced Air Striking
    Force, 31, 32, 33, 92, 94

Affleck, Flt Sgt, 82

air-sea rescue, 38, 67, 68, 86, 87, 134, 159

Alcock, Sgt, 90

Alexander, Mr A.V., 39

Armstrong, P/O, 132

Avern, Sgt, 19, 126

Babington-Smith, Constance, 50

Bain, Flt Lt, 130

Baldwin, AVM 'Jack', 31

Baldwin, Stanley, 27, 29, 46

Barling, Flt Sgt, 127-128, 137

Barton, Sgt, 95

Bassett-Wilson, 2nd Lt P., 106

Batteson, OS Ralph, 101, 103

Battle of Britain, 38-40, 88, 112,
    113, 115, 132

Bay of Biscay, 12, 40, 58, 61, 63-66, 69,
    106, 124, 127, 135, 160

Beart, Lt E.H., RNVR, 107

Beattie, VC, Lt-Cdr S.H., RN, 99, 103,
    150, 152

BEF, 49, 77, 87, 112, 113, 125

Bell, W/O, 66-67

Bennett, Wg Cdr D.C.T., 80

Birch, P/O, 83

Bircham Barrel, 38

Birney, Capt D.L., 104, 106

Blériot, Louis, 27, 39, 44, 45

Bletchley Park, 50

Bogarde, Dirk, 51

Bomber Command Operation Order
    No. 141, 12, 21, 24, 76, 172-175

Bonnar, P/O, 55, 64

Bonvin, Lt J.A., 106

Bordeaux, 58, 64, 78, 113

Bow, F/O W.D.S., RAFVR, 61, 62

Boyd, Lt Tom, RNVR, 99, 110, 111, 135,
137, 138

Bradley, Capt E.W., 105

Bradley, L/Sgt R., 106, 140

Bray, Flt Sgt C.L., 93

Bray, Sgt (103 Sqn), 93

Bray, Sgt Donald, 88

Breen, Air Cdre J.J., 32

Brest, 32, 50, 54, 55, 58, 60, 62, 78, 110,
    113-117, 128, 131, 134, 154

Brett, Lt G., 108

Briault, Lt D.L., RNVR, 105, 110, 136

Bridge D, 98, 105, 106

Bridge G, 107, 108, 109

Bridge M, 25, 98, 107

Britannia Royal Naval College
    (BRNC), 41

British Commonwealth Air Training
    Plan, 30

Broadhurst, P/O, 137

Broadley, Flt Lt Bill, 84

Bromet, AVM G.R., 41

Brookes, P/O, 92

Brown, Wg Cdr A.C., 132

Burn, Capt M.C., 79, 107

Burt, Lt E.A., RNVR, 107

Burtinshaw, Lt R.J.G., 108

Butt Report, 25

Campbell, F/O Kenneth, 60

Campbell, F/Sgt D., 93

Carr, AVM C.R., 33

Casa Maury, Wing Commander the
    Marquis of, 18-19

Central Interpretation Unit (CIU), 51-52

Chamberlain. Neville, 46, 51

Chant, Lt Stuart, 59, 100, 103, 109

CHAR ONE, 20, 22, 24, 25, 152, 160-171

Charpentiers Channel, 64

Cherwell, Lord, 25

Cheshire, Gp Capt Leonard, 71

chief of Combined Operations, 6, 16, 22,

24, 65, 119, 148, 150, 178

chief of staffs committee, 6, 23

chief of the air staff (CAS), 18, 31, 48, 148, 149, 150

Churchill, Sarah, 51

Churchill, Winston, 6, 10, 14, 16, 41, 46, 76, 91, 101, 153, 154

Clibborn, Lt W.C., 104

Clow, F/Sgt Ernest, 89

Coates, Sgt, 137, 138

Colditz, 59, 105, 107

Colledge, Sgt D.M., RAFVR, 83

Collier, Lt T.A.M., RNVR, 105, 106

Cologne, 26, 94

Combined Operations Headquarters (COHQ), 18, 19, 20, 53, 55, 84, 146, 148, 152, 154

Coningham, Air Cdre Arthur, 33

Constantine, Gp Capt Hugh, 75

Copland, Major Bill, 98, 103, 108, 109

Cotton, F/O, 65

Cotton, Sidney, 44, 46, 57

Craven, Sgt R.H., 89

Crossan, Sgt, 119, 126

Crozon peninsula, 8, 62, 63, 131, 139

Currie, Sgt A.Mc.G., RAAF, 20, 81, 142-143

Curtis, Lt D.M.C., RNVR, 110, 120

Danesfield House, 50-51

Daniel, Glyn, 51, 127

Davidson, Gp Capt A.P., 74

Dennison, Lt M.C., 108

director of combined operations (DCO), 14, 15, 16

director of naval intelligence (DNI), 14, 15, 53

Dolman, Flt Lt, 150

Dorrien Smith, Anne, 54-55

Douglas, Sgt, 87, 88

Douglas, Sqn Ldr, 132

Dowding, AVM Sir Hugh, 48

Downward, P/O A.C.R., 93

du Boulay, Wg Cdr J., 92

Due, Sgt E.E., RAAF, 142

Dulag Luft, 57, 140, 143

Duncan, P/O John, 88

Dunkirk, 13, 31, 32, 39, 43, 77, 87, 112, 125

Durrant, VC, Sgt Tom, RE, 111, 120

Earp, Flt Lt, 91

Elder, Sgt, 88

Elworthy, Wg Cdr Charles, 17-19, 21, 22, 23, 77, 148, 175

Endicott, P/O, 62

Engel, Sgt, 96

Essen, 26

expansion schemes, 28-29, 31, 32, 72, 73, 74, 86, 127

Fairhurst, Sgt G.B., 93

Falconar, Lt H.G.R., RNVR, 105, 106, 110, 111, 120, 136

Falmouth, 10, 20, 25, 53, 56, 58, 59, 61, 64, 65, 91, 98, 103, 105, 106, 110, 111, 120, 129, 131-136, 138, 155, 156

Fane, Flt Lt A.F.P., 57

Fenton, Lt L., RNVR, 107, 111, 117, 120, 126

Fern, Sgt, 126

Ferté, Sir Philip Joubert de la, 41

Figuera, F/O, 96

Fisher, Sgt, 82

Fokker, Anton, 45

Forbes, Admiral Sir Charles, 6, 14-16, 19, 148, 150-151, 171

Fox-Talbot, 45

French Resistance, 84, 87

Gallaway, Gp Capt Frederick, 70

Gillespie, Flt Lt R., 92, 93

Glover, Wg Cdr, 119, 123, 126

Godfrey, Sqn Ldr Oliver, 93

Goode, Col Paul 'Pop' (US), 146

Gorman, P/O, 92

Graham, Gp Capt Strang, 72, 73

Green, Lt Bill, RN, 64, 98

Greenhall, Sgt R.E., RAAF, 142

Gunn, Flt Lt Alistair, 57

Haines, TSM G.E., 108

Harris, ACM Sir Arthur, 18, 22, 23, 29, 31, 33, 80, 148, 149, 150, 176

Harrison, P/O James, 83

Harvey, Sqn Ldr, 90, 91

Haydon, DSO MC, Brig J.C., 15, 16, 19, 22, 23, 24, 53, 55

Hayward, Flt Sgt, 90

Helme, P/O, 85
Hill, F/O, 65
Hill, Sgt, 137
Hitler, Adolf, 13, 46,49, 50, 58, 77, 105,
    112, 113, 118, 141
Hodgson, Capt E.S., 105, 136
Holford, Sqn Ldr David, 92, 93
Hooper, Capt R.H., 107
Hopwood, Lt H.G.L., 109
Horlock, Lt K.M., RNVR, 106, 111
Houghton, Lt Joe, 105
Hughes-Hallett, Captain J., RN, 16, 18,
    19, 84, 149, 155
Hunter, P/O Jim, 40
Illingworth, Flt Lt, 130
Irwin, Lt S.B., RNVR, 99, 110, 121
Isles of Scilly, 58, 89, 136
Ives, Sgt J.H., RAFVR, 142
Jenkins, Lt M., 107
Jenks, Lt Cdr Robin, RN, 67
Johnstone, Flt Sgt, 127, 128
Jones, Sgt William, 89
Kelbling, Kptlt Gerd, 64
Kent, Sgt, 126
Keyes, VC, Admiral of the Fleet Sir
    Roger, 16
Kriegsmarine, 78, 112, 116
    22 Marine-Flak-Regiment (22 MFR),
        78, 81
    5th Torpedo Boat Destroyer Flotilla,
        56, 64, 123
    Altmark, 40
    Bismarck, 13, 14, 39, 40, 61, 115
    Botilla Russ, 104, 111
    Gneisenau, 55, 60, 93, 113, 131
    Hipper, 55
    Jaguar, 56, 120
    Marine-Artillerie-Abteilung 280
        (MAA 280), 98, 106
    Prinz Eugen, 13, 40, 55, 61, 113
    Scharnhorst, 40, 55, 76, 93, 110, 113, 131
    Sperrbrecher, 104, 110
    Tirpitz, 13, 14, 16, 57, 71, 80, 153
    U-593, 64, 111, 120
La Rochelle, 58, 78, 113
Lambe, Captain Charles, RN, 16

Lancastria, 13, 32, 43
Law, Sgt, 95
Laws, Sgt Major V., 46
Lawson, Sqn Ldr H.R., 90, 91
Lawton, Sgt, 119
Lewis, Sgt, 93
Lindholme Gear, 38, 74
Lloyd, Air Cdre L.T., 132
Lofoten Islands, 15
Lord, Flt Sgt, 91
Lorient, 58, 64, 78, 113, 114
Louthood, Sgt W.P., 83
Lown, P/O, 130
Lübeck, raid on, 22
Ludlow-Hewitt, AM Sir Edgar, 30, 31
Luftwaffe
    5./Aufklarungsgruppe 3.(F)/123, 114
    Arado, 115, 117, 122
    Blohm and Voss, 115, 135
    Dornier 217, 114, 133, 135
    Fliegerführer Atlantik, 114, 116
    Focke-Wulf Kurier, 130
    FW190, 84, 130
    Heinkel 111, 114, 115, 117, 126,
        131, 134, 135
    Heinkel 115, 115, 117, 121, 122,
        126, 135
    IX Fliegerkorps, 114, 116
    Junkers 88, 114-117, 122, 123, 135
    Kampfgeschwader 2 (KG2), 114
    Kampfgeschwader 40 (II/KG40),
        114, 115
    Kampfgruppe 506 (KGr 506), 114
    Küstenfliegergruppen 106 (KüFlGr
        106), 114, 116, 117
    Küstenfliegergruppen 406 (KüFlGr
        406), 114, 115
    Küstenfliegergruppen 906 (KüFlGR
        906), 114, 115, 117
    Luftflotte 2, 113
    Luftflotte 3, 113, 114, 116
Mackay, Sgt Sandy, 89
MacKenzie, P/O, 90
Maltby, Sgt Chris, 95-96
Marks, Flt Lt, 69
Martin, P/O, 92

Mason, P/O, 90
Mayo, P/O T.A., RAAF, 142-143
McKnight-Kauffer, Ann, 50, 55
McLeod, Sgt, 55, 64
McNichol, Sgt, 123
Mecke, KsZ Karl-Conrad, 78, 81, 101, 102, 103, 106, 151
Mellor, Wg Cdr, 95
Meteorological Section, 38
Miedecke, F/O, 68
Miranda, A.J., 47
Monro, P/O, 84, 85
Montgomery, Capt R.K., RE, 54, 109
Moore-Brabazon, 2nd Lt, 45, 46
Morgan, Lt R.F., 107
Morgan, Sgt, 82
Morgat, 9, 139, 140
Moss, RSM Alan, 107
Mountbatten, Vice-Ad Lord Louis, 6, 15, 16, 18, 19, 23, 24, 53, 149, 150, 176
Mullen, P/O, 136
Mullineaux, Sgt H.J., 131, 139, 140, 141
Nation, Sgt Brian, 9, 84-85
Newhall, ACM Sir Cyril, 48
Newman, Sgt L.K., RAF, 62
Newman, VC, Lt Col A.C., 19, 20, 23, 24, 53, 56, 99, 103, 107, 109, 110, 152, 153, 155
Nock, Sub-Lt Bob, RNVR, 99, 110
Normandie Dock, 14, 16, 25, 56, 71, 78, 98, 106, 109, 110, 153
O'Brien, L/Cpl Richard, 106
O'Connell, Sgt, 136
Old Entrance, 99, 106-111, 120, 164-166
Old Mole, 98-100, 104-109, 164, 165, 167
Ollivier, M. and Mme., 102
Operation:
    Archery, 15
    Biting, 84-85
    Exodus, 145
    Jericho, 84
    Musketoon, 105, 106
Oughtred, Lt N., 105
Parfitt, Sgt H.R., RAFVR, 9, 123, 125, 126
Parker, LMM T.G., 135
Parnell, Sgt A.G., 130-132, 139, 140,

141, 143, 144
Parsons, Flt Sgt, 90
Paton, Capt David, RAMC, 135, 156
Paul, Kapitänleutnant F., 120
Penhoët Basin, 23, 25, 77, 91, 93, 152
Pennington, Lt H., 107
Pickard, DSO DFC, Gp Capt P.C., 50, 84, 93
Pickering, Sgt, 123
Pierse AM Sir Richard, 31
Pike, Sqn Ldr, 31
Platt, Lt T.D.L., RNR, 104, 110, 135
Plymouth, 20, 37, 41, 54, 56, 67, 69, 86, 104, 120, 121, 122, 128, 132, 124-135, 148
Pockley, F/O, 69
Point T, 120, 135
Point Y, 111, 120, 121, 135
Point Z, 67, 98, 136
Pope, Flt Sgt, 63, 66
Portal, AM Sir Charles, 18, 31, 148, 150, 176
Potter, F/O J.W.G., RAFVR, 62
Pound, Admiral Sir Dudley, 16
Powell, P/O, 95
Powys-Lybbe, Ursula, 52, 53
Price, Sgt Arthur T., 129, 131, 139-141, 143, 144, 145
Prisoner of War Camps
    Marlag Nord, 107
    Oflag 64, Moosburg, 17
    Stalag IIIA (Luckenwalde), 141, 142, 145
    Stalag IXA (Ziegenhain), 143, 144
    Stalag Luft I (Barth), 141
    Stalag Luft III, 17, 57, 94, 139, 141, 143, 146
    Stalag VII-A (Moosburg), 146
    Stalag VIII-A (Görlitz), 143
    Stalag VIII-B (Lamsdorf), 140, 143
Pritchard, Capt W.H., RE, 54, 105, 106, 109
Pryde, Sqn Ldr, 91
Purdon, Lt Corran, 60, 107, 108, 109
Race, F/O, 136
Rankin, P/O, 123
Reeder, Sgt Harold, 88
Rennes, 82, 107, 113, 116, 122
Robb, AVM J.M., 150
Robinson, Flt Lt, 55

Roderick, Lt J., 64
Rodier, Sub-Lt M.F., RNVR, 108
Ross, P/O, 132
Roy, Capt D.W., 59, 108
Royal Aircraft Establishment, 48, 51, 52
Royal Air Force – Aircraft
    Avro Anson, 60, 61, 127, 128
    Beaufighter, 20, 60, 118, 119-126,
        128, 130, 131, 159
    Beaufort, 40, 60, 119, 133
    Blenheim, 9, 47, 48, 54, 121, 127,
        128-133, 139, 140, 147, 150, 159
    Catalina, 39, 40
    Fairey Battle, 31, 32, 51, 74, 92, 94, 96
    Fairey Swordfish, 39, 133
    Hampden, 17, 28, 73
    Hudson, 38, 39, 40, 80, 122, 126,
        127, 132-134, 136, 137, 158, 159
    Hurricane, 46, 58, 59, 69, 74, 118, 159
    Lysander, 38, 86, 87, 134, 159
    Spitfire, 21, 38, 46, 48, 50, 54, 55,
        57, 64, 73, 74, 86, 88, 159
    Sunderland, 39, 65, 67, 68, 128, 158
    Tiger Moth, 54
    Wellesley, 75, 79
    Wellington, 7, 22, 24, 28, 32, 33, 39,
        51, 61, 72, 73, 75, 76, 77, 81, 84,
        91-96, 101, 142, 149, 155, 158, 173
    Whitley, 20, 22-24, 28, 33, 37-39,
        59, 61, 63, 65-68, 70-79, 80-91, 96,
        137, 155, 158-159, 173
Royal Air Force – Commands
    Bomber, 6, 12, 16-25, 27-34, 39, 40,
        41, 57, 60, 73, 75, 76, 77, 80, 86,
        93, 96, 113, 148, 149, 150, 153,
        154, 155, 161, 162, 170,
        172-175, 176, 177
    Coastal, 20, 23, 35-42, 44, 49, 51,
        58, 60, 61, 68, 73, 75, 89, 90, 96,
        113, 117, 118, 120, 122, 127, 128,
        132-134, 150
    Fighter, 20, 28, 40, 48, 49, 113, 118,
        128, 133
    Training, 28, 125
Royal Air Force - Groups
    1, 24, 31, 32, 74, 75, 77, 91, 149

    2, 31
    3, 31
    4, 10, 24, 33, 73, 75, 77, 148, 149,
        173, 178
    5, 29, 31, 32, 74
    15, 36, 37
    16, 36, 49, 132, 133
    18, 36, 37
    19, 20, 37, 40-42, 86, 118, 119, 122,
        123, 127, 129, 132, 136, 137, 148,
        150
Royal Air Force - Squadrons
    10 (RAAF), 33, 67-68, 71-72, 80, 158
    51, 33, 70-73, 81, 83, 84, 85, 88, 89,
        90, 96, 149, 153, 155, 158, 177
    53, 133, 134, 158, 183
    58, 18, 33, 70, 71, 81, 84, 89, 90, 91, 158
    59, 133, 134, 158
    77, 33, 72, 79, 81, 83, 84, 91, 158
    103, 32, 51, 74-76, 91-94, 96, 158
    150, 32, 51, 73, 76, 81, 84, 89, 94,
        96, 158
    233, 126, 127, 158, 159
    236, 118, 120, 122-126, 128, 131, 135, 159
    247, 58, 118, 159
    254, 128-131, 139, 150, 159
    276 (ASR), 86, 87, 88, 159
    304 (Silesian), 32, 33, 74, 76, 96, 158
    305 (Ziemia Wielkopolska), 32, 33,
        74, 96
    407 (RCAF), 132-137, 159
    502, 60-62, 65, 66, 137, 158, 159
    612 (County of Aberdeen), 61, 62,
        65, 66, 137, 158-159
Royal Air Force - Stations
    Aldergrove, 60, 125, 127
    Benson, 51, 57, 94
    Boscombe Down, 23, 71, 76, 77, 133
    Carew Cheriton, 118, 128-129, 131,
        150, 159
    Catfoss, 118, 124, 125, 140
    Cattewater, 67
    Chivenor, 23, 72, 76, 77, 89, 129,
        132, 173
    Cottesmore, 72, 82
    Dishforth, 33, 70-72, 83, 90, 158

Elsham Wolds, 32, 51, 74, 92, 93, 158
Exeter, 23, 76, 77, 87, 88, 173
Harrowbeer, 86, 87, 88, 159
Heston, 43, 44, 47-49, 51
Leeming, 33, 70, 72, 80, 81, 83, 91, 158
Leuchars, 56, 63, 127
Limavady, 61
Lindholme, 32, 74, 96, 158
Linton-on-Ouse, 33, 70-71, 90
Medmenham, 50-54, 56
Mount Batten, 67-69, 158
North Coates, 118, 133-134, 158
Pembroke Dock, 67, 68, 69, 128
Photographic Reconnaissance Unit
  (PRU), 43-57
Portreath, 60, 86, 118
Pershore, 23, 76, 92, 96, 158
Predannack, 37, 58, 60, 118, 119,
  120, 122-125, 129, 132
Reykjavik, 61-62
Scampton, 74
Snaith, 32, 51, 73, 74, 94-96, 158
St Eval, 21, 23, 37, 39, 40, 49, 50, 54,
  55, 56, 59-67, 69, 76, 77, 91, 118,
  126-128, 131-138, 150, 158-159
St Mawgan, 60, 91
Stanton Harcourt, 23, 76, 94, 96, 158
Syerston, 74, 96
Thetford, 83
Thorney Island, 132-133, 136, 159
Warmwell, 86-88, 159
Wattisham, 118-120, 124, 125, 159
Wick, 49, 50, 57, 61
Royal Flying Corps (RFC), 18, 27, 30,
  35, 41, 45, 46, 72
Royal Naval Air Service (RNAS), 30, 35,
  41, 46, 47, 59, 67, 72, 73, 128
Royal Navy - Coastal Craft
  MGB 314, 15, 58, 59, 99, 101,103,
    104, 110, 111, 116, 120-123, 126,
    135, 160, 162, 164
  ML 156, 108, 111, 117, 120, 121,
    126, 135
  ML 160, 110, 111, 135
  ML 177, 108
  ML 192, 36, 107

ML 262, 107
ML 267, 107
ML 268, 107
ML 270, 110, 111, 121, 126, 135
ML 298, 99, 110
ML 306, 101, 106, 111, 120, 121, 123
ML 307, 105, 106, 111, 135
ML 341, 105, 136, 137
ML 443, 105, 106, 111, 135
ML 446, 105, 111, 120, 121, 126, 135, 136
ML 447, 104, 106, 135
ML 457, 100, 105, 106
MTB 74, 59, 99, 110, 160, 164, 165
Royal Navy - Ships
  HMS Atherstone, 56, 59, 64, 67, 98,
    117, 120, 121, 122, 123, 134, 135
  HMS Brocklesby, 56, 117, 121, 122,
    134, 135
  HMS Campbeltown, 10, 20, 37, 57, 58,
    59, 67, 84, 91, 99, 100, 103, 104,
    107-110, 129, 138, 150, 160-171
  HMS Cleveland, 56, 121, 122, 134-136
  HMS Foylebank, 88
  HMS Hood, 13, 14, 39, 40
  HMS Neil Smith (FY 529), 88
  HMS Tynedale, 59, 64, 65, 98,
    120-123, 134, 135
  HMSub Sturgeon, 67, 98, 100, 136,
    163, 171
  Princess Josephine Charlotte, 54, 56
Rudloe Manor, 85, 86
Rundstedt, F.M. von, 112
Ryder, Sgt Richard, 89
Ryder, VC, Commander R.E.D., RN, 19,
  20, 24, 53, 56-59, 61, 63-65, 67,
  99, 101, 103, 110, 116, 120-123,
  135, 138, 150, 151
Sanderson, P/O, 82
Saundby, AVM Robert, 18, 22, 23, 25, 90
Savage, VC, AB W.A. 'Bill', 104, 111, 120, 122
Saxelby, Flt Lt Clive, 92-94
Sayer, Cdr G.B., RN, 121, 135
Scott, P/O Arthur, 89
Scrivens, Flt Sgt, 91
Searson, L/Sgt A.C., 106, 140
Seymour-Price, Sqn Ldr, 82

Schaefer, P/O, 119

Sheahan, F/Sgt G.J., RAFVR, 142

Shepherd, Sgt, 95

Silva, Sgt, 82

Sise, Flt Lt G.D. 'Bill', 130-132

Skarsynski, F/O, 96

Skellon, Sgt, 87-88

Small, Sgt, 90

Smalley, Lt C.J., 107, 109

Smith, P/O (103 Sqn), 92

Smith, P/O (236 Sqn), 125

Smith, P/O P.D., 88

Smith, Sgt (276 Sqn), 82, 88, 119

southern caisson, 57, 84, 91, 98, 104,
    108, 109

Sperrle, Generalfeldmarschall Hugo,
    113-115

St Nazaire, 6-9, 10, 12-23, 28, 30-32,
    37, 39-42, 43, 50-58, 60-64, 68-70,
    72-74, 76-86, 89-96, 101-106, 110,
    113, 115-117, 120-121, 123, 127,
    129, 130, 133, 135, 149, 151, 153,
    154-157, 160-164

Staniland, Sgt, 92

Stein, P/O D.M., RAFVR, 62

Stephens, Lt Cdr W.L., RNVR, 107, 108

Stirling, F/Sgt, 95

Stokes, Flt Lt, 68, 69

Stoney, P/O, 90

Swayne, Lt R.O.C., 106, 120

Sykes, F/Sgt, 96

Tait, Gp Capt J.B. 'Willie', 71

Target for Tonight, 50, 84

Taylor, Sgt A.W., RAAF, 123-126

Taylor, Sqn Ldr Alastair, 56

Tedder, The Lord, 43

Ten-Year Rule, 29

Tett, P/O, 92

Thornaby Bag, 38

Tibbits, Lt N.T.B., RN, 98, 104

Tillie, Lt A.B.K., RNVR, 107

Tookey, Sgt H.M., RAFVR, 62

Treadwell, Sgt, 125

Trenchard, MRAF Sir Hugh, 27, 28, 46

Trondheim, 56, 57

Tuttle, Wg Cdr Geoffrey, 44, 48, 49

Ushant, 59, 63, 123, 131-134

Vaagso, 15, 17, 20, 150

Vanderwerve, Lt J.E., 106, 120

Veal, Sgt, 82

Versailles, Treaty of, 46, 112, 113, 115

Victoria Cross, 60, 71, 84, 120, 153, 154

Wallis, Barnes, 71, 75, 87, 118

Wallis, Lt N.B.H., RANVR, 105, 106, 111,
    135, 137, 138

Walton, Lt P., 105, 106

Watson, 2nd Lt Bill 'Tiger', 100, 105, 106

Webb, Gp Capt Eric, 95

Wheeler, Cpl G., 106

Whitley, Gp Capt J.R., 70

Whyte, Sgt George, 89

Willetts, Group Captain A.H., 6, 10, 15-25,
    84, 85, 146, 147, 148-149,
    152-155, 176

Wilson, Lt A.D., 106

Wilson, P/O, 90

Wingfield, Lt-Cdr Mervyn, 98

Women's Auxiliary Air Service
    (WAAF), 36, 50, 52, 54

Women's Royal Naval Service
    (WRNS), 36

Wood, Sqn Ldr, 119, 123

Woodcock, Lt M., 107

Wright, P/O, 130-132

Wynn, Sub-Lt Micky, RNVR, 99, 107, 110

Young, Sgt D.A., RAFVR, 62